The Return of the State

The Return of the State

Restructuring Britain for the Common Good

Edited by

Patrick Allen, Suzanne J. Konzelmann and Jan Toporowski

First published in 2021 by Agenda Publishing

Agenda Publishing Limited
The Core
Bath Lane
Newcastle Helix
Newcastle upon Tyne
NE4 5TF
www.agendapub.com

ISBN 978-1-78821-329-5

British Library Cataloguing-in-Publication Data
A catalogue record for this book is available from the British Library

Typeset by Newgen Publishing UK
Printed and bound in the UK by CPI Group (UK) Ltd, Croydon,
CR0 4YY

Contents

Contributors

Patrick Allen is founder and Chair of the Progressive Economy Forum and founder and Senior Partner of Hodge Jones & Allen Solicitors.

Craig Berry is Reader in Political Economy at Manchester Metropolitan University.

Robert Calvert Jump is a research fellow at the University of Greenwich.

Danny Dorling is Professor of Geography at the University of Oxford and a Council member of the Progressive Economy Forum.

Marc Fovargue-Davies is a research associate at the Centre for Business Research, University of Cambridge.

Stephany Griffith-Jones is Financial Markets Director at the Initiative for Policy Dialogue at Columbia University, Emeritus Professorial Fellow at the Institute for Development Studies, University of Sussex, and a Council member of the Progressive Economy Forum.

Louisa Harding-Edgar is a Glasgow GP and Academic Fellow in General Practice at the University of Glasgow.

Susan Himmelweit is Emeritus Professor of Economics at the Open University, coordinator of the policy advisory group of the Women's Budget Group and a Council member of the Progressive Economy Forum.

Will Hutton is co-chair of the Purposeful Company, an associate of the London School of Economics' Centre for Economic Performance, a columnist for *The Observer* and a Council member of the Progressive Economy Forum.

Suzanne J. Konzelmann is Reader in Management at Birkbeck, University of London, a research associate of the Centre for Business Research, University of Cambridge, co-executive editor of the *Cambridge Journal of Economics* and a Council member of the Progressive Economy Forum.

Stewart Lansley is a visiting fellow at the School for Policy Studies at the University of Bristol, and a Council member of the Progressive Economy Forum.

Jo Michell is Associate Professor in Economics at the University of the West of England.

Johnna Montgomerie is Reader in International Political Economy at King's College London and a Council member of the Progressive Economy Forum.

Ann Pettifor is a Director of Policy Research in Macroeconomics (PRIME) and a Council member of the Progressive Economy Forum.

Kate Pickett is Professor of Epidemiology and Deputy Director of the Centre for Future Health at the University of York and co-founder of the Equality Trust.

Allyson M. Pollock is Clinical Professor of Public Health, Institute of Population Health Sciences, at Newcastle University.

Josh Ryan-Collins is Head of Finance and Macroeconomics and Senior Research Fellow, Institute of Innovation and Public Policy, University College London.

Robert Skidelsky is Emeritus Professor of Political Economy at the University of Warwick and a Council member of the Progressive Economy Forum.

Guy Standing is a Professorial Research Associate at SOAS University of London, a founding member and honorary co-president of the Basic Income Earth Network (BIEN) and a Council member of the Progressive Economy Forum.

Geoff Tily is a senior economist at the Trades Union Congress. This follows 25 years in the government statistical and economic services, mainly at the Office for National Statistics but also HM Treasury.

Jan Toporowski is Professor of Economics and Finance at SOAS University of London, Visiting Professor of Economics at University of Bergamo, Professor of Economics and Finance at International University College, Turin, and Visiting Professor of Economics at Meiji University, Tokyo.

Richard Wilkinson is Emeritus Professor of Social Epidemiology at the University of Nottingham Medical School and co-founder of the Equality Trust.

Preface

The Progressive Economy Forum (PEF) was founded in 2018 to highlight the dangers and failings of austerity, provide alternative progressive policies to rebuild the economy, deconstruct economics myths, explain economics to a wider audience and help coordinate the response of the economics profession to the failure of government policy. At the heart of PEF is a Council of leading economists and academics. Since its foundation PEF has produced policy papers, held workshops and delivered public lectures on current economic problems. Many PEF policies were included in the 2019 manifesto of the Labour Party, including proposals for shorter working hours and a pilot of Universal Basic Income.

In May 2020 the Covid-19 pandemic had already caused many deaths and major damage to the economy as the lockdown measures took effect. Temporary measures were put in place to preserve jobs and business; but it soon became clear that this is the time for a major reappraisal of British economic policy and management, to deal with the legacy of austerity, Covid-19, Brexit and climate change all at once. PEF therefore decided to produce this book to help shape the debate for a new economy.

When we embarked upon the project, our friend and colleague John Weeks, coordinator of PEF, enthusiastically embraced the idea and agreed to be an editor. We had already begun working with him on sketching out the book and choosing authors when, tragically, he died, on 26 July 2020. On hearing of John's death the PEF Council decided without hesitation to dedicate this book to his memory.

John Weeks was Emeritus Professor of Economics at SOAS University of London, and a founder member of PEF. He was the first coordinator of the PEF Council and worked assiduously to promote its success. He attended all the Forum's meetings, lectures, events and workshops; and he contributed many blogs to the website.

John was born in Austin, Texas. He gained an undergraduate qualification in economics at the University of Texas in 1963 and then enrolled at the University of Michigan for a PhD, studying Nigerian industrialization. After completing his doctorate, in 1969, John taught at Ahmadu Bello University in northern Nigeria. In 1971 he moved to the University of Sussex to become a lecturer in economics, and then to the newly established Economics Department at Birkbeck University of London, in 1973. In 1990 SOAS University of London asked him to create an MSc programme in development studies. He accepted with enthusiasm, and remained there until retirement in 2006, holding joint appointments in two departments, development studies and economics, and chairing each at various times. He also helped SOAS set up the Centre for Development Policy Research.

Development economics remained a lifelong focus. John worked on projects funded by United Nations organizations, national governments, central banks and trade unions in many countries across Asia, Africa and Latin America. John was a brilliant and passionate macroeconomist. He believed that macroeconomics was the tool to create a fairer and better society. He worked hard to promote reform of the UK economy and to overturn the damaging ideology of neoliberalism and austerity. His last book, published a few months before his death, *The Debt Delusion: Living within Our Means and Other Fallacies*, was written to explode commonly believed myths about balanced budgets, tax and public debt. It is a model of clarity and scholarship.

In preparing this book, we invited members of the PEF Council and other academics to submit essays in their areas of expertise. The idea was to consider, in each case, the reasons why the British economy is failing – and to propose pragmatic solutions for a better economy and society. We have tried to cover the most important areas of policy as well as the public services the government needs to deliver.

We commend all the contributors for their ideas and for preparing and delivering their essays in a very short period of time, despite their many other commitments.

We fervently hope that this volume will be of service to progressive policy-makers and that it will make a significant contribution to the debate. Our aim is to help create a fairer, more prosperous and stable economy that is of service to British society.

Patrick Allen
Suzanne J. Konzelmann
Jan Toporowski

1

Introduction

Patrick Allen

The UK economy is in crisis. As a result of the economic policies of recent decades, the lives of millions are insecure. Inequality and poverty in the United Kingdom have risen to levels not experienced since the 1930s. Growth has stuttered and productivity stagnated. Despite numerous promises and eye-catching headlines to "level up" and help those "just about managing", there has been no concerted economic policy to address the increasing gap in income and wealth in the country. Since 2016 the economy and politics have been paralysed as all other issues have been sidelined by Brexit negotiations, arguments and disagreements. When matters could not have got worse for the United Kingdom, the Covid-19 pandemic brought many sectors of the economy to a standstill.

Between February and August 2020 the lockdown of society to prevent the spread of the virus caused the economy to shrink by an unprecedented 17 per cent. At the same time, the government's furlough scheme, under which it assumed responsibility for 75 per cent of furloughed workers' wages, was implemented at a cost of £14 billion per month. The government has also lent substantial amounts to companies postponing their VAT and income tax payments. For the first time, people are being paid not to work, unlike unemployment benefit, when people are paid a far lower amount under the condition that they look for work.

The effect on government finances has been predictable. By November 2020 public debt had risen to £2,099 billion, or the equivalent of 99.5 per cent of GDP – a level not seen since 1961.

As the Covid-19 pandemic intensified towards the end of 2020 lockdowns were reintroduced and the furlough scheme extended, but this was too late to save many jobs. There were record redundancies, 370,000, from August to October 2020 and unemployment is expected to rise steadily as companies give up trading or reduce their workforce as a result of Covid-19.

Recovery to pre-pandemic levels is unlikely before the end of 2022, but the economy will also be affected by Brexit arrangements, which commenced on 1 January 2021. The Office for Budget Responsibility (OBR) expects that the effect of this relatively hard Brexit will be to reduce GDP by 4 per cent in the long run. Already businesses are struggling to adapt to the new barriers to trade with the European Union. Furthermore, the government has no detailed and credible plan to deal with the climate emergency, which has continued to grow unchecked while the government has been distracted by the immediate public health crisis and Brexit negotiations.

The revelations of Covid-19

The experience of the Covid-19 pandemic has laid bare many aspects of our society, exposing its shortcomings and failures as well as some resilience and triumphs.

Public services. Covid-19 has revealed the abject state of public health and other services. Ten years of austerity have left all public services severely underfunded, hollowed out and ill equipped to cope with the emergency. During the early stages of the pandemic the National Health Service (NHS) struggled with insufficient staff, beds, personal protective equipment (PPE) and ventilators. The pandemic has revealed just how reliant we are on the state to protect and look after us – as well as how inadequate the safety net of the shrunken welfare state has become.

The importance of key workers. The "Clap for Carers" initiative was indicative of our seemingly sudden realization that we rely on front-line workers – bus and train drivers, care workers, nurses and doctors – for our well-being and health. These workers, poorly appreciated and poorly rewarded in the past, have precarious and insecure jobs but they kept working during the pandemic even when it put their own lives at risk, because inadequate protective clothing and equipment meant that they were exposed to the virus, and many died while doing their jobs.

The spending power of the state. Just as in wartime, the pandemic demonstrated that the government can spend and borrow money to cover whatever is required to sustain the economy during a national emergency. This has been done without inflation or a collapse of the pound; and it has demonstrated that only the coordinated efforts and power of the state can save us at a time of war, global crash or pandemic.

Centralization, not local provision. As evident in the response of some local authorities and institutions, when global supply chains for critical medical equipment broke down, they are in the best position to assess local needs and deal with local pandemic hotspots and to implement effective track and trace measures. But they have for the most part been marginalized by central government, and sidelined in favour of private company solutions.

Privatization of key services. For ideological reasons, the government outsourced virus testing contracts worth millions to favoured private contractors, such as Serco and Deloitte, companies with no previous experience in public health. This was done without adequate scrutiny, tendering or transparency; and the results have been fragmented and dire in delivery. Tests have gone missing, results have been too slow, tracing poorly done. The Public Accounts Committee report in March 2021 found that NHS Track and Trace is budgeted to spend £37 billion by May 2022. The Chair Meg Hillier said "despite the unimaginable resources thrown at this project Test and Trace cannot point to a measurable difference to the progress of the pandemic". Experienced public health staff were sidelined; and, without any evidence, Public Health England (PHE) was blamed for failures in the pandemic response and replaced by the National Institute for Health Protection, whose new head has no experience in public health. Scotland has appeared to do rather better and launched its own contact-tracing app on 10 September 2020. Northern Ireland's StopCOVID NI became available in late July, using the same platform as the Republic of Ireland's app.

How did we get here?

Austerity is the immediate cause of the problems in the British economy. This was the chosen tool of the Conservative-led coalition government elected in 2010, headed by Prime Minister David Cameron and Chancellor of the Exchequer George Osborne, to deal with the aftermath of the 2008 crash. But our problems go back much further: to the ideology of neoliberalism, which has been the key force driving economic policy in the United Kingdom since 1979 – in effect, a long-running economic experiment.

To see how policy-makers got the drivers of our economy so wrong, it is essential to look back over the entire twentieth century to see where economic mistakes were made and what the consequences were, how economists learned from those mistakes and how, tragically, politicians came to make the same mistakes again.

During the 1920s and 1930s Western economies were weakened by stresses caused by debts incurred in the First World War and by the Versailles Treaty's punitive provisions against Germany. In the United States, an economic boom combined with wild speculation to produce the 1929 Wall Street crash, the Great Depression and high unemployment. Policy-makers applying the rules of classical economics sought to balance their budgets and cut spending in the depths of the recession. This was the first modern application of austerity, and it was an abject failure in all countries that tried it, including Britain, the United States, France, Germany, Sweden and Japan.

Austerity caused the stagnation of the UK economy for 20 years. It prevented a speedy recovery from the 1929 crash, leading to mass unemployment, poverty, political instability, extremism and – ultimately – war.

The economist John Maynard Keynes concluded that the lack of demand resulting from consumer and business uncertainty at a time of recession could be cured only by increasing government spending and investment, targeted at unemployment. This policy eventually turned around the US economy, under the New Deal of President Franklin Roosevelt, although it was spending on rearmament before the Second World War that finally ended the recession in both Britain and the United States.

From 1950 until 1979 economic policy in the United Kingdom, and the rest of the Western world, was influenced and shaped by the ideas of Keynes. Postwar politicians were determined to learn from the 1930s. The collective effort to win the war provided the conditions and support for a new economic framework. Henceforth full employment would be the target of macroeconomic policy, and government action was devoted to achieving it.

This policy was supported by a new international architecture, agreed at Bretton Woods in 1944, which created a system of exchange rates linked to the dollar, convertible to gold at a fixed rate, and transnational organizations such as the World Bank, the International Monetary Fund (IMF) and, later, the General Agreement on Tariffs and Trade. Governments in the United Kingdom and other Western countries actively managed their economies to maintain demand and keep unemployment low. There followed a period of unprecedented growth and stability, so successful that the quarter-century from 1951 to 1975 has been described as the "golden age" of economics.

Despite emerging from the war with the highest public debt in history, growing prosperity enabled the United Kingdom to create the modern welfare state and the NHS. Year on year the economy grew; and the debt to GDP ratio steadily declined. Unemployment was kept low, inflation was modest, there were no significant recessions and no financial crises. The British state was a major investor in the economy. It nationalized key industries, such as coal and the railways. Over 7 million workers were employed in the UK public sector by 1975, including 2 million in the nationalized industries and over 3 million in education, welfare and local government services. Unions played an active role in securing wage rises to match the increase in national income. Inequality fell dramatically at the same time as health and life expectation steadily improved.

The system came under strain during the late 1960s and early 1970s. Excess demand in the United States, fuelled by spending on the Great Society programme and the Vietnam War, spilled over, via the growth of the US trade deficit, into the rest of the Organisation for Economic Co-operation and Development (OECD) countries, leading to rising inflation. The United States was unable to maintain the dollar–gold peg, and in 1971 abandoned the fixed exchange rate mechanism of Bretton Woods. The quadrupling of oil prices in 1973/74 magnified inflation. Trade unions sought to protect the living standards of members, which led to industrial unrest and, in the United Kingdom, the "winter of discontent" in 1978/79, when low-paid public sector workers went on strike.

High inflation and the trade union action prepared the ground for a counter-attack based on the ideas of economists such as Friedrich Hayek, the principal influence on Margaret Thatcher, who became UK prime minister in 1979 and Ronald Reagan, who was elected president of the United States in 1980. Both had a similar plan.

On her election, Thatcher rapidly implemented the "neoliberal agenda", which championed free markets, deregulation, privatization of state assets, removal of higher-rate income taxes and the introduction of curbs on trade union activity. Keynesian economic management was abandoned and the target of economic policy shifted from unemployment to inflation. The state was seen to be a burden on free enterprise, so its role was to be diminished. Reagan did the same in the United States from 1981 onwards.

Interest rates were raised to drive out inflation. The resulting high exchange rate of sterling damaged the international competitiveness of UK manufacturing. Unemployment shot up to over 3 million as large swathes of industry were destroyed. The economy went into a self-inflicted recession, the deepest in UK industrial history, with a 20 per cent loss of manufacturing capacity and the destruction of 1.7 million manufacturing jobs, To this day, many parts of the country have never recovered from these losses. Between 1983 and 1991 more than 70 state-owned enterprises were privatized, including telecoms, water, gas, electricity and the railways.

Unemployment remained high for the remainder of the 1980s. But the loss of manufacturing was not mourned. Instead, services – especially financial services – were now the preferred drivers of the economy. High unemployment was explicitly used as a tool to control both trade union and working-class bargaining power and inflation. As Norman Lamont, the Chancellor of the Exchequer from 1990 to 1993, put it in a speech in the House of Commons in May 1991: "Rising unemployment and the recession have been the price that we have had to pay to get inflation down. That price is well worth paying."

This came at considerable social cost; and there was a dramatic rise in inequality and poverty, as wealth was diverted from wages to profits, and to the higher-paid and wealthy. Reforms to trade union law made it more difficult for unions to protect their members. The share of income going to the top 1 per cent returned to levels not seen since the 1930s.

It was claimed that wealth incentives with low taxes, and the unrestrained free market, would be a spur to growth, and that this would in turn "trickle down" to raise the income of the lower-paid. But all indicators during the period following 1979 were worse than during the Keynesian postwar period.

Some of the ill effects were mitigated by the New Labour government from 1997 to 2010, with increased public spending, tax credits and benefit improvements. But there was no challenge to the overall direction of a slimmed-down state, privatization, deregulation, increasing financialization and rising inequality.

Deregulation of the ever-increasing and powerful financial services sector was a contributory factor in the Global Financial Crisis of 2008, the worst global recession since 1929. A massive property bubble had been created by deregulated banks in the United States and Europe, driven by sub-prime lending and the sale of bundled mortgage derivatives. Many banks went bust and had to be rescued by their governments. The United Kingdom – with its large financial sector – was particularly badly affected. GDP dropped by more than 6 per cent between 2008 and 2009. It was a spectacular failure of the private sector.

The policies that had produced the 2008 crash should have been met with a new approach to policy. But Cameron and Osborne used the crisis to intensify the neoliberal agenda. They claimed that the deficit and rise in public debt that had followed the crash were attributable to excessive public spending. The reality is that they were consequences of the crash – and the government's rescue of financial institutions deemed "too big to fail".

Austerity, the failed policy of the 1930s, was reapplied. Public spending was cut, allegedly to reduce public debt and the deficit and achieve a long-held aim of Thatcher's heirs: to shrink the state still further.

Just as in the 1930s, the programme was damaging and futile. The economy stuttered, with the loss of many public sector jobs. The recovery from recession was the slowest in history and, instead of falling, public borrowing increased – from an amount equivalent to 65 per cent of GDP at the start of the austerity programme to 88 per cent in March 2020. At the same time, poverty, insecurity and inequality all increased, as the cuts in public services and benefits affected the poorest and most vulnerable. By contrast, in the United States there was a rapid recovery from the crash, thanks to the $787 billion stimulus programme introduced by President Barack Obama, despite the fact that the ambitious level of the programme was cut back by a misguided Republican-led Congress.

There has been no let-up in austerity since 2010. After ten years the long-term effects of the underfunding of local government, public services and infrastructure have been exposed by the pandemic.

Some of the effects were summed up by Professor Philip Alston, United Nations Special Rapporteur on extreme poverty and human rights, in November 2018:

> Libraries have closed in record numbers, community and youth centres have been shrunk and underfunded, public spaces and buildings including parks and recreation centres have been sold off. 14 million people, a fifth of the population, live in poverty. Four million of these are more than 50 per cent below the poverty line, and 1.5 million are destitute, unable to afford basic essentials. […] For almost one in every two children, to be poor in twenty-first century Britain is not just a disgrace, but a social calamity and an economic disaster, all rolled into one.

The UK record on the climate emergency

The world is facing its greatest ever collective challenge in the shape of climate change. The evidence for global warming is incontrovertible. The year 2019 was the 12th warmest year in a series from 1884. The world is about 1°C warmer than before widespread industrialization, according to the World Meteorological Organization (WMO). The 20 warmest years on record all occurred in the past 22 years, with 2015 to 2018 making up the top four. At the time of writing, September 2020 was the world's warmest month on record. Across the globe, the average sea level increased by 3.6mm per year between 2005 and 2015.

The United Kingdom desperately needs a cogent, effective and detailed climate change policy. The country will host the UN climate change conference, which commences on 1 November 2021. To have any credibility as an authority at these talks, the UK must have the best possible strategy on climate change to demonstrate global leadership on the issue. So far, rather than leading from the front, the government's policies have been vague and lacking in ambition.

The Committee on Climate Change (CCC), an independent statutory body established under the Climate Change Act 2008, heavily criticized the government in 2019. Lord Deben, the CCC chair, said: "The whole thing is run by the government like a *Dad's Army* operation … We can't go on with this ramshackle system … but the system is not fit for purpose, and doesn't begin to face the issues." Action to reduce greenhouse gas emissions lags far behind what is needed, even before the government set a tougher new target to cut pollution to zero overall by 2050. In May 2020 the Committee called on the Conservative government headed by Boris Johnson to take immediate steps "to support reskilling, retraining and research; to build a climate-resilient economy; to scale up housing retrofits and build new homes that are fit for the future; to invest in low-carbon, resilient infrastructure such as improved broadband instead of new roads; to make it easy for people to work remotely, walk and cycle and to expand tree planting, peatland restoration, green spaces and green infrastructure".

It is essential that all future UK economic policy embeds action to combat climate change and incentivizes companies to act.

What next?

As yet, there has been no convincing long-term plan to deal with the current economic crisis, although we can detect elements of a new strategy in the emergency. The March 2020 budget suggested the end of austerity, but with no plan to reverse the cuts of the last ten years. The spending taps were to be turned on, with some spending and infrastructure programmes. The government discovered the power of public spending to avert the worst of the pandemic but, even before the end is in sight, cuts and tax rises to pay for the increased debt are on the table for discussion. Nothing has been suggested to address the economic fallout from Brexit or the inequality, poverty and cuts to public services resulting from a decade of austerity. Nor are the recent announcements on an expansion of wind farms enough to deal with climate change. The government has not announced an enquiry into its handling of Covid-19 nor sought to explain why the United Kingdom has the highest death toll in Europe.

It is clear that we need to find a new, evidence-based consensus to rebuild our economy in the face of the combination of problems caused by neoliberalism, austerity, Covid-19, climate change and Brexit. Nothing less than a complete rethink of macroeconomic policy is required. To this end, PEF commissioned Council members and other experts to contribute essays that, together, provide a blueprint for a post-Covid, post-austerity, green economy that will correct the mistakes of the last 40 years and rebuild the economy on a better base.

Neoliberalism and the golden age compared

To guide future policy, it is essential to compare the years of neoliberalism with the golden age of the economy – and to learn the lessons that this comparison reveals.

The golden age was marked by steady growth, year on year. The government's commitment to full employment gave businesses the confidence to invest. There was great economic stability, an absence of financial crashes, no severe recessions. Unemployment remained low. Inflation was under control until the final years of the period, and then, due to a unique combination of factors, it increased. The level of national debt to GDP fell dramatically, wages steadily increased, investment by businesses was high. The welfare state and the NHS were developed and expanded during this period.

The golden age was by no means perfect. Policy suffered from "stop-go" interruptions and a worsening, constant pressure on the balance of payments and the level of sterling. But, for Britain, it represents a time when the economy was working for the good of society and not the other way around.

Under neoliberalism, the target of economic policy shifted from unemployment, economic stability and stable prices to the rate of inflation alone. Growth stuttered, although, overall, the trend was lower than during the golden age. Unemployment rose sharply and remained high; but this was considered useful in the battle against inflation, which during the 1970s was very high. It was later reduced, probably as a result of cheap money and inexpensive goods from China. There were recurring severe recessions, the most recent of which, in 2008 – the greatest financial crash since 1929 – we have yet to recover from.

During the golden age, national wealth was shared and inequality fell to an all-time low. Under neoliberalism, the sell-off of national assets, reduced taxes for the wealthy, reduced benefits and restrictions on trade unions led to wages falling as a share of national output and a massive rise in inequality.

The situation has worsened with austerity, to the point where life expectation is now falling for the first time in decades as a result of poverty and cuts in services for the poor, sick and vulnerable. The state safety net is no longer adequate to prevent hunger and destitution in our First World economy. The building of social housing has more or less ceased. Millions lead precarious lives of insecurity, near or below the breadline. Households living on wage levels that are inadequate to sustain a normal life are routinely topped up with debt. This situation is not sustainable – and it will lead to further economic instability. The neoliberal experiment has failed.

The lessons of the golden age are clear; and they confirm the insights of Keynes: that the free market on its own cannot reach equilibrium at full employment without active government management of demand. The state should therefore take the lead and actively pursue full employment policies, and regulate the private sector to bring this about. Government-managed fiscal and monetary policy should be directed away from fighting inflation to fighting stagnation.

The universally accepted law of economics is that saving equals investment. But because of uncertainty – and the fact that savers and investors are two different groups of people – the volume of private investment will normally be less than what the public would save at full employment. When this is the case, the state should spend what is required to make up the gap.

The reduction of inequality in society is essential, not just because of the harm it causes to the poor and vulnerable but because it impoverishes the whole of society. Excessive inequality reduces the purchasing power of workers and the middle class, whose spending is required to keep the economy growing and to generate employment. By contrast, wealthy people have a lower propensity to spend; instead, they save or use wealth for speculative purposes, which leads to a lack of demand and investment.

Control of inflation should not involve the maintenance of an army of unemployed workers on low benefits and the destruction of trade unions. However, inflation is not the current problem facing the economy, as the massive accumulation of savings and wealth has led to the lowest interest rates seen in decades and negative yields on government bonds.

Shrinking wages require people to go into debt to sustain their consumption levels, which is not sustainable in the long term. Eventually that debt has to be repaid, and spending has to cease to achieve this.

The key elements of our proposals are, therefore:

- the return of a strong, interventionist role for the state to manage, stabilize and direct the economy and achieve full employment;
- strategic plans for industry and regional development and infrastructure investment, assisted by a National Investment Bank;
- investment in high-quality services for healthcare, care and education in order to create jobs;
- universal provision of public services, to reduce poverty and improve physical and mental health and life expectation;
- strengthening of employment rights, common ownership and trade unions to ensure that workers share in the increasing prosperity of the nation;
- halting and in some cases reversing privatization of public goods and commons;
- regulation of companies so as to introduce a public purpose;
- redesign of the tax and welfare system to stabilize the economy, provide a safety net and assist in wealth redistribution;
- policies to target the reduction of inequality and poverty;
- control of inflation with fiscal and monetary policy, and a compact with representatives of labour; and
- all investment and economic activity to be based on rapidly decarbonizing the whole economy to tackle the underlying climate change emergency.

The essays are organized into five sections. In arguing for strong state intervention to manage the economy and public services, to reverse privatization and to reduce poverty by redistribution, the influence of Keynes can be seen throughout the contributions.

Foundations

The battle for ideas comes first; when it is won, we can turn to policy. This theme is developed by Robert Skidelsky, who, as the leading authority on Keynes, turns to his thought for clarification of the problem. Keynes (1973 [1936]: 372) wrote: "The outstanding faults of the economic society in which we live are its failure to provide for full employment and its arbitrary and inequitable distribution of wealth." The interventionist state will tackle both – spending public funds to reach and maintain full employment and redistributing the cake to reduce inequality.

Poverty and inequality lie at the heart of our health and social problems, as Kate Pickett and Richard Wilkinson have argued for some years. Substantially reducing inequality is a fundamental requirement for a progressive government's economic plan.

Geoff Tily sets out the roots of the current relationship of labour and capital in the international context, with a view to how resetting it is essential for the future well-being of society.

The public service sectors

The delivery of key public services – healthcare, social care, housing and education – is a fundamental task of the state. All have been run down by austerity and privatization.

Josh Ryan-Collins makes the case for housing to be a source of shelter and not a financial asset. First and foremost, housing must become a right for all citizens and not a means to securing wealth.

The pandemic has placed the NHS under severe strain. Allyson M. Pollock and Louisa Harding-Edgar examine how changes to the NHS and public health – its fragmentation and privatization, and the erosion of communicable disease control – contributed to the need to protect the NHS from collapse during the pandemic. The consequences of the lack of funding, understaffing and privatization have been made all the more apparent by the pandemic; and they need to be tackled to prevent unnecessary deaths now and in the future.

Susan Himmelweit explains how the privatized system delivers unsatisfactory social care by undertrained and badly treated workers. This contributed to the many deaths from Covid-19 in care homes. The task of transforming care into a high-quality universal system will not be easy; but it holds the promise of addressing many of the issues that plague society.

The United Kingdom squanders a high proportion of the funds for secondary education on the tiny minority of children who attend private schools. Danny Dorling shows that more equitable societies produce better educational outcomes, and argues for an end to the elitist system of private education that shuts the vast majority of young people out of a privileged education system.

Reform of corporate governance, industrial strategy and finance

A successful economy depends on businesses having a clear social purpose with long-term aims and a commitment to their workforce. In return, companies need to be able to rely on the state to provide the stable conditions that enable them to trade, the provision of enforceable law, healthy and well-educated workers, and infrastructure.

Will Hutton urges changes in company ownership rules and regulation in order to ensure that companies have a constitutionally entrenched purpose beyond making a profit.

The concept of corporate purpose and a UK industrial strategy is developed by Suzanne J. Konzelmann and Marc Fovargue-Davies. This has been largely absent from UK planning since 1979, as neoliberalism relies on the free market to allocate business activity. However, we know that government intervention can change results, as the efforts made to improve sport and our consequent Olympic achievements have demonstrated.

Craig Berry proposes a strengthened state-run defined contribution pension scheme that would take some of the risk from private pension provision and may be a more effective vehicle for green finance.

The United Kingdom also needs a National Investment Bank (NIB), to provide strategic direction, increase and channel investment to where it is needed and help the country out of the inevitable pandemic-induced recession. This proven policy is developed by Stephany Griffith-Jones.

Tackling poverty and inequality

British society has become increasingly impoverished since the advent of neoliberalism. The sell-off of national assets and the privatization of infrastructure and utilities has had long-term costs for consumers in the United Kingdom. It is well known that it is more expensive to be poor; and, with increasingly precarious and low-paid jobs, most working families have little choice but to turn to exploitative debt mechanisms to keep a roof over their heads and food on the table.

Guy Standing examines the consequences of the privatization of commonly owned assets. He argues for a Charter of the Commons and a mechanism to compensate commoners for the illegitimate acquisition of the commons via enclosure.

An effective anti-poverty and pro-equality strategy aimed at sharing the rising pool of wealth more equally could involve wealth taxation, and the creation of a Citizens' Wealth Fund, according to Stewart Lansley. This is a strategy that has proved successful in Norway through its sovereign wealth fund.

Burgeoning personal debt is a ticking time bomb in the UK economy. Johnna Montgomerie makes the case for measures to provide debt relief for households that are struggling with debt repayments as a result of the pandemic. The government has been willing to pay billions to bail out banks; but debt relief for consumers has been conspicuously missing. In generating a general uplift in the economy, reducing the debt overhang will facilitate economic stability and avoid another cycle of boom, bust, bailout and austerity.

The United Kingdom also needs a more effective system for social security. Millions of people fall through the patchy safety net that exists at present. Lansley proposes a non-means-tested income floor to boost the incomes of the poorest families, which would cut child poverty by more than a third and working-age poverty by over a fifth, reducing inequality and strengthening universalism.

A progressive recovery

Globalism is the problem for our age. Ann Pettifor looks critically at how it has to be reformed if the international financial system, future pandemics and climate change are to be stabilized. The climate emergency requires that the UK economy be decarbonized rapidly.

Many are worried about how the cost of Covid-19 will be paid back. The need to support consumption through furloughing, welfare payments and medical expenditure has raised public borrowing to an unprecedented level. Increasing taxes and/or cutting expenditure when the pandemic is back under control will undoubtedly hobble the economic recovery. We need to learn the lessons of the austerity following the financial crisis, which choked off growth and led to increasing hardship and suffering in our communities.

Jan Toporowski and Robert Calvert Jump suggest that the government could finance the cost of the crisis by issuing long-term bonds. Once the recovery is assured, any primary surplus required to stabilize the ratio of debt to GDP could be achieved by taxes on wealth and profits.

Jo Michell presents the arguments for rationalizing the tax system, with moderate increases in tax rates on higher incomes and the institution of a proper wealth tax. Above all, a Labour government needs to reverse the "race to the bottom" in corporate tax rates. Such tax increases will not disadvantage business enterprise, since tax revenue that finances government expenditure will, through that expenditure, find its way back into business coffers.

What will a progressive recovery look like? Toporowski argues that is not enough to pursue a programme of public works that draw in labour surpluses from eastern and southern Europe. A better way to create domestic employment is through the provision and extension of high-quality public services and training for the public sector jobs that the country needs.

Conclusion

In short, what is required for the United Kingdom to recover and reinvent itself in the twenty-first century is for the state to return to its role as manager of the economy. It needs to control demand, target full employment and achieve a rapid reduction of social inequality. A minimal state, with an economy driven by incentives for the wealthy, has to come to an end if we are to save lives and deliver an economy that works for everyone. It is only the coordinated power and wealth of the state that has enabled us to survive the health and economic ravages caused by the pandemic. Only the state has the power and authority to direct funds, to secure full employment and to provide the environment for a stable economy in which citizens and business can thrive.

The state is powerful, democratic, transparent and subject to oversight by Parliament. It has massive resources at its disposal and is the single most effective delivery mechanism for the public good. Private enterprise, by contrast, is profit- and rent-seeking and engineered for private gain. The private sector inevitably exploits government contracts to its own advantage, without considering the public good unless forced to by regulation.

Our hope is that this book of ideas will provide a starting point for debate. There is already much consensus in progressive circles as to what we need to do to mend the economy. The challenge is to find a government to adopt them.

The problems are immense. The 2007–09 financial crisis was avoidable and austerity unnecessary. The Covid-19 crisis was unforeseen. But, even here, our response has been poor compared to our international neighbours' – and involved yet another attempt to find private rather than state and local authority solutions.

We want future governments to adopt pragmatic policies that work. We need to banish the binary of private enterprise as an unalloyed good and state involvement as necessarily bad.

Let the debate start, and let us move swiftly to the implementation of policies that set our economy to rights, provide happiness, security, good health and prosperity for all and preserve our planet.

Further reading

Ainsley, S. 2018. *The New Working Class: How to Win Hearts, Minds and Votes*. Bristol: Policy Press.

Alston, P. 2018. "Statement on visit to the United Kingdom, by Professor Philip Alston, United Nations Special Rapporteur on extreme poverty and human rights". Office of the United Nations High Commissioner for Human Rights, 16 November. Available at: www.ohchr.org/en/NewsEvents/Pages/DisplayNews.aspx?NewsID=23881.

Coates, D. 2018. *Flawed Capitalism: The Anglo-American Condition and Its Resolution*. Newcastle upon Tyne: Agenda Publishing.

Keynes, J. 1973 [1936]. *The Collected Writings of John Maynard Keynes*, vol. 7, *The General Theory of Employment, Interest and Money*, D. Moggridge (ed.). London: Macmillan.

Konzelmann, S. 2019. *Austerity*. Cambridge: Polity Press.
Lansley, S. & J. Mack 2015. *Breadline Britain: The Rise of Mass Poverty*. London: Oneworld.
Skidelsky, R. 2019. *Money and Government: A Challenge to Mainstream Economics*. London: Penguin.
Wilkinson, R. & K. Pickett 2009. *The Spirit Level: Why More Equal Societies Almost Always Do Better*. London: Allen Lane.

PART I

FOUNDATIONS

2

Rentier capitalism: the role of finance in the macroeconomy

Robert Skidelsky

The battle for post-Covid-19 economic policy has to be won at the intellectual level before it can be won at the political level. Ideas always come first: intelligence can tame power. If there are no persuasive new ideas, politics will simply recycle the ideas of those who last had ideas. This recycling is in full swing.

The last set of ideas in economic policy were those associated with those of the rational expectations and monetarist schools, slightly modified by "new Keynesianism". From this mix of value and monetary theory came the proposition – rooted in Léon Walras and David Hume – that market economies are spontaneously self-adjusting to a full employment equilibrium provided money is kept in order. No fiscal policy is required to balance the economy's books. All government needed to do in the way of macropolicy was to set independent central banks inflation targets, leaving them free to choose appropriate bank rates.

It may be objected that, since 2008, policy has been nothing like this. Emergency measures have been applied twice: in the immediate aftermath of the banking collapse of 2008/9 and to offset the partial lockdown of the economy in 2020. But one can think of these events as exceptions to the rules, too rare to justify dynamiting the theory of the self-regulating market. As US economist Robert Lucas remarked in 2009, "I guess everyone is a Keynesian in the foxhole." In the foxhole – but not out of it: Keynes was for emergencies only.

We have the same reaction today. Impelled to close down 30 per cent of their economies to stop the spread of the coronavirus, governments have spent money freely, to support businesses and pay wages. They hope that, as the economy, reopens a V-shaped recovery will relieve them of their fiscal burden. This will not happen. To understand why, we need to start in a different place; that is, with Keynes.

Keynes's theory

For Keynes, "[t]he outstanding faults of the economic society in which we live are its failure to provide for full employment and its arbitrary and inequitable distribution of wealth and incomes". His theory dealt with the first failure, in the 1930s. Economies, he argued, have no spontaneous tendency to full employment. Faced with a severe shock, output and employment will keep falling till the growing poverty of the community reduces saving to the reduced amount people want to invest. At this point economies will settle down to an inferior equilibrium, marked by persisting underemployment. For government to increase its saving (cutting its budget deficit) while firms and households are increasing their saving (refraining from spending) will only deepen the downturn. It took a well-trained economist to believe that the way out of a slump was to stop everyone consuming. Rather, increased private saving must be offset by increased public spending. Increased public spending does not "crowd out" resources being used by private firms; it "crowds in" resources that are otherwise idle.

The demand-side analysis of Keynes's *General Theory* was independent of distribution. But Keynes hinted at two ways in which "arbitrary and inequitable" distribution contributed to the problem of deficient demand.

First, wealth stimulated "oversaving", because the wealthier society is the more likely will be its marginal propensity to save. Orthodox theory encouraged saving in order to increase investment, whereas his own theory suggested that it was an increase in consumption that was most favourable to investment. A "second, much more fundamental inference" from his argument is "our theory of the rate of interest". The *rentier* aspect of capitalism led to a rate of interest too high to secure continuous full employment. Just as the old landed class live off the rent of land, the new rentier class live off the rent of money. Their interest was to keep this rent as high as possible; the business interest was to keep it as low as possible. This was Keynes's "class struggle", and he used the term "rentier" with a full sense of the history behind it.

The conflict between those who lend and those who borrow money is the earliest class struggle. It long preceded the capitalist–worker struggle, and later coexisted with, and cut across, Karl Marx's theory. In the nineteenth century rentier power operated through the gold standard and control of government budgets. The gold standard determined interest rates and demanded a budget balanced at the lowest possible level of spending and taxes to make gold reserves credible. However, the rentier–business, creditor–debtor conflict was subdued in the nineteenth century, because investment opportunities were so large in Europe's expanding overseas markets. Besides, British control of the gold standard kept British and global interest rates low. The rentier got 3 per cent and the businessman 5 per cent, and everyone was happy (except agricultural workers, who took ship for the New World).

The large fluctuations of prices and exchange rates that accompanied and followed the First World War shattered the Antonine stability of the Victorian age. Debtors were temporarily in the ascendant, but the creditor class regained control by enforcing a return to the gold standard and the balanced budget rule. In the United Kingdom this came at the cost of the unemployment of 10 per cent of insured workers in the 1920s. Moreover, the misaligned exchange rates of the restored gold standard made the conflict between creditor and debtors worldwide, as some countries ran unyielding current account surpluses and others persistent current account deficits.

Keynes's three theoretical books of the interwar years – *A Tract on Monetary Reform* (1923), *A Treatise on Money* (1930) and *The General Theory of Employment, Interest and Money* (1936) – were an attempt to give analytic shape to this disastrous concatenation of events. In the first, he was mainly concerned with how deflation favours the rentier and hurts the businessman: "It is worse, in an impoverished world, to provoke unemployment than to disappoint the *rentier*."

The story in the *Treatise* was that a shock to investor confidence triggers a redistribution of wealth within the ownership class from the borrowers to the lenders, causing interest rates to rise rather than fall. This, in turn, causes prices and output to fall rather than recover, slowing down the growth of wealth.

In the *General Theory*, the "speculative demand for money" was firmly established as the central explanation of why slumps persist and remedial action by the state is needed. It is this "speculative demand" that prevents interest rates from falling to adjust the volume of saving to a fall in the marginal efficiency of capital. Put crudely, the rentier demanding 5 per cent for the rent of money and the businessman expecting a 3 per cent return on a long-term investment made producers, owners and workers unhappy. "The rate of interest which will allow a reasonable average of employment is one so unacceptable to wealth-owners that it cannot be readily established merely by manipulating the quantity of money." This speaks directly to our recent situation, when large "injections" of central bank money after 2008 failed to revive economies in face of increased "liquidity preference".

Keynes's nationalism

In the interwar years the conflict between business and "usury" arose between countries, with "hoarders" being those countries that did not apply their export surpluses to raising consumption at home or investing them abroad, but "hoarded" them in their central banks, imposing deflation and unemployment on the deficit countries, and eventually on themselves. As Keynes pointed out in 1941: "The process of adjustment is *compulsory* for the debtor and *voluntary* for the creditor. If the creditor does not choose to make, or allow, his share of adjustment he suffers no inconvenience ... The *debtor* must borrow; the creditor is under no ... compulsion [to lend]." Keynes's economics took a nationalistic turn in the troubled interwar years. In his *Tract on Monetary Reform* (1923) he called for "managed" national currencies. In "The Economic Consequences of Mr Churchill" (1925) Keynes attacked Britain's return to the gold standard at the prewar parity as a policy forced on society from the "top tier", oblivious to the social breakages it caused. In his *Treatise on Money* he argued that to allow fluid capital in a system rigid in other respects was "dangerous". In his essay "National Self-Sufficiency" he concluded: "Let goods be homespun whenever it is reasonably and conveniently possible; and, above all, let finance be primarily national." A floating exchange rate, Keynes still insisted in 1936, was the necessary condition of an expansionary domestic fiscal and monetary policy.

Keynes's turn to economic nationalism was a "second best" policy in a world in which international agreement to regulate money and trade had become impossible. He hoped for a reformed global monetary system, and drew up schemes for an "ideal" currency system under supranational management. However, his argument for greater national self-sufficiency was based not just on the absence of a feasible alternative but also on the positive benefits of a "complete" national life, which allowed people to display the full range of their skills and traditional ways of living.

The historical frame in which this analytic progression made sense arose once investment had not simply started to be financed by bank loans to customers or by reinvested profits but had come to rely on a disaggregated financial system. It became important to distinguish between two forms of capital: physical goods and money. In "real" theory, capital consists of physical capital (factories, offices, machines, tools) used to produce goods and services. Saving was originally thought of as stocks of such productive instruments. It made no difference if they were stocks of money committed to purchase such instruments.

But either money can be used to buy "machines" or it can be kept liquid. By virtue of their demand for liquidity, the rentier class had come to control interest rates. But the scarcity of money they created was not a *real* scarcity. Keynes observed that "our desire to hold wealth in liquid form [rather than investing it in physical assets] is a barometer of the degree of distrust of our calculations and conventions concerning the future".

Keynes's identification of financial power – the power to keep money scarce – as *the* flaw of contemporary capitalism neatly sidesteps the question (not to mention justice) of the distribution between the two "factors of production", capital and labour. In the Hobsonian/Marxist underconsumptionist theory, it is the maldistribution of wealth and income that leads to the "overinvestment" of physical capital, producing periodic crises of "realization". In the Keynesian system, the power of finance leads to capitalist crisis by keeping the rate of interest too high for full employment investment.

Keynes's policy conclusion was not to redistribute wealth and incomes from capitalists to workers but from rentiers to producers and consumers. Expansionary monetary policy designed to keep interest rates low and capital accumulation high would lead, in a generation or so, to the "euthanasia of the rentier".

The Keynesian revolution between 1945 and 1975 was an assertion of producer power over rentier power, debtor power over creditor power. Policy should not aim primarily to control the value of money but to secure full employment production. Inflation was a lesser evil than deflation. In the nationalist economics of the 1930s, international finance was severely repressed. The Bretton Woods system constrained the power of international finance to derail production by capital controls. But conditions for international trade were preserved, with the *Pax America* replacing the nineteenth-century *Pax Britannica*. However, with full employment, the working class started to gain at the expense of the business class, suggesting that the Hobsonian/Marxist analysis of capitalist crisis had always been more fundamental than the Keynesian one.

The two stories: finance and income inequality

The contemporary interest in unequal distribution starts with the polarization of income shares over the last 40 years. Wage shares in GDP have been falling across Europe and Japan, to a lesser extent in the United States and United Kingdom, which have, though, seen a big increase in the inequality of personal income. Median weekly wages in the United States grew a mere 2.8 per cent from 1980 to 2005; the bottom quartile fell by 3.1 per cent while the top 10 per cent increased by 21 per cent. (Engelbert Stockhammer points out that, if exorbitant management salaries in the United States and United Kingdom are considered as profits rather than wages, the wage share has declined equally across the developed world; see Stockhammer 2009.)

Growing inequality is correlated with declining macroeconomic performance. All the indicators suggest that the Keynesian era of managed capitalism was more successful for Western countries than the succeeding era of liberated capitalism. Given the importance of growing inequality, the difficulty is how to relate it to the simultaneous spread of globalization. Put simply, the question is: did inequality cause globalization or did globalization cause inequality? The policy response we favour depends very much on the answer we give to this question, even though there can be no simple answer.

The two main, sometimes competing, partly overlapping, explanations of income polarization have been new technology and globalization.

Paul Krugman has pointed out that, until the 1980s, productivity gains were matched by income gains (see Krugman 2013). Improvements in efficiency made possible the employment of a growing workforce at rising real wages. This no longer happens. Since the 1980s real wages have stagnated while profits have grown. Krugman has rejected globalization as the cause of stagnant wages. The offshoring of jobs has not been on anything near a sufficiently large scale to explain the observed effect of declining wages and/or rising unemployment: the cause is too small for the effect. His explanation is that recent technological change has raised the premium paid to highly skilled workers relative to the wages of the less skilled. This technologically driven shift in the demand for labour "has been a key cause of the growth of earnings inequality in the United States as well as much of the rise in unemployment in Europe". However, in the long run technology will devalue the work of "symbolic analysts" and favour talents common to all humans. This means that growing inequality is a passing phase that no deliberate changes in the distributional structure of capitalism are called for.

There are two gaps in Krugman's account. First, he fails to link up his story of technologically driven inequality with short-run failures of demand. There appear to be no crises of capitalism en route to the "golden age of equality" that is to come. Second, Krugman ignores the institutional context of technological innovation. Following mainstream growth theory, he treats technology as exogenous. He does not explain why these particular new technologies appeared at this particular time. But technological innovation may be, and usually is, an endogenous response to a growing shortage of labour relative to capital.

The other explanation for growing inequality lies in the liberation of finance from national controls. Inequality fell in all countries from the 1950s to the 1970s, when finance was repressed; it then increased between the 1980s and 2000. The explosion of "global finance" preceded the technological innovations highlighted by Krugman. The way to address inequality effectively, argues James K. Galbraith, "is to bring the forces of financial instability, debt peonage, and predatory austerity under control". The growth of inequality is tied to the most unstable and unsustainable element of the world system, which is global finance. The capacity to reduce macroeconomic shocks and inequality jointly "depends on the capacity of insulation from external financial pressures".

However, this story needs to explain the explosion of global finance. Why was the financial system progressively unshackled from national controls from the 1980s onwards?

The explosions of technological innovation and of international finance can be seen as an employer response to a trade union wage push in conditions of full employment. Put simply, employers started to cut labour costs by restructuring companies, replacing human workers by machines and offshoring production. A legislated emasculation of trade union influence over wages and conditions was a necessary part of the employer offensive. These institutional changes seem a more potent explanation of labour's failure to capture recent gains in productivity than the special premium attaching to highly skilled labour.

Technological innovation and globalization are twin responses to the crisis of profitability of the full employment Keynesian economy in the 1970s, both aiming to restore a "reserve army" of the unemployed or low-waged. However, in solving the crisis of profitability, the business class were faced with the crisis of "realization" – their inability to sell the goods they were producing. "Financialization" was their response: consumption was kept up by means of increased access to credit, resulting in the pile-up of debt. But this, in turn, made the system increasingly vulnerable to financial crises. According to Stockhammer, we now have a "finance-dominated accumulation regime that is one of *slow* and *fragile* accumulation" (Stockhammer 2009: 15, emphasis in original).

What is financialization?

The Marxist theory of finance capitalism deals with the process of the private monopolization of the means of production, not with the diversion of productive activities to financial intermediation. For example, Rudolf Hilferding contrasted monopolistic capital with the competitive and buccaneering capitalism of the previous liberal era. The unification of mercantile and banking interests reflected the investment by European banks in manufacturing industry. Socialism was an inevitable outcome of private monopolization. Once "finance capital" had brought the most important branches of industry under its control, the state did not need to expropriate thousands of firms or peasant holdings but only to seize a few giants to gain control over the means of production. In short, capitalism was making itself riper for plucking. Vladimir Lenin took over this idea in his pamphlet *Imperialism: The Highest Stage of Capitalism*.

In contrast, modern analysts mean by the "financialization of the economy" the increasing salience of its financial sector, and financial innovation as the preferred type of innovation. Mainstream economists regard financialization benevolently. They argue that the more liquid financial markets are, the more efficiently they will allocate capital. Financial instruments are developed to accommodate an increasing variety of risk and risk preferences. According to the IMF: "The dispersion of credit risk by banks to a broader and more diverse group of investors, rather than warehousing such risk on their balance sheet, has helped make the banking and overall financial system more resilient" (IMF 2006: 51).

But the future is inherently uncertain. In Keynes's view, no objective probability distribution of future outcomes exists, so many risks cannot be correctly priced. Consequently, the financial sector is a potent source of instability. One result of financial liberalization has been a very steep increase in the relative scale of financial activities within the economy (what Adair Turner calls "financial intensity") and a big increase in financial sector remuneration – one of the main drivers of inequality. Studies show a disproportionate increase in both financial employment and the rewards accruing to it. Turner argues that the mainstream case ignores the power of the financial sector to extract distributive rents from the rest of the economy. Krugman's skill premium is increasingly reserved not for industrial skills but for highly paid and skilled people engaged in a "zero-sum distributive" struggle for ever higher financial rewards.

In a financialized economy, capital is increasingly allocated through financial markets. Mechanisms such as securitization (turning debts into marketable securities) feed housing bubbles by converting mortgage debt into tradeable instruments, thus creating an inverted pyramid of debt on a narrow base of real assets. The orientation towards maximizing shareholder value has encouraged outsourcing and corporate disaggregation while increasing compensation at the top. Financialization has also shaped patterns of culture and social change in the broader society; making money rather than making things is the name of the game.

An account of capitalism's recent history would start with the crisis of profitability that struck the Western economies in the 1970s, the resulting rise in inflation as firms attempted to "pass on" the rise in costs to the state's money-printing machine and the failed attempts to contain inflation by "incomes policies": imposing or negotiating wage and price controls.

The Thatcher/Reagan revolutions of the 1980s, with their supporting economic doctrine of the naturally self-adjusting market, can be seen as attempts to restore business profitability by weakening the power of organized labour. The main prongs of the attack were abandoning the full employment commitment domestically (recreating the "reserve army of the unemployed"); freeing capital to create production facilities in cheaper-labour locations abroad; and importing cheap labour from abroad – all three exerting downward pressure on domestic wages. However, the compression of the wage share reduces consumption, and, with it, the demand for final goods. This leads to a "search for yield" through financial innovation. Financialization, apart from being a major new source of profit, has facilitated the financing of aggregate demand through consumer debt, including mortgages, credit cards and overdraft bank accounts. This led to a big increase in household debt ratios.

Financial liberalization has also allowed some countries to sustain current account deficits at higher levels, and for longer, than previously. But the capital inflows that finance their trade deficits may be abruptly halted or reversed, causing severe crises, as happened in East Asia in 1997/98.

To sum up: the old dynamic of class conflict has morphed into a new dynamic of creditor–debtor conflict, domestically and internationally, with debt bondage replacing wage bondage as the point of tension. With the drying up of older sources of productivity growth in manufacturing, profitability has become increasingly dependent on financial innovation. As a result, economies have become more fragile, more prone to crashes and subject to populist revolts against the "power of finance".

Today

Keynes wrote in 1933, "The decadent but individualistic capitalism [of today] is not a success. It is not intelligent, it is not beautiful, it is not just, it is not virtuous – and it doesn't deliver the goods … But when we wonder what to put in its place, we are extremely perplexed." This perplexity has returned, and bedevils all radical discussion. The political left vehemently rejects the nationalist road, briefly espoused by Keynes, and argues for the restructuring of the global economy on labour's terms (see Geoff Tily, Chapter 4 in this volume). But it is notably short of proposals on how this can be done. The obstacle, which it persistently fails to address, is that, while economics may be global, political legitimacy is national. This is why, when the international system ceases to "deliver the goods", the natural response is economic nationalism.

Keynes's failure to get his 1941 proposal for an International Clearing Union accepted by the United States is a cautionary tale. Keynes proposed to tackle the problem of creditor country "hoarding" by imposing penalties on countries running persistent current account surpluses, and, in extreme cases, transferring the surpluses to the accounts of the deficit countries. The Americans, predictably, rejected this attempt to limit their accumulation and use of foreign currency reserves, and the Bretton Woods system was set up in 1944 without any provision for creditor adjustment.

The fact that, nonetheless, the post-1945 international system was so much more successful than the non-system of the interwar years is attributable not to the Bretton Woods agreement but to the *Pax America*. The United States was able and willing to act as a surrogate economic (and, to some extent, political) government of the "free" world, its role legitimized both by its power and prestige and by perception of a common communist threat. The collapse of the Bretton Woods world of fixed but flexible exchange rates can be explained by the technical problem of the dollar glut. But its root cause was the emergence of a more plural power constellation, whose counterpart was the declining willingness and ability of the United States to take on hegemonic responsibilities. This is the current situation. The future of the global monetary and trading system, for good or ill, will depend on the relationship between the United States and China, the two truly sovereign states in today's world, with Europe having little impact on the outcome.

The reason for Europe's weakness is that the European Union is a giant economy but a pigmy sovereign. Its fundamental flaw, universally recognized, but so far unattended, is that it limits the economic autonomy of its members without replacing it with a Europe-wide system of economic and political governance. It cannot do so, because no European government exists able to take on Keynesian managerial functions. The construction of the Union, and especially of the eurozone, was tied to belief – or hope – in a self-regulating market, governed only by a common set of rules, and with no foreign policy to speak of. The European Union's responses to the 2008/9 and the current Covid-19 crises were emergency reactions, in violation of its own rules. But it is hard to see how the Union can change its rules without challenging the nation state's monopoly of political accountability.

This leaves the nation state. There is much that a British government can do to improve the welfare of British people without breaking international agreements.

First, a government genuinely committed to a "northern powerhouse" should ensure that money flowed north rather than south or out, or not at all. It should find a way of mobilizing the "hoards" of the banking system to invest in infrastructure and housing, especially in the "green" aspects of both. There are numerous historical examples of state or quasi-state vehicles through which such channelling of money could be done. Typically, they start successfully and then deteriorate as politics take over. They need a broad mandate that reflects an accepted national purpose, while insulating their commercial decisions from political meddling. This is easier said than done. But we should give the matter constructive thought, rather than surrender to deflationary first principles.

Second, the state should make itself responsible for all procurement policy that affects the health and security of society. The pandemic has exposed vulnerability to global supply chains, which might be cut off. As much as possible of what a nation's citizens *need* should be produced at home. The principle of any public procurement policy should be "just in case" rather than "just in time".

A third step would be to stabilize the economy by a public sector job guarantee. This would constitute a labour buffer stock, which would expand and deplete with the state of the private demand for jobs. It is the modern way of realizing the full employment commitment of postwar Keynesian governments.

Fourth, we should recognize the strength of the underconsumptionist argument that maintaining a high level of aggregate demand is easier with a more equal distribution of wealth and income. This means forgoing the expedient of keeping up consumption by means of a continuous expansion of private debt, which inevitably leads to crashes.

There is a large social democratic agenda here, which is a natural complement to Keynesian demand management.

Finally, governments need to reduce their dependence on international credit markets. It is not enough to be able to offset capital flight by quantitative easing. A state must have the power to limit what Keynes called "financial circulation", domestically and internationally.

To sum up: governments should follow a dual strategy. They should actively pursue the widest possible international agreement to make the global economy safe for their citizens, while at the same time taking all feasible national steps to secure their welfare. The case for domestic priorities at the present time is clear enough. In the absence of a regional or world government, national governments alone have responsibility for the welfare of their citizens. Experience has shown that they cannot safely outsource this responsibility to the financial system.

Further reading

Galbraith, J. 2019. "The unsustainability of inequality". Project Syndicate, 23 August.

IMF 2006. *Global Financial Stability Report April 2006: Market Developments and Issues*. Washington, DC: International Monetary Fund.

Krugman, P. 2013. *Exchange-Rate Instability*. Cambridge, MA: MIT Press.

Skidelsky, R. 2012. "Review of Turner, *Does Economic Growth Make You Happy?*" *Times Literary Supplement*, 27 September.

Skidelsky, R. 2019. "How to achieve shorter working hours". London: Progressive Economic Forum.

Skidelsky, R., F. Martin & C. Westerlind-Wigstrom 2012. "Blueprint for a British Investment Bank". London: Centre for Global Studies.

Stockhammer, E. 2009. "The finance-dominated accumulation regime, income distribution and the present crisis", Department of Economics Working Paper 127. Vienna: Vienna University of Economics and Business.

Turner, A. 2018. "The zero sum economy". Project Syndicate, 15 August.

3

Post-pandemic health and well-being: putting equality at the heart of recovery

Kate Pickett and Richard Wilkinson

As epidemiologists researching the social determinants of health and well-being, we study the impact of inequalities in income on physical and mental health, human development and social relationships. A very small silver lining to the coronavirus pandemic is that more people – and, crucially, more politicians and policy-makers – now understand the importance of epidemiology – i.e. the study of the distribution and determinants of health, and of public health research and practice. And, although it is the infectious disease epidemiologists and modellers who guided the government's immediate response to the onset of the pandemic, social epidemiology is critical to understanding the stark inequalities in health and well-being revealed by Covid-19 and the longer-term impacts of the responses, including lockdowns, recessions and depressions. Socio-economic and ethnic inequalities have shaped the demographics of Covid-19 and the severity of illness and mortality in different groups, a perspective also sharpened amid the pandemic by the Black Lives Matter movement. Rapidly rising rates of mental illness and of insecurities of income, employment, food and housing urgently highlight the need for routes to an inclusive recovery that could lead us to a much better new "normal". More equal societies have weathered the storm better, benefiting from levels of trust and solidarity that have heightened resilience, whereas more unequal and authoritarian societies have suffered more illness and death. Equality really is at the heart of the matter.

Economic inequality, and its intersection with inequalities related to ethnicity, gender, disability, language, religion and more, is not just a health issue, of course. All the problems that are more common at the bottom of society, revealing a social gradient, get worse with greater inequality. In addition to shorter life expectancy, higher death rates and levels of chronic disease, increased obesity, mental illness and poor child well-being, more unequal societies suffer from more violence, including homicides, domestic violence, child maltreatment and bullying. Children and young people do less well in school and have lower chances of social mobility and higher rates of dropping out and teenage births. Drug and alcohol abuse, gambling, status consumption and consumerism also rise with inequality, while civic and cultural participation decline. Social comparisons become toxic, status anxieties increase and some go under with depression and anxiety, whereas others respond with self-enhancing narcissism. Societies that tend to do well on any one of these measures tend to do well on all of them, and the ones that do badly do badly on most or all of them. Inequality has always been regarded as divisive and socially corrosive; and for some time now the data have shown not only these wide-ranging effects but also that differences between countries are large, that even small differences in the amount of inequality matter and that, although the poor are affected the worst, inequality affects almost everybody.

Our vision for change, then, is that central and local government policy recognize the criticality of greater equality for better population health, better life chances for children, higher-quality social relationships and engagement in civil life and greater collective efficacy for a better quality of life for all. There are other cases to be made for greater socio-economic equality – a moral case, a business case and a sustainability case – but, as we write in the midst of a pandemic, well-being and quality of life feel paramount. Stark inequalities in deaths and disease existed before Covid-19, and they have been ignored and exacerbated by the Conservative and coalition governments. Worldwide, we were already in the middle of other inequality-related pandemics of diseases related to air pollution, climate change, obesity and depression. If we are going to take the lessons of Covid-19 to heart, we need to get serious about reducing inequality.

And how do we do that?

Here we outline six policy proposals, which would go a long way towards realizing the vision of a more equal society.

Enact the socio-economic duty of the 2010 Equality Act. UK governments already have a powerful potential tool that they could use to reduce inequality: the socio-economic duty, section 1 of the Equality

Act 2010. The Act has been brought into law, but the socio-economic duty has not. It imposes a duty on any public sector body, to the effect that it "must, when making decisions of a strategic nature about how to exercise its functions, have due regard to the desirability of exercising them in a way that is designed to reduce the inequalities of outcome which result from socio-economic disadvantage". Section 1 requires public bodies to adopt transparent and effective measures to address the inequalities that result from differences in occupation, education, place of residence or social class. Passed by the last Labour government in 2010, the succeeding coalition and Conservative governments have refused to enact section 1 as law, despite the recommendation of the United Nations Committee on Economic, Social and Cultural Rights that it should do so. Other UK policy-makers have been bolder: in 2018 the Scottish Parliament enacted the Fairer Scotland Duty, the name given to the socio-economic duty in Scotland. The Welsh government, after a period of consultation, had planned to enact the socio-economic duty in September 2020, but this was postponed, because of the coronavirus crisis, to March 2021. The Welsh government sees the duty as a key mechanism for an inclusive recovery from Covid-19. Some local authorities in England have adopted aspects of the duty, including Newcastle City Council, which decided to act as if the duty was already in force, and Oldham City Council, which developed equality impact assessments. As the 2010 Equality Act is already enshrined in law, any new government could exercise its power to introduce the socio-economic duty (section 1) on day one – a powerful symbol of intent to create a more equal society.

Tackle wealth and top incomes with financial transaction taxes, wealth taxes and progressive income taxes, and boost low incomes with a universal basic income and a proper living wage. Other chapters in this volume are very relevant to this proposal. Stewart Lansley (Chapter 16) describes how a basic income floor strengthens social protection in fragile times, empowers citizens and creates well-being. Here we focus on why it is important to tackle both the top and bottom ends of the income and wealth distributions simultaneously to create public sanction for radical reforms.

If progressives want to counteract the anger that has been fuelling right-wing populism, and gain support for the changes needed to realize their vision of a socially just and equal society, they need to convince citizens that they will no longer be left behind, excluded or voiceless. Because greater equality is so enabling for social solidarity, it has been prioritized when governments need to get people to pull together in difficult circumstances. Pioneering social researcher Richard Titmuss described after the Second World War how the public cooperation needed for the war effort was fostered deliberately by the introduction of egalitarian policies. Income differences were reduced by taxation, essentials were subsidized, luxuries taxed and food and clothing were rationed. An example of how perceived injustice can block the introduction of sustainability policies comes from France, where the *gilets jaunes* protested against a proposal for an additional tax on petrol after years of increasing discontent with growing inequality and a perception that government and taxation were biased in favour of the rich.

Promote fair work and economic democracy. We view forms of economic democracy and policies that promote fairness at work as necessary to take a major step forward in human emancipation; it is at work that so many of us experience the pain of hierarchy, including discrimination, lack of respect and recognition, as well as the injustices of low pay and lack of job security. Embedding fairness and democracy into the workplace will lead to smaller income differences and help to future-proof greater equality against fickle fiscal policies imposed by future governments. Evaluations also suggest that companies with more democratic models of governance have higher productivity.

Important policy steps include requiring, by law and as a condition for public procurement, (a) that all except the smallest companies have employee representatives on company boards and remuneration committees, with a higher proportion in larger companies and increasing over time to majority control; (b) increasing employee ownership, by requiring that a small proportion of shares be transferred each year to employee-controlled trusts until they have majority control; (c) promoting, incentivizing and offering training and legislative support, within government, for employee ownership, co-operatives and alternative business models (and see Will Hutton's chapter in this volume, Chapter 9); and (d) that companies meet democratic company standards, such as living wage accreditation, or "fair work" charters.

There are excellent models, examples and case studies for government and local authorities to learn from, including the Greater Manchester Good Employment Charter, Scotland's Fair Work Action Plan and

Australia's Fair Work Ombudsman. The Equality Act could be updated to include a "right to know" the pay of potential comparators, and to make equal pay audits mandatory when data suggest that unequal pay exists.

Government also needs to champion a fresh public recognition and valorization of trade unions and grow support for unionization in new sectors of the economy and those that have not traditionally been unionized. Covid-19 has taught us to appreciate our health, care and other key workers; and, just as we need to continue to appreciate them with higher wages and more job security, we also need to relearn an appreciation for the institutions that have fought for our human rights and social justice at work.

As part of the strategy for reducing inequality, government should always aim to keep unemployment to a minimum. Both modern monetary theory and Keynesian economics suggest that governments should normally be able to control the level of unemployment. However, some forecasts of the levels of job loss that might result from automation may pose more fundamental problems about how to share the proceeds of production and maintain demand. Universal basic income may be part of the solution here too.

Put children and young people at the centre of an inclusive recovery plan: end child poverty; end selective education; properly fund a comprehensive education system; enshrine in law universal free school meals and free holiday meals for families on benefits; and close the digital divide. The pandemic has changed the lives of children across the world, disrupting their education and daily routines and increasing their anxieties and mental health problems; many come from families that have experienced the loss of loved ones, work and income and that face an uncertain future. Just as for adults, the coronavirus crisis brings into sharp focus the pre-existing vulnerability of too many children to the politics, policies and practices that perpetuate inequality. In the United Kingdom, poor children, children with special educational needs and disabilities, children from Black, Asian and minority ethnic (BAME) groups and children experiencing maltreatment have all suffered more from the impacts of lockdown, including the loss of support from school and nursery closures and the fiasco caused by the cancellation of GCSE and A level exams (see Danny Dorling's chapter in this volume, Chapter 8). But it is important also to remember that the average – and, indeed, the more affluent – UK child has worse well-being than the average child in more equal societies, and is more likely to have parents and carers with longer working hours, more debt, more mental illness and addiction problems.

There are examples of good practice that could be implemented at multiple scales. Internationally, the OECD published *Changing the Odds for Vulnerable Children* in 2019 and the Foundation for European Progressive Studies, in 2020, called on the European Union to create a Child Union to build upon the Child Guarantee, which focuses on child poverty, to improve access to early childhood education and care, and better integrate this with other welfare provisions. Nationally, Wales has the Well-being of Future Generations (Wales) Act 2015, requiring public bodies in Wales to consider the long-term impact of their decisions and to help children grow up happy and healthy; and Scotland has the Children and Young People (Scotland) Act 2014, which aims to improve well-being for all children in Scotland by aiming to make them feel safe, healthy, active, nurtured, achieving, respected, responsible and included.

At a local level, in a city with high levels of deprivation and ill health, an example of good practice that one of us works closely with is the Born in Bradford programme, wherein ten years of collaborative work has created a rich research environment and the collaborations needed to co-produce, implement and evaluate early-life interventions to promote well-being and reduce inequalities. Just as the coronavirus hit, we were building the ActEarly City Collaboratory to provide a whole-system environment in which the public, scientists, policy leaders and practitioners can work with each other to develop upstream preventative solutions for a healthier, fairer future for children. Since the pandemic hit we have been using those resources to respond to the immediate crisis and help put children at the heart of local recovery planning.

Policy-makers also need to listen to children and young people and be alive to what they are telling us – about how we have failed them in the past, how we appear to be limiting their futures, how we are letting them down now as they live through the pandemic. There are millions of potential Greta Thunbergs in the United Kingdom; they can tell us what we need to do to build their opportunities and their resilience.

Make well-being society's goal. Calls for a "new economics", a post-GDP world, circular economies and "Green New Deals" (and see Ann Pettifor's chapter in this volume, Chapter 17) are rife, and a broad movement of heterodox economic thinking has spread worldwide. For us, these concepts can be crystallized into the idea of a well-being economy, one focused on delivering human and ecological well-being rather than economic growth. Recognition of the limits of orthodox economics and criticism of the enshrinement of GDP growth as society's main aim are nothing new. In 1968 US Senator Robert Kennedy made the point:

> The gross national product does not allow for the health of our children, the quality of their education or the joy of their play. It does not include the beauty of our poetry or the strength of our marriages, the intelligence of our public debate or the integrity of our public officials. It measures neither our wit nor our courage, neither our wisdom nor our learning, neither our compassion nor our devotion to our country; it measures everything, in short, except that which makes life worthwhile.

A well-being economy meets the needs of all within planetary boundaries; it is fair, sufficient and ecologically sustainable. And it need not be a distant utopia; around the world there are nations, states and cities successfully pursuing well-being goals. The Wellbeing Economy Governments (WEGo) partnership is a collaboration of national and regional governments with a shared ambition of building well-being economies. So far Scotland, New Zealand, Iceland and Wales have committed to WEGo – to collaboration in pursuit of innovative policies, to progressing towards the United Nations Sustainable Development Goals and to addressing the economic, social and environmental challenges of our time. There are other examples of good practice elsewhere. Costa Rica runs completely on renewal energy much of the time, while actively reforesting and punching above its weight on the Social Progress Index. Slovenia, with low income inequality and a small gender pay gap, also has a societal vision for 2050 that focuses on learning for life, an innovative society, trust, the quality of life and an identity that is inclusive and outward-looking. Bhutan works towards Gross National Happiness. Rwanda has made huge strides on a long path from genocide to well-being, cracking down on corruption, investing in health and promoting women's rights and equality. How much more inspiring these visions are than the tawdry ambition of the current Conservative government in the United Kingdom, with its emphasis on being tough on crime, tough on immigration, tough on public spending and timid on tax.

Build on positive aspects of the solidarity epidemic. Alongside the deep suffering caused by Covid-19, many communities have seen a rise in neighbourliness, sociability and a desire to take care of one another. Britain is now home to an unofficial network of community-based mutual aid groups; set up to identify and provide support for the shielded and the vulnerable, they have brought people together in sustained solidarity. We have also gained a new appreciation of health and care sector workers, and the "key workers" who kept the streets safe, the lights on, the rubbish taken away and the supermarkets stocked. We can all feel benefits that we get from contributing to a friendly, functioning community: the five ways to well-being are connecting, being active, learning, giving and taking notice. We have also seen improvements in air quality, active government encouragement to the public to be physically active and lose weight and – for some people – a freedom from stressful and/or unsafe environments at work or school and an opportunity to spend more time with family. This is not to negate the suffering, but we need to find ways to sustain the positive aspects of our new world and make sure they extend to everyone.

The What Works Centre for Wellbeing, after systematically reviewing the evidence, suggests that community hubs, meaningful participative decision-making and participative community development can bring people together and increase social capital. The government could also learn from the model of the People's Health Trust, which uses proceeds from the Health Lottery to fund community-led projects to reduce health inequalities. Instead of relying on lottery funding (drawn disproportionately from the working class), progressive taxation of the wealth and incomes of the rich could provide grants and supportive advice to fund innovative and inclusive community-based groups, networks and projects.

What is stopping us?

The evidence that inequality is destructive of the well-being of both people and planet had been growing in breadth and depth for a long time before Covid-19; it is not a lack of robust data that is the problem. From a government that now claims to be always "led by the science" and determined to "save lives" we have had to put up with a great many years of austerity and cuts to public spending that were never evidence-based or backed by any scientific consensus. Public health researchers and practitioners have known for decades that poverty and inequality lie at the heart of health and social problems but have been unable to get the attention or commitment of ideologically driven politicians. Covid-19 can focus attention, change mindsets and shift political ground; it creates the space and consensus for a radical agenda for equality.

Further reading

Equality Trust n.d. "The Equality Trust works to improve the quality of life in the UK by reducing socio-economic inequality". Available at: www.equalitytrust.org.uk.

Wellbeing Economy Alliance n.d. "WEAll is a collaboration of organisations, alliances, movements and individuals working towards a wellbeing economy, delivering human and ecological well-being". Available at: https://wellbeingeconomy.org.

Wilkinson, R. & K. Pickett 2018. *The Inner Level: How More Equal Societies Reduce Stress, Restore Sanity and Improve Everyone's Well-Being*. London: Penguin.

4

A second internationalism of labour

Geoff Tily

An alternative analysis of economic and political dysfunction requires an internationalism of labour operating on three levels, with international arrangements supporting domestic change.

- Micro: trade union recognition and rights, collective bargaining, other domestic/international industry-level agreements, facilitated and promoted by the International Labour Organization (ILO) and other international institutions.
- Macro: Bretton Woods 2.0/clearing union exchange mechanism to permit domestic autonomy (including permanently low interest rates and increased government spending) and facilitate international trade but contain speculation; global fund to support economic development.
- Meso: industry and regional strategies, investment to meet climate emergency, global tax reform, with international coordination as relevant.

The agenda challenges the false opposition between globalization and nationalism. With globalization understood as an internationalism on the terms of capital, internationalism must instead be conducted on the terms of labour.

The relevant interplay of class forces, politics and economics is shown by events over the past century, in particular, the progressive and left debate in the interwar period. The associated policy changes amounted to a first internationalism of labour (IOL), devised as an alternative to *both* the disastrous internationalism of capital (IOC) implemented in the wake of the First World War and the subsequent degeneration to nationalism. Today's economic, social and political crises are understood as the inevitable consequences of a renewed IOC, most obviously but imprecisely traced back to Thatcher, Reagan and the "Volcker shock" (the sharp rise in US interest rates introduced in 1981/82 by Paul Volcker, the then chairman of the Federal Reserve).

A second internationalism of labour is the correct – and viable – alternative to resumed nationalist degeneration. In November 2018 international trade union economists and officials concluded: "Populism and anti-politics are a reaction to this but instead of an inward-looking agenda the solution must come from the global stage. To foster a global debate on an alternative approach, the global Trade Union movement has a key role to play."[1]

Nationalist poison makes such change seem far-fetched. It is less far-fetched against the scale of the crisis.

In this chapter the present internationalism of capital is outlined, showing how class forces have led to excess rather than deficient supply, and the consequent threat from private debt.[2] This analysis is then situated in interwar socialist and trade union debate, substantially informed and refined by Keynes during the first internationalism of labour. The resumed IOC can be traced back more precisely to the termination of the European Payments Union of the 1950s. A second internationalism of labour would undo this undemocratic and ultimately disastrous change of direction.

Diagnosis

From 1979 class relations were decisively reset – back – in favour of wealth and away from labour. Over time purchasing power has become increasingly deficient against increasingly excessive production, in relative not absolute terms (i.e. supply is excessive). The imbalance has emerged as a systemic tendency to borrow among firms that are unable to sell products, and households unable to afford a basic standard of living. Wealth accumulation has also fostered other speculative cycles, not least in property.

The results at a global level are an ongoing but unsustainable inflation of private (and public) debts, economic instability and international

1. The "Lessons from the financial crisis" conference marked the 150th anniversary of the Trades Union Congress (TUC) and the 70th anniversary of the Trades Union Advisory Committee (TUAC) to the OECD.
2. The views are the author's own, not those of the Trades Union Congress.

competition to reduce wages and working standards. The financial crisis and recession of 2007–09 reflected the fundamental and inevitable failure of these arrangements, triggered by the implosion of private debt. Vast resources were deployed to protect financial institutions and arrest collapse; afterwards, the IOC was simply intensified.

Since that crisis economic policy has operated with a wrong diagnosis, and so a wrong cure. The wrong diagnosis follows from governments' inflation-targeting frameworks, and the usual judgement of deficient production against excessive purchasing power (i.e. supply is deficient, not excessive). The framework endures despite its incompatibility with private debt, and at least a decade of price disinflation that is at odds with policy judgements. Official commentary identifies symptoms as the cause of the problem. The prolonged reduction in productivity growth is regarded as evidence of a supply deficiency, when it is simply a consequence of a price rather than a quantity adjustment in the labour market to weak demand growth. As the Trades Union Congress argue, any fourth industrial revolution is serving further to disadvantage labour. Technology cannot advantage society when demand is deficient. Increased inequality is inevitable given the wider rebalancing to wealth from labour. Taxing wealth is, plainly, necessary, but the main concern here is to address cause.

In the meantime, austerity policies contain households and governments "within their means", and, 40 years down the line, still more "flexibility" is demanded of workers, including the toxic politics of Conservative Party trade union reform. With excess production, further reductions in purchasing power exacerbate rather than resolve the problem. Hence private (and public) debt crises remain unresolved.

Corresponding to the policies to contain labour are policies supporting wealth, with quantitative easing (QE) the most prominent of various subsidies to banks and related institutions. These have supported productive activity to the extent that money has been directed into new and riskier markets:[3]

3. QE supports wealth in asset markets. But it is also integral to increased risk, as financial institutions sell their government debt to the central bank, and use the credit that they receive in exchange to buy riskier assets, intermediating between borrowers and wealthy individuals/pension funds seeking high returns. The risk arises from borrowers being unlikely to be able to repay these high returns (e.g. Turkish corporations repaying debt). Furthermore, risk is shifting from financial institutions to households.

- a global bubble in high-end residential and commercial property;
- sub-prime auto loans;
- emerging market economies (EMEs);
- leveraged lending and corporate takeovers; and
- technologies and businesses (the five corporations that dominate the US capital market: Facebook, Amazon Apple, Netflix and Alphabet) associated with the fourth industrial revolution (with overblown claims around artificial intelligence and robots taking over the workplace).

Lending to EMEs replays overproduction processes, with vigorous excess giving way to even deeper austerity (Turkey is a recent example). The consequences are increased rather than reduced reliance on trade, intensified overproduction at a global level and the race to the bottom in pay and working conditions.

Nationalism thrives in these conditions. In international trade, the consequence is "dumping" and protectionism. Migrant victims of the resulting global deflationary pressures and wider economic dysfunction are attacked. Nationalist governments reduce labour protections and rights, at worst tolerating modern slavery, child labour, violence and murder. The International Trade Union Confederation speaks of "the dismantling of workplace democracy and the breakdown of the social contract". This is how the internationalism of capital gives way to nationalism. Fundamentally, of course, power relations are left intact; instead, labour is set against itself.

Nationalism cannot resolve the underlying economic dysfunction. Ongoing economic imbalances threaten a resumed and intensified crisis, with new dangers as the risk is shifted from banks to pension funds and to households.[4] Ultimately, two means of resolving or realigning production and purchasing power are possible. Either production collapses in renewed recession, or purchasing power rises. The former is the present course. The latter requires deliberate action under the internationalism of labour.

---

4. Their pension funds also make workers in the North capitalists to those in the South.

A first internationalism of labour

In a 1919 speech, Ernest Bevin, the dominant figure in British trade unions, foresaw that "[t]he crude black international of trade will inevitably go for the real international of the great peoples of the world". Trade union economic thinking is naturally concerned with the basic imbalance between what workers produce and what they can afford to purchase. By the time Bevin was engaged, the imbalances were already global. His observation from a century ago could have been written today: "The great fields of exploitation of China, Japan and the East generally will inevitably attract capital from the Western World ... [The] world ... will over-produce in an intensified degree in less than five years from now ... [and] will produce a world stagnation." He saw how to reverse the logic, challenging the employers in his audience: "You think the only avenue to progress and success is overseas markets. You give little or no consideration to the home market ... You have not realised that if you can raise the standard of life by 100 to 200 per cent that inevitably makes it better for all the producers concerned within your borders."

These overproduction/underconsumption arguments were critical to the left debate of this era. The writings of liberal economist John Hobson at the turn of the century were a key influence. In 1932 Léon Blum, the leader of the French socialists, wrote "[T]he world produces more goods than consumers are able to acquire. It is an excess of production relative, not to the needs that no one knows, but simply to the general inadequacy of purchasing power." Critically, the argument was prominent in the Labour Party's 1945 general election manifesto: "Over-production is not the cause of depression and unemployment; it is under-consumption that is responsible. It is doubtful whether we have ever, except in war, used the whole of our productive capacity." Over a century after Hobson, Matthew Klein and Michael Pettis have revived these arguments in their aptly titled 2020 book *Trade Wars Are Class Wars*.

In his (1936) *General Theory*, Keynes paid a major tribute to Hobson, although he argued that the thinking was incomplete, especially around the rate of interest. The disastrous and chaotic policy failures of the 1920s had already brought the role of finance and interest into sharp relief. Bevin in particular was struck that immense interest payments to finance from firms and government (as a result of high-interest war loans) were sacrosanct, leaving firms and government needing to force wage cuts on workers. The left considered that this need not be the natural order of things.

The economics profession by and large denies, ignores or misses Keynes's conclusion that high interest rates are the fundamental cause of economic dysfunction. The authorities can set interest rates across the spectrum, from rates on government debt through to the bank rate; and it is imperative that they operate a permanent policy of cheap money. Somewhat obliquely, Keynes also affirmed trade union thinking: only "inexperienced", "unjust" or "foolish" persons would advocate "flexible wages over flexible money". These arrangements would not only improve labour's share of the pie, they would also mean a bigger (and more stable) pie – from which industry would also benefit. The "euthanasia of the rentier" would extinguish any disproportionate reward to wealth, but retirement incomes would still be more secure and fairer.

In the final chapter of his masterpiece, Keynes appealed to the logic of the internationalism of labour:

> [I]f nations can learn to provide themselves with full employment by their domestic policy ... there need be no important economic forces calculated to set the interest of one country against that of its neighbours ... International trade would cease to be what it is, namely, a desperate expedient to maintain employment at home by forcing sales on foreign markets and restricting purchases, which, if successful, will merely shift the problem of unemployment to the neighbour which is worsted in the struggle, but a willing and unimpeded exchange of goods and services in conditions of mutual advantage.[5]

In response to the later Bretton Woods agreement, Hugh Gaitskell, then a Labour MP, put it best (writing in 1946 in the *Daily Herald*): "It is recognised at last that the expansion of international trade depends on the maintenance of Full Employment – and not the other way round ...

5. In 1977 British economist Richard Kahn observed: "The world still has to accept this simple lesson taught by Keynes."

From this follows the ideas of an undertaking by each nation … that it will not seek to maintain employment through measures that are likely to create unemployment in other countries."

If countries cooperate for full employment and do not compete for trade they will advance together rather than engage in competitive deflation. This amounts to a clear and distinct practical approach, with policies operating on the three dimensions given above. As early as the Macmillan Committee (1929–31), trade unions in Britain regarded public ownership of the central bank as the critical means by which labour could assert power over wealth, and begin to reset the position on wages and interest. In practice, the timing of political change meant that Roosevelt (1934), Michael Joseph Savage in New Zealand (1935) and Blum in France (1936) acted before Clement Attlee (1946). However, cheap money began (under the National Government) when Britain came off gold in September 1931, leading to a sustained reduction in short and long interest rates across the world.

Roosevelt then gave the decisive global lead at the World Economic Conference in 1933. His action is usually portrayed as anti-internationalist, but he was rejecting the internationalism of capital and looking to the monetary system for an internationalism of labour: "Old fetishes of so-called international bankers are being replaced by efforts to plan national currencies with the objective of giving to those currencies a continuous purchasing power which does not greatly vary in terms of the commodities of modern civilization."

When Blum took office as French prime minister in 1936, France, the United Kingdom and United States signed the tripartite agreement – really a fundamental next step, allowing the French socialist programme to be protected from speculators. Following Roosevelt's National Labor Relations Act (Wagner Act) of 1935, Blum implemented the Matignon Accords: wage increases of 12 to 15 per cent, the 40-hour week, holidays with pay and the right to full union recognition and collective bargaining. In his 1937 book *The Labour Party in Perspective*, Attlee reported similar initiatives under socialist governments in Sweden and New Zealand. Their actions preceded by 85 years the contemporary call for wage-led growth by post-Keynesian economists.

The same governments extended public ownership into (variously) transport, energy, armaments, mining and forestry. But collective ownership of all means of production was no longer necessarily the ideal.

Labour's 1945 manifesto concludes: "There are basic industries ripe and over-ripe for public ownership and management in the direct service of the nation. There are many smaller businesses rendering good service which can be left to go on with their useful work." An "industrial programme" of public ownership of fuel and power, inland transport and iron and steel was proposed and implemented.

The disastrous failure of the interwar years was not a failure of internationalism, but a failure of internationalism on the terms of capital. Trade unions and democratic socialists stood for an internationalism on the terms of labour. They refused and recognized nationalism as a degenerate form of capitalism. In the same book Attlee baldly stated that fascism was "a cloak for capitalism".

Political economy

In his 1902 work *Imperialism*, Hobson warned: "The selection and rejection of ideas … and the propagation of them in the intellectual world, have been plainly directed by the pressure of class interests." On this view, the internationalism of labour could not endure. By regarding the interwar years as synonymous only with nationalism and the postwar age as a single sweep of accelerating globalization, the internationalism of labour is written out of history.

To the extent that any changed policy approach is recognized today, the (domestic) state rather than (international) class interest is seen as the dominant factor. Finally – and only after the Second World War – "society" chose to place less reliance on market forces and more emphasis on the state and other non-market mechanisms. In the United Kingdom technocrats like William Beveridge have the credit for an era-defining welfare state. Trade unions and the left are associated mainly with the disarray at the end of the era, rather than the constructive thinking and committed action that set a far greater change in motion.

The place of class interest under the internationalism of labour also cuts across left thinking. Conventionally, a Marxist left is opposed to a reformist or "opportunist" centre. But class forces were inherent to socialist thinking and Keynes's analysis; instead the means of resolving the conflict was democratic and reformist.

In practice the resolution was concerned with payments to – rather than ownership of – the factors of production. This means rebalancing between the return on wealth and the return on labour. Moreover, the interests of labour and industry are not inherently opposed: rebalancing payments towards labour strengthens consumer demand and so production (and even increases the amount, if not the share, of profit). On the other hand, the interests of finance and wealth are opposed to both labour and industry. Lastly, improved public services are only one feature of a wider agenda, with the increased spending both supporting production and facilitating the rebalancing of returns to labour: private and public activity were understood as complementary, not rival.

Of his theory, Keynes observed

> [N]o obvious case is made out for a system of State Socialism which would embrace most of the economic life of the community. It is not the ownership of the instruments of production which it is important for the State to assume. If the State is able to determine the aggregate amount of resources devoted to augmenting the instruments and the basic rate of reward to those who own them, it will have accomplished all that is necessary.

He perceived a key political question as the balance of market and the state, but his naivety was to think that vested interest would permit the realignment of class forces. In reality, socialism (of various forms) was necessary to make the changes his theory (and what he saw as "reason") demanded. After the Second World War the technocrats permitted the IOL only in greatly compromised form.

Outcomes

The broad political shifts of the past century are familiar, but economic statistics offer a more accurate bearing on the balance of class forces: the real interest rate for the return to wealth (Figure 4.1); and the labour share for the return to labour (Figures 4.2a and 4.2b).

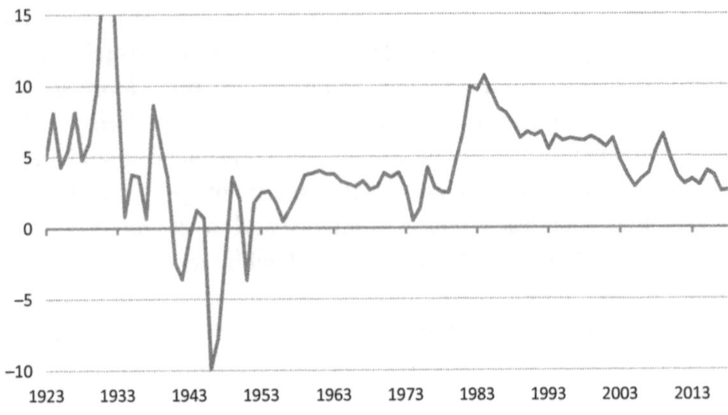

Figure 4.1 US (and hence global) real interest rate, 1923–2018
Note: Y axis cut off for years of severe deflation.
Sources: Federal Reserve BBA graded corporate debt; Bureau of Economic Analysis (BEA) for GDP deflator.

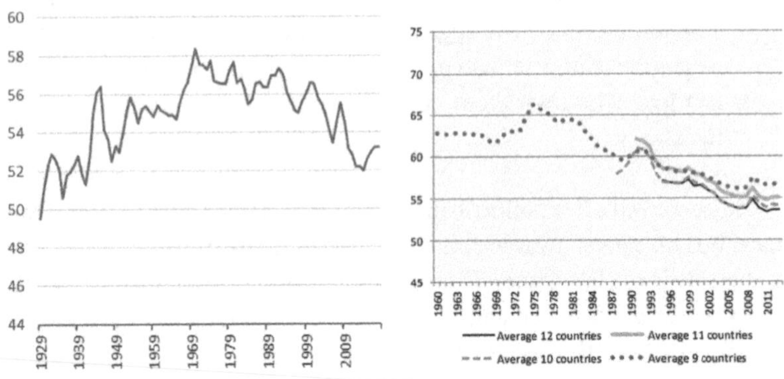

Figures 4.2 **a** US labour share, 1929–2018; **b** G20 labour share, 1960–2012
Sources: BEA; OECD, ILO and IMF.

Both show material rebalancing from the 1930s and for the first decades after the Second World War. The gains are undone from the 1980s, with the return to wealth an uncannily close match to that of the 1920s.

From the turn of the millennium there has been some reduction in the real interest rate, but this is unlikely to reflect the wider return to wealth – with portfolios increasingly allocated to higher-yielding but more risky lending. Tellingly, over the same period the labour share has not recovered.

The unrivalled prosperity of the three decades after the Second World War was the outcome of changed thinking and policy, not, as normally portrayed, good fortune. The subsequent reversal in outcomes was due to discredited thinking and policy. Some important points emerge from this.

First, production has been driven by domestic demand. In the golden age stronger domestic demand drove higher economic growth; under globalization, the dominant factor is the weakness of domestic demand. As Gaitskell predicted, trade growth was stronger in absolute terms when domestic demand was stronger.

Second, the shared interests of labour and industry in the golden age economy worked better even on the conventional productivity measure. The Bank of England's chief economist, Andrew Haldane, has observed: "From 1950 to 1970, median global productivity growth averaged 1.9 per cent per year. Since 1980, it has averaged 0.3 per cent per year." However, fundamentally, the left's goals were full employment and a decent standard of life. Over the 1950s and 1960s most major economies secured unemployment rates of between 1 and 5 per cent. Chasing growth became a preoccupation only when capital recovered lost ground, and is not a necessary feature of the internationalism of labour. Reviving the understanding that the economy is not something apart from the efforts of workers must be critical to addressing the climate emergency.

Third, the decades after the Second World War were more stable, with the incidence of banking crisis at zero effectively from 1940 to the mid-1970s. The stability was first disrupted by the recession of the mid-1970s. Inevitably, the renewed internationalism of capital has meant constant instability, and, from 2007–09, the most severe financial and economic crisis since the Great Depression.

A Europe of labour

In Britain the most prominent manifestation of the consequent nationalism is the Brexit process. Supranational institutions are no less subject to the interests of capital or labour. The League of Nations played an important role in setting the internationalism of capital of the interwar years. The Bretton Woods institutions were devised to support the internationalism of labour, but were soon co-opted by rival interests (the first head of the World Bank was Eugene Meyer – one of Roosevelt's bitterest opponents). But the International Labour Office has helped to establish and affirm the tripartite approach between government, trade unions and businesses.

In the original form of the Western European Union, European initiatives were closely aligned with labour internationalism. From his first trip to the United States in 1919, Bevin had been attracted to the (demand) potential of a single market within Europe. As foreign secretary in the Attlee government from 1945 to 1951, he led the European countries' response to the US offer for Marshall Aid. He sought both to unblock the wider reliance of the global monetary system on too scarce dollars; and to set a socialist/social democratic Europe as a counterbalance to nationalist conflict between the United States and Soviet Russia.

Gaitskell led on the practical arrangements. Much later he gave the following succinct explanation of the European Payments Union to the House of Commons: "As a matter of fact, the system was directly based on an idea of the late Lord Keynes which was worked out in a famous paper called 'The Clearing Union'. It was far more in line with Lord Keynes's ideas than the International Monetary Fund which emerged from Bretton Woods."

Keynes's scheme applied the principles of banking to international exchange, so that countries with trade surpluses would automatically lend to those with deficits. On this approach currencies were no longer subject to the vagaries (not least the political prejudice) of the foreign exchange market; instead, limits to deficits and surpluses were set by the operational rules of the scheme. The ideal system is multilateral by definition, with national currencies convertible into a notional world money (strictly, a world money-of-account) issued by a world central bank.

Tragically, Gaitskell made the above remarks in a (January 1959) debate on the ending of the regime. The Bank of England had intrigued constantly against the arrangement, and, along with other central banks (and the Bank for International Settlements), ensured that the (1957) Treaty of Rome would be secured on more orthodox monetary territory (specifically, the European Monetary Agreement). Gaitskell saw clearly the implications, namely the effective ending of the first internationalism of labour:

> [W]hat we are emphasising by this step [is] that we are determined to be … a world finance centre … We are always talking about sterling as a world currency … The whole basis of the doctrine of convertibility is, of course, to build up and to give as much freedom as possible because on that basis we can get the most business to the City … We shall be told that we must cut back; that we are trying to do too much; that there is overfull employment. We shall be warned that we must delay expansion; not because of anything that is done, but because of what might be thought by speculators.

British economist Andrew Shonfield offered a no less clear-sighted assessment:

> Here in fact is the vicarious reassertion of the political power of the owners of wealth – not businessmen or people active in any way, but just owners – which the postwar social revolution in Britain had set out to prevent. The Conservatives, when they came to power, gave no hint that it was part of their purpose to undo the *fait accompli*. It was certainly not the conscious purpose of the party leaders, either then or later.

His class analysis makes plain the inherent conflict between wealth and industry in the Conservative Party. On this vital occasion, "the political power of the owners of wealth" was exerted through officials at the Treasury and Bank of England and their counterparts in other countries.

Conclusion

The internationalism of capital has served the interests of the few at the great expense of the many. Remedying this situation is not only an economic imperative but a democratic necessity. The postwar golden age gives a sense of what has been denied to society. A second internationalism of labour will restore prosperity through domestic policies for full and decent employment, facilitated by a changed and progressive international infrastructure. Above all, at present, local initiatives must put the world in a better position to address the climate emergency.

Further reading

Attlee, C. 1937. *The Labour Party in Perspective*. London: Victor Gollancz.

Tily, G. 2007. *Keynes's General Theory, the Rate of Interest and 'Keynesian' Economics: Keynes Betrayed*. London: Palgrave Macmillan.

Trade Union Advisory Committee to the OECD 2018. "Lessons from the crisis: joint TUAC–TUC anniversary conference". 23 November. Available at: https://tuac.org/news/lessons-from-the-crisis-joint-tuac-tuc-anniversary-conference.

TUC 2019. *Getting It Right This Time: Lessons from a Decade of Failed Austerity*. London: Trades Union Congress. Available at: www.tuc.org.uk/research-analysis/reports/lessons-decade-failed-austerity.

PART II

THE PUBLIC SERVICE SECTORS

5

Affordable housing and a stronger economy

Josh Ryan-Collins

The UK housing market is broken. The accepted affordability ratio for house price to incomes is around 4:1. In most major cities in the United Kingdom the ratio is double this, and in London, where the most jobs continue to be created, it is currently 14:1. A recent survey by Santander found that 70 per cent of 18 to 34-year-olds now believe that homeownership is over for their generation.

The first Covid-19 lockdown brought into stark view the plight of those unable to buy a home in a country with some of the weakest regulations protecting renters in the Western world. In cities such as London, renters pay over half their income to landlords. As incomes collapsed due to the lockdown, many have fallen behind with their rent (an estimate by Shelter put the number at 230,000 in England alone). The fear of eviction and homelessness has been ever present over the course of the pandemic, with the government having to repeatedly extend its ban on evictions at the last minute every few months.

Prospective home-buyers may have hoped that the virus-induced recession would finally lead to a sustained fall in house prices. There were a few months of gradually falling prices. But then, in July 2020, the government intervened, offering a stamp duty holiday on all properties under £500,000. Coupled with increasing demand for larger properties as people choose to work more from home because of the virus, the result has been the fastest rise in house prices in 16 years. The average price of a home – £240,000 – is now at its highest level ever.

The current government – like so many governments before it – is convinced that the housing affordability crisis is fundamentally a market failure on the supply side. The recent White Paper "Planning for the future" (see MHCLG [Ministry of Housing, Communities & Local Government] 2020) is a case in point. It proposes to overhaul an "outdated" planning system and "cut red tape" by largely removing the role of local authorities in approving planning applications and replacing it with a zoning system. The hope is that, with less regulatory oversight, the market will be set free to build more homes.

This is the wrong diagnosis. Politicians, policy-makers and many economists consistently seem to forget that housing has a dual economic role. It is a consumption good – providing shelter – but also a financial asset: a source of collateral and a store of wealth. Over the past four decades the latter role has come to dominate the former. The UK housing market suffers from excessive speculative credit and investment flowing into an inherently limited supply of locationally desirable housing.

Once we accept that the supply of housing is intrinsically limited, we must accept the need for state intervention to shape the land and housing market to ensure that the use value of housing is given priority over its market value. This leads to bigger questions about the social and economic structure of the UK economy and what can be done to reform it.

The true drivers of high house prices

The increasing political preference for homeownership over other forms of tenure, coupled with the liberalization of the financial system, has led to two important developments in the UK housing and land market. First, the capital gains that naturally accrue to land- and homeowners in a growing economy – generally referred to as "land rents" – have been allowed to grow as taxes on property and the public provision of affordable housing have withered. Second, and more significantly for explaining the rises in house prices in the last two decades, the deregulation of the financial system has created a positive feedback cycle between finance and house prices. Finance has become addicted to property just as citizens in many capitalist economies have come to expect to own a home.

In the act of lending, banks also create new money. When a bank makes a loan, it creates both an asset (the loan) and a liability upon itself in the form of a new deposit in the bank account of the borrower. This money is not borrowed from elsewhere in the economy. The main limit on bank money creation is the bank's own confidence that the loan will be repaid. If mortgage lending supports the building of new homes, this new money can be absorbed into the economy. However, in most cases in the United Kingdom mortgage finance enables people to buy existing property on existing land. As households, supported by banks, compete to purchase, the result is increasing land and house prices. Higher prices lead to more demand for mortgage credit, which further pumps up prices, and so on. Rising house prices means rising collateral value, encouraging banks to make ever bigger loans

This housing–finance feedback cycle runs against standard economic theory, whereby an increase in the supply of goods, all else being equal, should eventually lead to a fall in prices. The explanation lies in the unique nature of housing as an economic commodity. Housing is a composite good, made up of the structures (the bricks and mortar) and the land underneath it. "Location" might be a better word than "land", since, in economic terms, it is *where* a property is situated that determines its value more than anything else. Desirable locations – such as homes in successful cities, homes near green space or good schools – are *inherently limited* in supply. More and more credit and investment chasing a limited supply of housing is inevitably inflationary.

Figure 5.1 shows the enormous growth in mortgage credit – from 20 to 60 per cent of GDP – in the United Kingdom from the 1980s

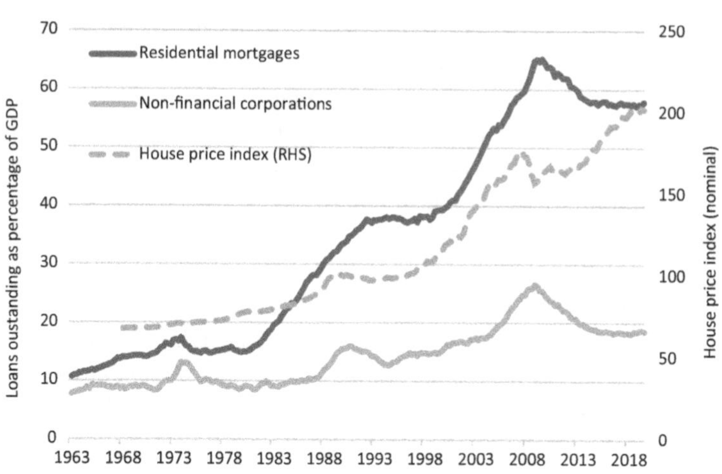

Figure 5.1 Loans outstanding as a percentage of GDP and house prices, 1963–2019

onwards, following Margaret Thatcher's liberalization of the financial sector. House prices have more than doubled in the same period. In contrast, the textbook role of the bank, business lending, is equivalent to just 20 per cent of GDP. UK banks today lend on average just £1 in every £10 to businesses. Since the late 1990s mortgage rates have also fallen dramatically. Inflation-adjusted interest rates on five-year fixed-rate mortgages have tumbled from 8 per cent to under 2 per cent today. This means that households and investors are more prepared to take out bigger loans as their debt servicing ratio falls.

Instead of acting to reduce the flows of credit into property, governments have subsidized it. A range of financial support products have been offered to first-time buyers, most recently the "Help to Buy" scheme. Buy-to-let-mortgages were introduced in 1996, making petty landlordism an attractive option for Britons who otherwise might have put their savings into businesses. Ten per cent of UK adults, or 5.2 million people, own a second home, while four in ten adults own no property at all, according to the Resolution Foundation.

But it is not just credit that contributes to excessive demand. Property is very lightly taxed in relation to other financial assets. Homeowners pay no capital gains tax on their primary property and Council Tax has not been revalued since 1991. Given the tripling of house prices that has taken place since then, this amounts to an enormous tax break for homeowners.

Demand-side factors help us answer another puzzle about the UK housing market. Outside London and the south-east, rents have not been increasing more rapidly than incomes, in contrast to housing. If the demand for housing was limited to its role as a consumption good, we would expect rents to rise at a similar rate to house prices. But falling interest rates have made housing much more attractive as a financial asset – in terms of both capital gains and a source of rental income for landlords – relative to other "safe" assets, such as government bonds.

Tumbling interest rates on government bonds, driven by central bank quantitative easing programmes, have also led domestic and global investors – ranging from pension funds, insurance companies and real estate investment trusts (REITs) – to plough money into real estate since the financial crisis of 2007–09. This helps explain why tougher mortgage regulation since 2008 has not been effective in reducing prices. It also explains the large regional variation in UK house prices. As research for the IMF has found (see IMF 2019), global investors have increasingly focused on globally integrated cities such as London, Sydney, Amsterdam and Hong Kong, resulting in house prices in these megacities synchronizing away from their hinterlands. London offers huge attractions to global real estate investors in terms of legal frameworks, generous taxation arrangements, language and time zone.

Reforms to the UK housing market

How have policy-makers allowed such a parlous state of affairs to emerge and continue? The United Kingdom is perhaps the canonical example of what has been described in the comparative political economy literature as "residential capitalism". Property wealth in the country constitutes 35 per cent of all wealth, while 91 per cent of all household debt is property debt. Once you become a property owner, rising house prices can be translated into cash via home equity withdrawal, which has been permitted in the United Kingdom since the 1980s. This has propped up consumption, fuelling home renovations and other large purchases. In addition, many UK banks are prepared to lend to smaller businesses only if property (usually belonging to the business owner) is put up as collateral.

All of this means that policies that would drastically reduce house prices would be economically and financially catastrophic and politically disastrous. A more gradual downward adjustment in house prices relative to increasing incomes – as described elsewhere in this book – is a much more attractive policy approach. There are three areas policy-makers should focus on.

Financial reforms

First, financial policy-makers – in central banks and ministries of finance alike – should now have the confidence to more explicitly regulate the quantity and allocation of credit for different purposes. During their history almost all advanced economies, and many emerging economies, have employed forms of formal and informal quantity-based credit regulation under various terms, including "credit guidance", "window guidance" and "moral suasion". The easiest way to introduce such a scheme might be to have some form of productive credit ratio, whereby a minimum ratio (e.g. 30 per cent) of a bank's assets should support non-financial firms (currently it is around 10 per cent on average in the United Kingdom). A gradual shift towards this kind of target would give banks time to either reduce their mortgage lending or increase their business lending depending on their preference.

Domestic regulations of this type would be more effective if they were complemented by supportive international regulation. International regulators, including the BIS and the IMF, need to reverse the strong favouritism shown towards property lending in terms of capital and liquidity requirements. Regulations should support banks that are able to de-risk their loans via methods other than property-based collateral, most obviously via the building up of long-term relationships with non-financial businesses.

This brings us to structural changes to the banking system. A good model is Germany, where two-thirds of bank deposits are controlled by either cooperative or public savings banks, most of which are owned by regional or local people and/or businesses. These "stakeholder banks" are more focused on business lending, do not have such stringent collateral requirements and devolve decision-making to branches. They de-risk their loans not by requiring property as collateral but by building up strong and long-lasting relationships and an understanding of the businesses they lend to. A second way of supporting non-collateralized lending to support productive activity and priority infrastructure (including affordable housing) would be the creation of a sizeable UK State Investment Bank, as suggested in Stephany Griffith-Jones's chapter in this volume, Chapter 12.

Taxing unearned land rents, not income

Reversing the fiscal favouritism for homeownership and treating landed property in the same way as any other financial asset would appear a logical step if we are to bring house prices back to levels closer to incomes. One proposal, supported by economists from across the political spectrum, would be a tax on the increasing value of land, or a land value tax (LVT), most famously proposed by the journalist and campaigner Henry George. This would involve an annual tax on the incremental increase in the unimproved market value of land, which would fall upon the landowner. The advantage of the tax is that it would accurately capture the economic gains deriving from public and private investment in a location – such as a new school or better transport infrastructure – that were not attributable to the landowner's own efforts; in other words, the tax would capture for the public purse economic rent.

By attaching a cost to owning land, LVT diminishes the incentive to buy land for speculative purposes to realize capital gains. Knowing that any increase in the value of a property would be taxed should lead to a shift towards households purchasing a house purely on the basis of its value as a place to live – i.e. a consumption good – rather than as a financial asset. There would also be less incentive for developers to hoard undeveloped land. Such a tax would probably end the practice of "land banking" or "slow release", which, as the 2018 Letwin Review revealed, is a major issue in the United Kingdom. With rising land prices, developers have reduced incentives to build and sell property efficiently, because the capital gains on their assets are rising, despite the shortage of housing the country faces. There is nothing in the current White Paper (MHCLG 2020) that deals with this problem.

There are major political challenges with implementing property taxes in Western democracies where homeownership and the idea of wealth generation from the home have become culturally entrenched. There are genuine fairness issues in some cases – in particular when households or individuals are asset-rich but cash-poor, meaning a tax would significantly reduce their income. Any land tax should be introduced as part of a wider tax reform that would reduce other unpopular and regressive taxes, such as income or sales taxes. Exemptions for low-income homeowners, or allowing homeowners to defer payment until sale, may reduce the unfairness criticism. Alternatively, homeowners could give up a percentage of their equity in the property each year that was not paid to the state, enabling the community to gain from any capital appreciation.

Rethinking tenure

Is homeownership really the superior form of tenure, from either an economic or a social welfare perspective? There is little evidence that higher rates of homeownership support stronger economies. Rather, empirical studies have found that higher rates of unemployment correlate with high homeownership, on account of less mobile workforces. High levels of homeownership reduce the efficiency of the distribution of labour and raise up the particular interests of property owners in opposition to community development.

The United Kingdom used to have one of the largest public housing stocks in the developed world. But the combination of mass privatization, via the "Help to Buy" and similar schemes, and an insecure and low-quality rental market has led to homeownership becoming the de facto superior tenure. This now needs to be reversed. Only a developer protected from the profit motive, such as the state itself, could ever have any incentive to produce houses at a rate that would lower the cost of housing overall in the area in which they are being built. Building affordable housing to the highest environmental standards should be a key part of the "Green New Deal", given the huge economic multiplier effects involved in constructions at a large scale. Local authorities – perhaps supported by a National State Investment Bank – should be freed up to borrow in capital markets for socially rented housing that will provide a secure flow of income. Such a policy would also reduce emergency housing costs, which have been mounting since the austerity policies of the Cameron/Osborne government.

The private rented sector should be made as secure as possible, with long guaranteed tenancies, limitations on rent rises and strong tenants' rights. Government should take steps to boost the stock of non-market housing, including homes with social rents, community-led schemes and co-operatives to ensure that different housing types and sizes are available in all tenures, and to make housing supply less dependent on the volatile private market in land and homes. Finally, decent investment alternatives and secure pensions should be provided, so that households are less prone to invest in the housing market to pay for their retirement or to rely on it to fund their care in old age.

To ensure that the costs of public housing are kept down, local authorities must be given compulsory purchase powers to buy up sufficient land for entire new settlements. By capturing the planning gain for the public purse, the cost of the original land purchase can be made up and exceeded, with profits put into further upgrades to infrastructure. This is the model that was used successfully in the development of new towns in the United Kingdom in the 1960s. This is standard practice in East Asian economies such as Singapore and South Korea, and in European countries such as Germany and the Netherlands. Such powers enable the public sector to shape the land market in a way that prioritizes housing's use value over its market value.

Conclusion

Political leaders must be brave enough to stand up to vested interests and make the case for housing to return to its primary function as providing shelter rather than being a financial asset. A new narrative focused on secure, affordable housing for all citizens as a right must be established, as opposed to housing as a means to securing financial wealth. As homeownership increasingly moves out of the reach of young and poorer households, this process should become easier.

The key will be to find a way of delinking our financial system and wider economy from where we live without causing financial havoc. Banks need to be weaned off their dependence on the housing market. Governments should be taking steps now to direct finance towards more productive ends, not least the creation of new housing and transport infrastructure that would boost economic growth and consumption but ease pressure on our cities. A gradual, managed rebalancing of house prices relative to income is required, with demand coming from investment and production, not off the back of rising asset prices. Then we can begin to break free of the housing–finance feedback cycle.

Further reading

IMF 2019. *Global Financial Stability Report April 2019: Vulnerabilities in a Maturing Credit Cycle*. Washington, DC: International Monetary Fund. Available at: www.imf.org/en/Publications/GFSR/Issues/2019/03/27/Global-Financial-Stability-Report-April-2019.

MHCLG 2020. "Planning for the future", White Paper. London: HMSO. Available at: www.gov.uk/government/consultations/planning-for-the-future.

Monbiot, G. (ed.) 2019. *Land for the Many: Changing the Way Our Fundamental Asset Is Used, Owned and Governed*. London: Labour Party. Available at: https://landforthemany.uk.

Ryan-Collins, J. 2018. *Why Can't You Afford a Home?* Cambridge: Polity Press.

6

Post-Covid national health and care policies to ensure universal services

Allyson M. Pollock and Louisa Harding-Edgar

Perhaps the most surprising aspect of the British Covid-19 crisis is the extent to which the Scottish, Welsh and Northern Irish governments, and the English regions, allowed strategy to be decided by Westminster, delaying the implementation of public health measures until the first UK-wide lockdown was declared on 23 March 2020. Health and social care are devolved, and this national epidemic is not homogeneous. It has been and continues to be made up of hundreds, if not thousands, of outbreaks, each at a different stage, ongoing in different local areas throughout the country. England had its first confirmed case on 30 January, Wales on 28 February and Scotland on 1 March. Some areas – such as Rutland, Hartlepool, Blackpool, the Isle of Wight, Tyneside, Durham, Orkney, the Western Isles – had no reported cases until late March; and London in the second phase, until December 2020, had relatively few cases compared with other areas, such as the north-west and south-west, which had far fewer cases six months ago but now appear to have more cases.

Because infection is transmitted between individuals, local knowledge of both communities and their living circumstances and individuals is key not only for understanding and managing the risk of spread but also for putting in place protective measures.

We are all vulnerable to Covid-19, but income levels, housing, living conditions, ethnicity, age, overall health and gender are all significant factors in determining the impact of the virus on different people. The conclusion is clear: as well as a revised approach to the NHS, the United Kingdom also needs revised policies in social care, housing and poverty, and – perhaps most importantly of all – better understanding of the realities of living beyond the "Westminster bubble".

Vulnerability

National lockdown in March 2020 emptied cities and streets of almost all people, the vast majority having retreated to their homes, where they awaited – with some trepidation – the government's daily press briefings. However, the reality is that the risk of dying or becoming seriously ill from Covid-19 is not the same for everyone in the country. We have also seen stark differences in infection rates and mortality between countries. This suggests that our pandemic response, and our national health and care systems, have failed.

Covid spares the young, especially children and infants, for whom the risks of illness are very low and the risks of death are negligible. The risk of death from Covid doubles with every decade. In the United Kingdom, older people are more likely to have serious illness when they contract Covid-19 compared to younger groups, and death rates are far higher – with those aged over 80 being 70 times more likely to die than those under 40. Fewer than 2 per cent of the population with symptoms are admitted to hospital; and most people get better, although some people may go on to have enduring post-viral symptoms.

Poverty is also a risk factor for serious illness and death from Covid. People living in areas of deprivation have significantly higher rates of infection – and double the mortality rates from Covid – of those in the least deprived areas. Analysis of UK admissions found that over a half of hospitalized patients had other health problems, such as diabetes, chronic cardiac or pulmonary disease, dementia or obesity, and that these were all associated with increased mortality. Obesity, for example, increases the risk of death from Covid by 48 per cent.

Both poverty and obesity correlate with socio-economic status – the better off are more likely to have healthier diets than the poor – so Johnson's current focus on a plan for addressing obesity is at least partly wide of the mark; dealing with interrelated issues demands joined-up policy, so an anti-poverty strategy needs to be part of the package too.

Ethnicity and Covid-19

The virus also impacts ethnic groups in different ways. Antibody surveillance data has shown that people from BAME groups are between two and three times more likely to have had Covid-19 than White people. Not only are ethnic minority groups more likely to contract the virus, they are more likely to die. Office for National Statistics (ONS) data show that Black males are 4.2 times more likely to die a Covid-19-related death and Black females are 4.3 times more likely than White ethnicity males and females. There is also a raised risk of death for people of Bangladeshi, Pakistani, Indian and Mixed ethnicities compared with those of White ethnicity. These differences were smaller, but persisted, after taking factors such as age, body mass index (BMI), smoking, deprivation, hypertension and other health issues into account.

Increased exposure of BAME groups to Covid goes some way to explaining these figures. Factors such as poor housing conditions, multigenerational living and crowded households may also be significant factors in the spread of disease and exposure to higher viral loads. People from BAME groups are also overrepresented in key worker, health and social care roles, as well as in less secure, lower-paid employment, in which defensive strategies such as social distancing are more difficult.

Review of the impact of Covid-19 on BAME communities found delayed presentation for testing and care, because of stigma and fear. Those from BAME backgrounds also had a worse experience of the pandemic than White people, and were more likely to be worried about the impact on their finances, as well as their physical and mental health. They were also less likely to trust information from the NHS, the government or scientists.

Care home residents: the most vulnerable group of all

The people most affected by illness and death from Covid-19 are older people, those receiving domiciliary care and care home residents. The initial lockdown in March was effective at slowing transmission of the virus overall, but huge failings in our social care system led to shocking infection and death rates in the elderly population. The early data from China, Spain and Italy made it abundantly clear that death rates from Covid-19 are far higher among older people, particularly those over 80. By June 2020 56 per cent of nursing homes in England had reported cases. By 23 June the majority of the 64,000+ excess deaths in the

United Kingdom had occurred among those aged 75 and over – many in care homes.

Government policy, then, failed to protect over 1.5 million disabled, elderly and chronically ill people, many of whom were, essentially, in solitary confinement for almost six months, and continue to have very restricted visitor rights. A crucial issue was lack of access to high-quality primary care and hospital care for care home residents. GPs in some parts of the United Kingdom were instructed not to visit and video calls substituted for care; many hospitals were instructed to empty their wards of older people (even if they were Covid-positive) and some refused to admit older people. Hospitalization rates for older people were very low. And all this was compounded by low staffing levels, poor staff training and a lack of PPE, which further undermined the quality of care.

As a result, between 28 December 2019 and 12 June 2020 there were 93,475 deaths in care homes in England and Wales, 45.9 per cent more than the same period a year earlier. Of these, 19,394 were registered as being caused by Covid-19. In Scotland, by September 2020 46 per cent of Covid-19 deaths had been in care homes.

The high death rates were the result of the state not being in control of social care in the United Kingdom, which is among the most privatized and fragmented in the Western world. In the UK there are around 410,000 residents in care homes, with around 5,500 different providers operating 11,300 care homes for older people. For-profit providers own 83 per cent of care home beds and social services are underfunded; between 2010/11 and 2017/18 local authority spending on social care fell by 49 per cent in real terms.

Underfunding, coupled with a diversion of resources to shareholders, means understaffing – which all leads to poor-quality care. Care services in England employ roughly 1.5 million staff, of whom 79 per cent are employed by the independent sector. Pay is low; 24 per cent of the workforce are on zero-hour contracts, and in March 2019 around a quarter were being paid the national living wage of £7.83 per hour or less.

In England the sector is over 120,000 workers short, further contributing to inadequate care, and the use of agency staff, who move from one home to another, increases the risk of disease transmission. Worse still, staff on zero-hour contracts do not get sick pay, so they often go to work with infectious diseases. A University College London (UCL) report has demonstrated that lower ratios of staff to patients are a risk factor for infection. We also now know that the risk of infection for staff in care homes using agency staff was twice that of other care homes. Residents in these homes were therefore also more likely to become infected. Having more staff caring for fewer patients would have minimized this transfer of infection between individuals and allowed for infection control procedures to be more strictly observed.

Social care has remained a low priority despite the high mortality associated with Covid-19 among frail older adults, not to mention the increased risk for social care staff. With residents in care homes also denied visits from relatives, as well as having minimal interaction with staff, and healthcare, when delivered, often done remotely – even when they are gravely ill or dying – these residents have an increased risk of neglect, or even abuse. The government should have doubled staffing levels, redeploying medical students, nursing students and clinical staff from quieter parts of the NHS and then planning for higher staffing levels in the long term.

As the Covid-19 pandemic has shown us, looking after a population made up of people in so many different situations needs local knowledge and well-informed, joined-up policies. Unfortunately, in spite of the all too clear impact of Covid-19 in the United Kingdom's privatized and fragmented care sector, not to mention the continuing exhortations to "protect our NHS", government policy has continued to develop along the usual lines, with centralization and privatization, rather than localism and the public sector, being the default approaches.

Testing

As a result, when it came to increasing the United Kingdom's capacity for Covid-19 testing, instead of boosting the underfunded NHS, university and PHE laboratories, the government set up a parallel privatized system for testing and tracing. The testing strategy published on 2 April 2020 supported the development of a UK diagnostics industry by expanding commercial testing for polymerase chain reaction (PCR) and antibody tests. These are being delivered by an alliance that includes Deloitte, Thermo Fisher Scientific, Amazon, Boots, Royal Mail and Randox, alongside the Wellcome Trust, Lighthouse labs and a few universities.

These commercial labs were set up in partnership with GSK and AstraZeneca, albeit with the support of NHS and university staff and equipment. There was also a large public subsidy. Astonishingly, though, neither GSK nor AstraZeneca had any experience of diagnostics, so, unsurprisingly, they ran into problems from the start.

Tests were not processed and returned, were poorly labelled and could not be linked to patient identifiers or postcodes; so they did not connect into the system. Commercial labs did not publish their standards and were unable to meet their contracts, leaving people without tests. There were also issues with the performance of the labs and the tests themselves. At the time of writing we still do not know how many people have been tested, and how many tested positive; and, of those testing positive, we do not know how many are infectious and how many have evidence of past infection.

Despite the failings of this largely private, highly centralized NHS test and trace system, it has been reported that the government intends to scale up testing to deliver weekly tests for the whole population. Deloitte and a slew of commercial companies are being contracted to deliver them under Operation Moonshot, a plan to ramp up tests to 10 million a day, at a cost of £100 billion – 70 per cent of the annual NHS budget for England. Ten million tests a day will generate 10,000 people testing false positives a day and result in unnecessary isolation and hardship for them and their contacts.

Lack of clinical integration

One of the key failures in responding to the pandemic was the government's decision to take testing out of health services. Normally, it is not possible to order a test without going through a health professional, whose role is to report suspected cases through the statutory notification system, order tests and bring together clinical symptoms with the test results. A test is simply a diagnostic tool. However, the current PCR Covid test is not a test of infectiousness, as it cannot distinguish between those who have the virus and are transmitting and those who have remnants of the virus but are not infectious. This is why symptoms are such an important part of the diagnosis.

However, primary care and GPs have been cut out of the testing system. As a result, the statutory notification system for reporting suspected cases was not followed, which delayed outbreak control and left the country without good data on cases. It also resulted in healthy symptomless people ordering tests and home kits, thereby adding to the demand for tests and the chaos and confusion over the interpretation of results. Matt Hancock, the United Kingdom's health minister, in September took to blaming the public for inappropriate use of tests when the system they set up was designed for self-referral. The only way to tackle this is for the government to integrate Covid services back into health services and resource primary care.

Privatized contact tracing loses its way

When people test positive for Covid-19 they are asked to self-isolate and give details of their contacts over the last two days. Contact tracing, testing of contacts, case finding, isolation and quarantine are classic public health measures for controlling communicable diseases. They require local teams on the ground, meticulously tracking cases and contacts to snuff out the reservoirs of infection. This approach is recommended by the World Health Organization (WHO) at all stages of the pandemic. It was painstakingly adopted in countries such as China, Singapore and Taiwan, with a high percentage of close contacts identified and many housed in hotels. Germany has traced contacts throughout. The leaked UK national risk register proposes it.

However, just like the public laboratories, the existing public system for contact tracing, which is operated through Public Health England and run by 21 local public health protection teams, had also been badly eroded by decades of cuts and closures. Again, instead of rebuilding its capacity, the government decided to create a parallel, centralized and complex privatized system. Like parts of the privatized testing system, it would be managed by the outsourcing giant Serco and the call centre company Sitel, neither of which has any experience in contact tracing.

The results, predictably, are not encouraging: the 27,000 workers employed by Serco and Sitel reached and advised an average of around two cases and two contacts per call handler over a 12-week period – the equivalent of around £900 per person traced. They reported having nothing to do, with some having no calls to make at all, claiming that they were, effectively, being paid to watch Netflix. Test and trace data also show that, in the 12-week period leading up to 5 August 2020, between them, the privatized national call centres and online services reached just over half the close contacts of those diagnosed with Covid-19, leaving local health protection teams and local councils to mop up the rest.

The failures of the privatized centralized system and the need to deal with outbreaks locally saw a few local councils and groups across England – from Sheffield to Suffolk – setting up their own test and trace schemes out of sheer frustration at the failures of the centralized private system.

Meanwhile, PHE and its local public health protection teams, working with local authorities, are already proving exceptionally effective, despite under-resourcing and the fragmentation inherent in the system. As of 5 August 2020 the PHE workload for complex contacts was one and a half times that of Serco and Sitel; and PHE teams were reaching and advising 95 per cent of the contacts.

The government appeared to recognize that there were problems, but only after appointing the management consultancy firm McKinsey – at a cost of £560,000 – to review the contact tracing service, rather than asking PHE, which was, clearly, doing the same job, but rather more effectively. The result was that, although the system was reorganized and relaunched, it did not take long for things to unravel once again.

This was mostly because, in spite of the apparent push to localize the system, the same companies – Serco and Sitel – did the contact tracing. Having already received £200 million, their contracts were extended by a projected £528 million. By contrast, PHE's budget for control of all infectious diseases came to a total of £87 million in 2018/19, about an eighth of Serco and Sitel's funding. Worse still, none of their staff will be moved to work with local authorities, as a result of the "new way of working" to strengthen local systems. As a result, although private companies make the initial call, if they fail to reach the contact, the obviously underfunded, but more locally aware, council teams must still take up the slack.

It is hardly surprising that this approach is not fit for purpose, and, once again, government would get far more "bang" for its "buck" by empowering the local authorities, local public health teams and local health services (including GPs and NHS laboratories) and giving them the resources to get the job done.

It is also important to recognize that these services are not all about money, and a large part of the reason for the higher success rate of the underfunded PHE staff is that contact tracing is skilled and sensitive work, which involves asking the right questions and building trust. It is hardly surprising, therefore, that it is experienced healthcare teams, rather than raw recruits, that deliver the best outcomes. Not only that, but local contact tracing, integrated with NHS labs and primary care, is the best building block of an effective test, track and trace programme. It would also be a programme the public – in all its many forms – could have confidence in.

The marginalization of public health and operational expertise

The marginalization of local influence in the United Kingdom's Covid-19 response and health policy is also apparent in the lack of formal recognition for the role of "hands-on" operational expertise in public health and communicable disease control and decades of expertise. The country's attitude towards other forms of knowledge when "following the science" is thus best illustrated by the sidelining of "real" experts in handling outbreaks and epidemics. Important knowledge about the established systems for pandemic control has therefore been squandered, and critical skills and insights wasted, with even PHE officials being almost completely invisible throughout the pandemic so far.

An influential factor in this is likely to be the fact that neither England's chief medical officer (CMO) nor the United Kingdom's chief scientific adviser (CSA) has a public health background. Until 2010 CMOs were drawn from a cadre of public health doctors whose unique training included expertise in health systems administration, health services planning, communicable disease control and monitoring population health. Public health doctors worked first as clinicians and then as public health doctors, gaining experience in the different administrative tiers of the NHS. The last CMO with a public health background retired in 2010. Chris Whitty, at the time of writing England's current CMO, was appointed only in October 2019 and is not a public health doctor. He held a number of clinical and academic posts in the United Kingdom, Africa and Asia, and is head of the National Institute for Health Research (NIHR) and a hospital consultant in infectious diseases. However, expertise in clinical infectious diseases is not the same thing as expertise in communicable disease control and outbreak control. The former is patient-oriented, whereas the latter is oriented towards populations.

Similarly, the CSA, Patrick Vallance, is a hospital-based clinical pharmacologist, who was a professor of medicine and consultant physician at UCL Hospital before moving into industry for five years at GlaxoSmithKline. He was appointed as CSA in 2018.

Both were therefore fairly new appointees to their roles, and neither would have lived through the changes to the NHS, its fragmentation, privatization or the erosion of communicable disease control and public health – let alone the impact of the 2012 Lansley Health and Social Care Act, which left health services fragmented, eroded and struggling to respond.

A further problem was the extraordinary faith in modellers over communicable disease epidemiologists. None of this might have mattered but for the clear marginalization of public health and lack of operational knowledge in the policy responses to the Covid crisis. To illustrate, Neil Ferguson's Imperial College model, which precipitated the government's decision to implement the first national lockdown on 23 March 2020, on the basis of a projected 400,000 or more deaths and the NHS being overwhelmed, simply did not take sufficient account of the impact of public health interventions such as contact tracing, quarantine, travel restrictions and social distancing. Moreover, the behavioural scientists at times seem more concerned with implementing policies than the lack of science and evidence behind them.

Policies must match population needs

Pandemic control needs tried and tested methods – so called "shoe leather" epidemiology – including on-the-ground community surveillance, the monitoring of cases, clusters and outbreaks, relentless enquiry and the careful pursuit, isolation, quarantine and monitoring of cases and contacts. It is all hands-on. There is no fancy modelling needed, just straightforward epidemiological analysis of new cases, incidence rates, prevalence rates and clusters, and painstaking enquiry and understanding of the local community, barriers to isolation and support required. Contact tracers and communicable disease control experts must know their communities.

This is why the local PHE staff, who understand their communities and are not profit-driven, are so much more effective than their freshly recruited opposite numbers in the private sector. They do not get paid to watch Netflix at work, either. There is a huge expertise in contact tracing, with environmental health officers and those working in sexually transmitted diseases seeing over 400,000 cases a year. These experts, who are also often trained as counsellors because of the sensitive nature of their work, were also marginalized and not asked for advice. But, for the CMO, CSA and government, it seems that what counted as "scientific knowledge" (in so far as there is such a distinct form of knowledge) was accompanied by a disregard for local, experiential and practical knowledge.

Failure to recognize that a pandemic is made up of thousands of outbreaks, each of which has to be dealt with locally, the sidelining of local authorities and the absence of a clear system for communicable disease control with well-defined responsibilities and clear lines of accountability did not serve us well before the pandemic, let alone during it. The disinvestment in health – and social care in particular – has had shameful consequences. Although the current government has pledged £31.9 billion for the NHS, much of this will go straight out to commercial providers; a staggering £15 billion will go to PPE, £10 billion to test and trace and just £5 billion to the NHS, including some private hospitals, even though these have already been underwritten by the government during Covid. The plans to give them a further £10 billion of contracts to ease waiting lists in the NHS over the next four years suggest both further privatization ahead and that the current government has still not learned its lesson.

With unemployment rising – and projected to rise further – instead of furloughing staff for jobs that may not exist in a year's time, the government could be putting in a major re-employment plan to fill the major gaps in public services, whether it be teaching, housing or health and social care. It is projected that a 50 per cent increase in staffing levels for care homes will be required by 2035 – just for the workforce to maintain its current ratio to the number of people aged 75 and over in England. But staffing levels are too low, so many more are needed.

A forward-looking policy would be to reinstate and reinvest in the NHS as a public service, nationalize care homes and integrate social care into the NHS as locally run services.

Finally, we need to take a leaf out of the Attlee government's book. It recognized the problems and addressed them. But the crucial insight was that health was not just about treating sick people; it was also largely about trying to facilitate jobs that paid a solid living wage and providing proper accommodation at an affordable cost. Policies that will address the problems that Britain has now, as well as some of those we have yet to see, will not be tackled by the enrichment of a few people – whose businesses are often not even up to the job anyway. It requires policies that recognize the causes of what we see around us and seek to address them.

Further reading

Bottery, S. 2020. "How Covid-19 has modified some of social care's key problems". The King's Fund, 25 August. Available at: www.kingsfund.org.uk/publications/covid-19-magnified-social-care-problems?

Deeks, J., A. Brookes & A. Pollock 2020. "Operation Moonshot proposals are scientifically unsound". *British Medical Journal* 370:m3699. Available at: www.bmj.com/content/bmj/370/bmj.m3699.

Macfarlane, R. & A. Pollock 2020. "Getting back on track: control of Covid-19 outbreaks in the community". *British Medical Journal* 369:m2484. Available at: www.bmj.com/content/369/bmj.m2484.

Pollock, A. 2005. *NHS plc: The Privatisation of Our Health Care.* London: Verso.

Pollock, A., L. Clements & L. Harding-Edgar 2020. "Covid-19: why we need a national health and social care service". *British Medical Journal* 369:m1465. Available at: www.bmj.com/content/bmj/369/bmj.m1465.full.pdf.

7

Reforming social care through a care-led recovery

Susan Himmelweit

Covid-19 has exposed and exacerbated the failings of a precarious, underfunded, privatized social care sector. Privatization has created a social care system that delivers unsatisfactory care by undertrained and badly treated workers. The pandemic has showed up the false economy of years of neglect, which has taken a huge toll on the lives and well-being of those the care system should be protecting.

The shocking number of deaths in care homes has highlighted key failures in the government's approach to managing the pandemic. Not only was it generally unprepared, callously dismissive of the interests of the most vulnerable and committed to an unwarranted belief in the ability of the private sector to prepare for and respond to risks. The government also misused the public sector, by both giving out large contracts to private sector firms instead of using local public health services and fixating on the popular institution of the NHS rather than the public good the NHS is designed to serve.

Thus, protecting and strengthening social care services were given far lower priority than protecting the NHS – hence the fateful discharging of untested patients to care homes ill equipped either to care for them or to protect their other residents. Reserving testing and personal protective equipment for the NHS meant that those both using and providing social care were unprotected, consequently suffering unnecessarily high death rates. These attempts to "save the NHS" may have stopped the institution from going under, but only by sacrificing the health and lives it was set up to protect.

The social care system that entered the pandemic was underfunded, understaffed, undervalued and at risk of collapse. Any response to Covid-19 – however fast or comprehensive – would have needed to contend with this legacy of political neglect. When it comes to rebuilding the economy, it will be important to learn from the current crisis and commit to genuine reform. It should now be clear to everybody that an economic and social system is only as good as the quality of care that it provides.

The current system

Whether an individual will need social care, and how much he or she will need, is unpredictable. This is the classic type of risk that the welfare state was designed to provide for collectively, in order to ensure that the costs do not fall disproportionately on the individuals unlucky enough to be affected. It is the same principle that underpinned the founding of the NHS.

However, unlike medical care, most social care is not provided free at the point of need. Instead, heavily means-tested support for social care is provided only to those on very low incomes and with few or no assets. People who do not meet the needs threshold, or who have incomes or assets above very low thresholds, are required either to find and pay for their own care in the market or to rely upon others to provide unpaid care. And, unlike the nationally funded NHS, it is a local authority responsibility to fund social care.

Since 1990 local authorities have been forced to tender for the care services they provide. As a result, they are now purchasers of care services from the private sector. Providers include some third sector non-profits; but most are for-profit providers. These range from small family-run care homes or domiciliary care providers to large commercial chains of much larger homes and businesses, many owned by private equity and hedge funds based overseas.

This mandatory privatization of care services was justified on two grounds. First, it would give care recipients choice and control of the services they received, which would in turn allow market competition to ensure quality and value for money. Second, through improving value for money, the cost of social care provision would be contained.

Containing the costs of social care to the state had become an obsession of successive governments. This is because medical success in preventing disability failed to keep pace with advances in keeping people alive, at the end of life and at younger ages alike. As a result, the numbers of both frail older people and working-age people with disabilities needing support steadily increased. Growing numbers of people needing care combined with rising employment rates of women, the traditional providers of informal unpaid care, to create a steadily rising demand for formal care. This is despite the vast majority of care still being provided unpaid by family carers, mostly, but not entirely, women. This has fundamental effects throughout the economy, because gendered assumptions and behaviour around the provision of unpaid care, for children as well as adults, are at the root of gender inequality in the economy more widely. The current system – which relies on traditional norms and roles for women, and on paying them poorly – is showing signs of strain and will not be sustainable in the long run as women's other opportunities change.

The effects of privatization

Care is a particularly bad candidate for privatization and quality improvement through competition. It is a highly labour-intensive sector, and must remain so to maintain standards. Indeed, the ratio of staff to care recipients is generally seen as a measure of quality in care provision. Although technology can often improve the quality of care, it cannot in general substitute for workers without cutting care quality. This means that the only way for providers to compete on costs is to reduce quality, by cutting staff numbers or employing workers whom they can pay less, notably women, people from BAME backgrounds and immigrants.

Consumer choice is supposed to limit harmful cost cutting by encouraging competition over quality. But exercising choice is difficult in a market in which changing providers is difficult and disruptive (certainly in residential care), quality is hard to judge prior to experience, and turnover among badly paid and poorly qualified workers is high. Although some in need of care have the resources to pay for excellent-quality care, most care is still paid for by local authorities or by individuals with very limited resources (given the severe means-testing applied to be eligible for state funding), with price competition fuelling a race to the bottom in terms of quality, in both the care provided and the employment conditions of workers. Rather than making the market work to the benefit of care recipients, insufficient resources and political will have invested in regulating care providers, with large providers – many of which are now parts of large "too big to fail" financialized chains – being favoured.

Care has always been underfunded. This is in large part a consequence of the failure, over more than 50 years, to use enough of the extra revenue generated by increased women's employment to finance a replacement for the care they previously provided unpaid. Even in 2006 the Wanless Report pointed out that social care was a crisis waiting to happen. Since 2010 austerity has exacerbated the problem, bringing the system to breaking point, with local authorities facing a 38 per cent cut in their central government grant between 2009/10 and 2018/19 at the same time as needs for social care have kept rising. In practice, these cuts have meant two things: (a) reductions in the amount local authorities pay care providers and cross-subsidization by self-funders, who are charged 41 per cent more than someone funded by their council; and (b) the needs threshold for receiving care has risen, with the government now spending 25 per cent less on social care for each individual over 65 years old than it did in 2009, leaving an estimated 1.5 million older people with unmet care needs.

Additional government funding to cover local authorities' Covid-19 costs was far too little and came too late. The fragmentation of our privatized social care system led to inadequate preparation for such an emergency by care providers themselves and made it difficult for local authorities to coordinate support. Although there was eventually some focus on care homes, those receiving and giving domiciliary and unpaid care have been almost entirely neglected.

What we need instead

A capabilities approach to running the economy

The aim of policy should not be to grow the economy, however measured, but to make the economy enhance the well-being of people and society in an equitable and sustainable way. Doing so equitably requires assigning priority to improving the well-being of the worst off; sustainability requires that policies, norms and behaviours reinforce rather than undermine each other, with respect not only to the physical environment but to our social infrastructure too.

There are many measures and interpretations of well-being, based on different principles. One that is particularly suited to validating care suggests that the pursuit of GDP growth should be replaced by the goal of enhancing the equitable and sustainable development of "capabilities" – that is, what people can choose to do and be. Under this interpretation, an equitable well-being economy would prioritize ensuring, as far as possible, that a set of basic capabilities was available to all. If we define people as needing care when their basic capabilities are reduced in comparison with those needed to function in society, this would make the provision of high-quality care the first priority of such an economy's government.

What those prioritized basic capabilities are would need to be decided democratically, by some deliberative process. They are likely to cover more of Martha Nussbaum's ten core capabilities (see Nussbaum 1988), which include being able to experience emotions, affiliation, play and control over one's environment, than our current low-aspiration notion of social care, which tends to focus only on the physical capabilities needed to achieve specified activities of daily living. Good-quality care can contribute to far more.

Using the capabilities approach, a society does better if its population is more educated, healthier and better cared for. By contrast, in focusing on GDP growth, all that matters is what is produced and can be sold. In practice, these things matter to us only in so far as they enable us to do or to be what we want. They should be seen simply as a means to such an end. If pursued as ends in themselves, priorities will inevitably be distorted.

Develop a universal care service

A publicly and centrally funded universal care service, free at the point of need, should be set up to take collective responsibility for care needs. It would cover domiciliary and residential care as well as everything in between (e.g. care services in sheltered housing, assisted living or retirement homes/villages). The basic capabilities to be covered as the criteria for receiving support would be nationally agreed, by some form of deliberative democracy, as would the forms of help available to enable everyone to have those basic capabilities as far as possible (and might well include other services besides personal care).

The universal care service would work closely with the NHS. It would be primarily a public sector service, but one that would make good use of services provided by non-profit third sector organizations. It would also invest heavily in preventative care, care that improves future well-being by avoiding preventable increases in health and care needs.

The range of basic capabilities for whose provision the universal care service would take responsibility should be decided at a national level. However, decisions about the mechanisms for enhancing capabilities should be decentralized: those receiving support would participate in the design of the whole system and have control over how their own care would be delivered. This is very different from the current notion of personal choice – as that which the market can deliver – which has led to the demise of many day centres and other collective forms of care.

Value care and care workers properly

There were 122,000 vacancies in the care industry in October 2019. Paid care workers' pay, working conditions and career opportunities will have to be improved if the universal care service is to be able to recruit and train men and women willing to learn and deliver good-quality care. Care workers would become capability facilitators. As such, they would require far more extensive skills than those that are currently required of care workers, who are seen as unskilled – just doing what the rest of us do anyway and/or women do unpaid for others in the family – even though, in practice, many care workers acquire unrecognized skills and do much to enhance capabilities.

Contracts would also have to be improved. It is a measure of the depths to which delivering high-quality care has fallen as a policy goal that, in work in which the quality of relationships is critical, zero-hours contracts are now the norm. Many people receiving care do not even know who will be coming to care for them each day. Care recipients and care workers both deserve better.

This is an opportunity to transform employment in care in a much-needed positive direction. Up to now, long-term care work has often been a job of last resort, for those who cannot get a "proper" job. Instead, all care work should be well-paid, skilled work with good conditions, so that both men and women are proud to choose it as a profession.

Mainstream care by organizing society around those who need care and worker/carers

The professionalization of paid care described above should greatly improve standards and, provided it is universally available, relieve the necessity of people depending on or having to provide unpaid care. However, paid care will always work in tandem with the care that families and friends freely provide. But, for this to be able to foster equal relationships, those receiving unpaid care and their carers will need to be better supported by good-quality, reliable professional services. Carers and those they care for should never be left without support; and both must be able to take a break from each other and have time to do other things with their lives.

Society should be organized around the assumption that it is normal for people, including workers, both to give and to receive care. This is not just about employment; but it is, above all, in employment that conditions need to change if carers and those they care for are to be treated equally. Good conditions in employment might then spill over into other activities, so that they, too, become more adaptable to the specific needs of those who give and receive care.

Normal conditions of employment for everyone, including working hours and the notice given of shift changes, should be compatible with reasonable care responsibilities and disabilities. Individuals should also have rights to take leave, without loss of income, for periods when care needs or demands are exceptionally high.

Currently, the people meeting demands for care are more likely to be women, perpetuating gender inequality. But, even if that were not the case, closing off opportunities to those with caring needs or responsibilities sends the wrong signal about the place of care in society. No job should be considered so important that it cannot be combined with carrying out the normal duties of a carer or be done by a person with a disability. Nor should those with care needs or responsibilities have to pay for the conditions that they need in lower wages.

Similar requirements should apply to the providers of services, both private and public, and to policy-makers, so that care is mainstreamed into all aspects of thinking about and being in society. Policy-makers should be required to consider the impact of any policies they propose and/or implement on those receiving and those giving care, both paid and unpaid; and they should change those proposals if their impacts are negative or discriminatory.

Invest in care to lead the post-pandemic recovery

The pandemic is expected to bring massive rises in unemployment, particularly in some sectors where women predominate, such as hospitality and retail; and any recovery will undoubtedly require government spending to generate jobs. Any type of spending should encourage employment, but most proposals focus on investment that would provide benefits in the future as well as jobs now. Recognizing that this is a chance to rebalance the economy in a more desirable direction, various spending proposals have been made to "build back better", including various "Green New Deals". One obvious candidate for rebalancing the economy is to invest public money in a new universal care service that can, as outlined above, rectify the problems caused by our underfunded privatized care system. Such an investment would also rebalance the economy in another way, by significantly tackling both the causes of gender inequality and their manifestation in the gender employment gap.

Nearly all other proposals, even the green ones, focus on investing in the construction industry, such as, for example, improving the carbon footprint of existing buildings. The gender impacts of these proposals are rarely considered. But, unless there is a specific mandate to give the majority of newly created jobs to women, investing in construction will inevitably worsen the gender employment gap, by employing more men than women.

Government spending works to stimulate employment by creating jobs not only in the industries directly targeted but also indirectly in industries down their supply chain. Jobs are also generated by the spending of the wages of any newly employed workers. Analysis by the Women's Budget Group (WBG) has shown that any investment in care would produce far more jobs in total than a similar-sized investment in construction. This remains true even when wages and hours are matched in the two industries, showing that the greater employment stimulus effects of investing in care do not depend on the newly created jobs being worse paid or of shorter hours than those in construction.

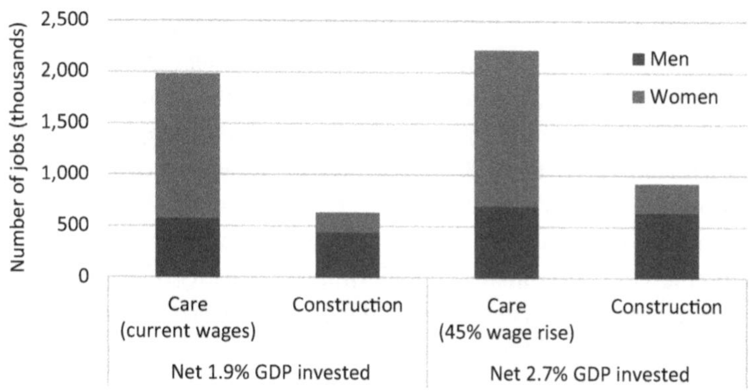

Figure 7.1 Employment effects of investing in care and construction
Source: Calculations by Jerome De Henau for WBG, based on 2015 data from Eurostat.

Since investment in care produces more jobs overall, it also results in more revenue being recouped through increased taxes, making the relative gains of employment from investment in care even greater when net costs are compared.

Figure 7.1 shows the number of jobs created by investing in a care system that has 10 per cent of total employment in care in the United Kingdom (roughly the same as in Denmark) in two scenarios: on the left with unchanged wage levels, and on the right with wages raised by 45 per cent (roughly to match those of Denmark as a proportion of average wages). Figure 7.1 also shows how many jobs would be created by investing the same *net* amounts in construction.

It can be seen that investment in care produces far more jobs overall (under either scenario). And, although investment in construction increases the gender employment gap, by creating far more jobs for men than for women, investment in care narrows it. However, because of the greater total employment generated, investment in care still provides almost as many jobs for men.

From here to there: strategy and implementation

One of the most difficult issues in developing a universal care system will be how to make the change from here to there. Private sector care is by now well embedded in the UK social care system. And there are some excellent private for-profit care providers, although it can be argued that they are excellent despite their for-profit status, rather than because of it.

There are also many care recipients, particularly among the younger disabled, who value the freedom that being able to employ their own care assistants gives them. Any universal system will need to allow space for care recipients to have at least the level of control that the market now gives them, to choose who supports them and how, without allowing market forces to dominate and undermine the quality of the system as a whole. Hopefully, real autonomy can then be achieved, not just the very limited autonomy of the market.

The first steps would have to be to invest in care workers: improving their pay and conditions and ensuring that sufficient numbers are recruited to meet the need. This would require setting up new training programmes and a new professional qualification for care workers, based on the skills needed to enhance capabilities. Similarly, a proper career structure, comparable with that of other skilled professions, would be required, with entry-level care workers paid above a realistic living wage and prospects for substantial progression. Special training and fast-track qualifications for current care workers should recognize and build upon their undervalued skills and experience.

Existing care providers could be funded to employ more staff, provided that they conform to stringent quality and training requirements. Most would need help with meeting the increased costs of doing so. Such funding should be given only in return for a public stake in the business of any provider over a certain size. The economies of scale of large providers, which tend to make care less personal, might disappear under such regulations; and many large providers would find continuing to provide care unprofitable. They could be bought out and turned over to local authorities, with their staff re-employed to form the nucleus of the universal care service, setting high standards that any remaining providers would have to meet to stay in business. At the same time, new forms of social ownership, such as cooperatives of care workers and receivers, should be developed and existing providers given help in transitioning to them. Capacity would also need to be built within the public sector, at national and – primarily – local levels, to administer the universal care service.

Further reading

Button, D. & S. Bedford 2019. "Ownership in social care: why it matters and what can be done". London: New Economics Foundation. Available at: https://neweconomics.org/uploads/files/Ownership-in-social-care-report.pdf.

De Henau, J. & S. Himmelweit 2020. "A care-led recovery from coronavirus: the case for investment in care as a better post-pandemic economic stimulus than investment in construction". London: Women's Budget Group. Available at: http://wbg.org.uk/wp-content/uploads/2020/06/Care-led-recovery-final.pdf.

Nussbaum, M. 1988. "Nature, function and capability: Aristotle on political distribution". *Oxford Studies in Ancient Philosophy* 6 (Supp.): 145–84.

Unison 2020. "Care after Covid: a UNISON vision for social care". London: Unison. Available at: www.unison.org.uk/content/uploads/2020/06/A-UNISON-Vision-for-Social-Care-June-2020.pdf.

Women's Budget Group 2020. *Creating a Caring Economy: A Call to Action*. London: Women's Budget Group. Available at: https://wbg.org.uk/wp-content/uploads/2020/10/WBG-Report-v10.pdf.

8

The post-pandemic provision of education in the United Kingdom

Danny Dorling

Education in England has been increasingly privatized. The result has not been good. It has not produced a better educational service. When international comparisons are made this becomes painfully clear. It has not become more efficient, because of a proliferation of private nursey classes, the academization of state schools, all new schools being free schools, university student number competition, and so on; it has not resulted in young people in England becoming more able – although it may have persuaded many to believe that they are very able and very clever despite not being able to speak and write in as many languages as children can do elsewhere in Europe – nor to show imaginative ability in mathematics and science (as well as many other subjects), as other young people in Europe can demonstrate when international comparisons are made.

Figure 8.1 gives a summary of the problem. It shows results for mathematics, but much the same can be seen for reading and problem solving. It uses data from 2012, as the repeat OECD organized international surveys taken in 2015 and 2018 did not measure ability up to age 24 but only around age 16. Schools in the United Kingdom are quite good at priming young people to produce an expected answer at age 16 or 18. However, by age 24 a great deal of what was taught in a UK school has been forgotten (greater than is the case in most other European countries, as Figure 8.1 makes clear).

As the figure implies, this *may* be related to economic inequality. The higher the economic inequality in a country, the worse the real educational performance.

What Figure 8.1 shows is not that economic inequality directly *causes* poor educational outcomes, but that a country such as the United Kingdom, which has become so economically unequal in recent decades, will tend to move in the direction of other very unequal countries, such

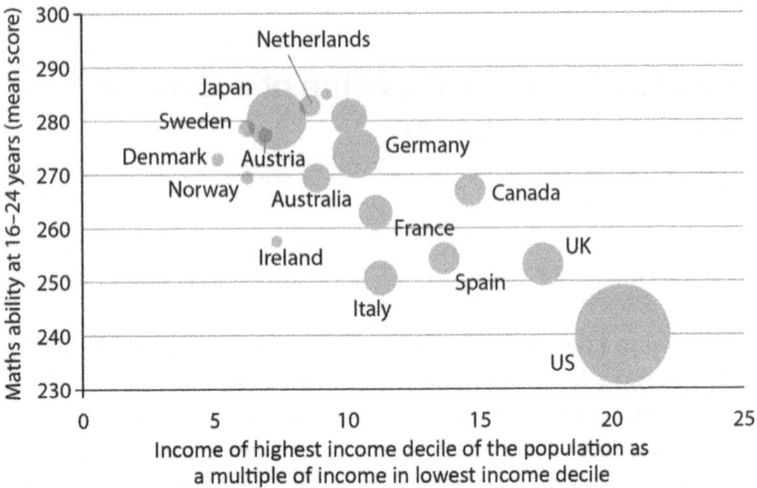

Figure 8.1 Economic inequality and the mathematics ability of young adults up to age 24, 2012

Notes: Countries are shown as circles sized by their respective populations. All countries for which there are data are included.

Sources: OECD (2013: tab. A2.7); income data from Dorling (2017).

as the United States. In contrast, in more equitable countries, such as Japan, Sweden, the Netherlands and Denmark, education at school is carried out in such a way that, when young adults are later tested in their early twenties, they are still – on average – quite competent in mathematics. The figure for ability at age 16 is not shown here, but it demonstrates a looser association than that shown in Figure 8.1 between inequality and educational outcome, implying teaching to the test – to get what appear to be good educational outcomes, but which (by age 24) have become obviously less clearly good.

As education in the United Kingdom, and especially in England, has been transformed from a service to a commodity that can be bought and sold, it has lost a great deal of its real, transformative, value – while often becoming a very expensive commodity. Annual private school fees in England are the highest in Europe. In fact, most of Europe has almost no private education. Similarly, English university fees are the highest in Europe; many countries in Europe have no such fees, or, if they do, these fees are negligible. The United Kingdom in the past was not this exceptional, and it need not be in the future when education is considered. We also need to understand that the United Kingdom is not just extreme when it comes to the European context. Private schools are less common and less costly in the richer US states; and, although Scotland still has free university tuition fees on average, in England the fees for attending university are even higher than those found across the United States. Affluent students avoid paying these fees, and the much larger loan repayments required if they are paid through a loan, by asking their parents to pay their university fees up front. Thus, in the United Kingdom, the poor who go to university pay more for an education.

The 2020 pandemic provides an opportunity to begin to take stock. It has highlighted inequalities in education in England in all kinds of ways, from the expenses of parents trying to look after their children when they were sent home from nurseries and schools in the spring of 2020 through to the fiasco of attempting the award of A level and GCSE grades in the late summer by a computer algorithm.

The debacle of August 2020

On Thursday 13 August 2020 A level students in England were awarded their exam grades. These were not grades for exams they had actually sat, but predictions of what they would each have achieved had they sat them. A government agency called Ofqual had invented an algorithm to try to predict what grades the students would have received, had they sat the exams that had been cancelled because of the pandemic.

When the results were released anger began to mount. It quickly became apparent that young people attending private schools had been awarded a much higher uplift in marks than those attending state schools – marks that were closer to what their teachers had predicted they might get. This was because of the way in which the algorithm had been designed. If a school in England had a relatively small number of students sitting A level exams then the predictions of their teachers were chosen over a model based on past school performance. Private schools very often have small class sizes. The algorithm resulted in the number of top grades in private schools being inflated overall by 5 per cent on the previous year, and 10.4 per cent in one subject (classics), as compared to almost no inflation for large sixth-form colleges and larger state schools.

The algorithm was published on the same day as the results were released, in a 319-page report (Ofqual 2020). The report used the phrase "independent school" rather than private school. Use of language is important here. Private schools are private in the same way that private healthcare is private: you have to pay for it; access is dependent on ability to pay. One reason for the mounting anger was that it became apparent that the children of richer people were now being awarded much higher grades simply because their parents were rich, not because of anything the children had done. Each of the four other nations of the United Kingdom overturned the use of such predicted grades in the days before England did (at 4 p.m. on Monday 17 August).

The rest of Europe avoided any drama because schools in other European countries held exams or based the marks awarded to young people on continuous assessment. They tended to award higher-than-average grades in other European countries, as finally happened across all the United Kingdom by late August 2020. This may have been a result of students across Europe studying more before the exams as there was little else they could do under the various lockdowns; it may also be a consequence of greater leniency from the examiners, aware of the conditions under which students were working in the spring of 2020. Issues of fairness did not come to the fore elsewhere in Europe to anything like the extent to which they did in England, partly because other European countries have far fewer private schools than there are in the United Kingdom.

Imagine how students would have performed at their A levels had the exams actually been held in June 2020, as happened in other European countries. Would those from schools that were better resourced have done worse, as they would not have had the advantage of the school keeping them "keen" up until the very last minute? Would the very small minority who attended a boarding school have done particularly badly, taking their exams in some local assessment centre near their parents' home instead of at that school? Almost all boarding schools had sent their children home when the pandemic began. Most importantly, would children from poorly resourced schools where few take A levels have actually done better than average, as they always had to rely disproportionately on their own ability and drive – even in the best of times? We will never know.

What we do know is that a rebellion led by students after they were unfairly awarded incorrect grades has resulted in far fewer being failed in 2020 than ever before; and a very large number of GCSE grades are also now being revised upwards. The students who were most vocal on Twitter and on television were often those predicted an A* who had been given an A or a B, and denied entry to their university of choice; but by their actions they helped grade hundreds of thousands of their contemporaries up, almost all who had been awarded much lower grades. The contrast with the past could not be greater. Almost four decades ago, in a typical English state school, those few children who did take A levels took and largely failed them. Incidentally, it is worth remembering that almost every academic and researcher who attended a state school, but went on to study at university, did not attend a typical English state school (such are the inequalities between English state schools).

It is very fortunate that the results of the GCSE grades modelled by Ofqual in 2020 were never released, as the model used to predict them explicitly treated private schools differently. Within the 319-page report it suggested that, for those schools, "they have a different relationship between prior attainment and outcomes" (Ofqual 2020: 25). That "different relationship" is called coaching, and it results in far higher GCSE grades and then A levels being awarded than any model would predict based on actual ability or flair.

Figure 8.2 shows how dramatically the funding of state and private schools varies across OECD countries and how the United Kingdom is the most extreme outlier in Europe on this measure. Note that Finland is highlighted in Figures 8.2 and 8.3, as it is the European country most dissimilar to the United Kingdom in terms of educational achievements. Private school funding as a percentage of GDP is given in brackets at the end of the bars in the figure. The United Kingdom sits between Colombia (one of the most economically unequal countries in Latin America) and the United States (the most economically unequal large rich country in the world).

What was so wrong before the pandemic?

Why does it matter economically if young UK adults are worse educated than in other affluent countries; or if the United Kingdom squanders such a high proportion of the funds it manages to find for secondary education on the tiny minority of children who attend private schools?

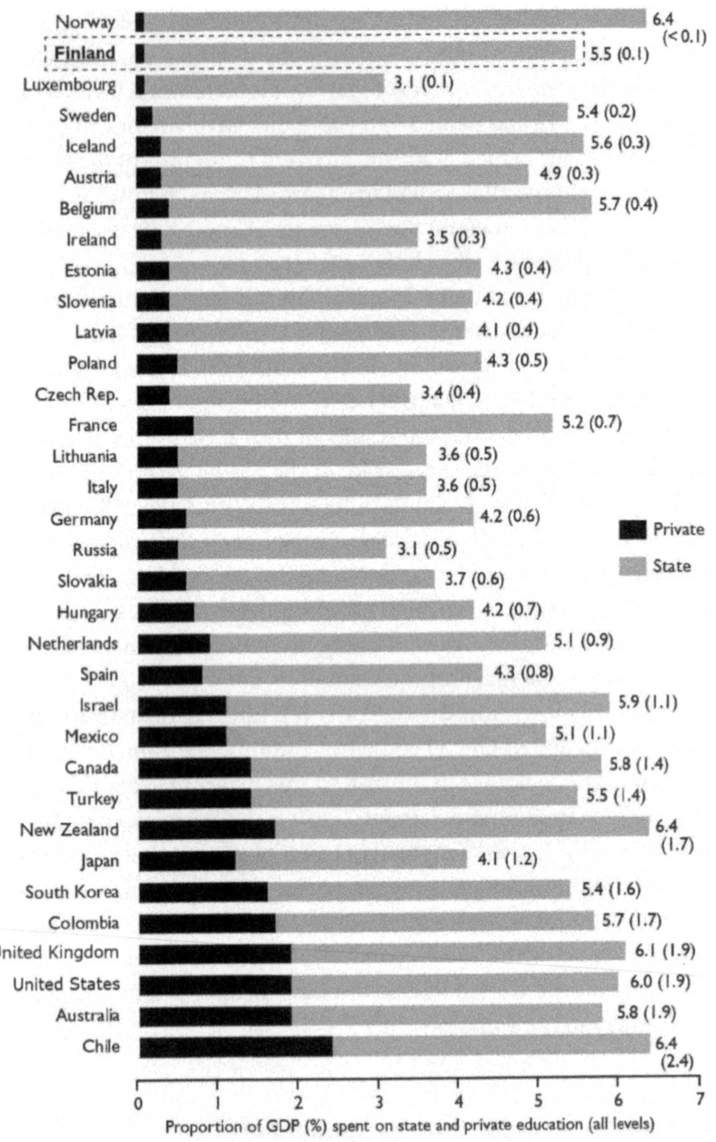

Figure 8.2 State and private school spending, OECD countries, 2016
Notes: Data for Denmark, Greece and Switzerland are missing from OECD (2019). Countries are sorted by the private percentage of the total amount.
Source: OECD (2019).

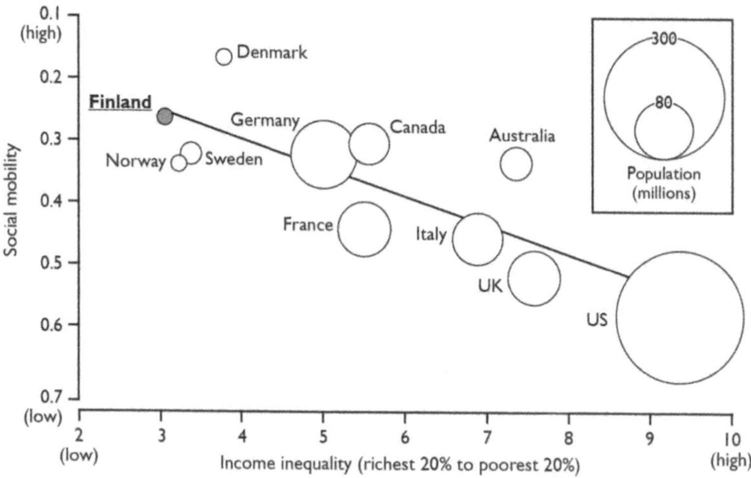

Figure 8.3 Social mobility and income inequality, by affluent country, 2009
Notes: In this version the area of each circle is made proportional to the population of each country. The horizontal axis is the ratio of the income of the richest fifth of households to the poorest (Wilkinson & Pickett 2009: 17), and the vertical axis is the measure of elasticity as reported in Blanden (2009: tab. 1).
Sources: Redrawn from data provided in Wilkinson & Pickett (2009), based in turn on intergenerational mobility data in Blanden (2009).

Superficially, this creates inefficiencies, such as those created when private healthcare spending is high. Health overall then suffers, just as education overall suffers when private education is so dominant in a society. More importantly, the maintenance of such a system holds people back from doing what they could do best and forces others (the children of the affluent) to take jobs they might not be well suited to or enjoy. This results in much lower social mobility in the United Kingdom compared to other countries, as is demonstrated in Figure 8.3.

By academic subject, the narrowing of options becomes even more stark when viewed in terms of who studies what in a UK university at age 18. Table 8.1 shows those 86 degree-level subjects that 500 or more students studied in 2019. Human geography is studied by 12 young people from the most educationally affluent fifth of backgrounds for every one young person who studies it from the equally populous fifth of areas where young people are least likely to go to university. In the past human geographers often went into banking as a profession. In the

United Kingdom we have not been drawing our bankers from a wide cross-section of society. Economics ranked fifth out of the 86, finance 18th, marketing 34th and business studies 35th.

The UK education system as currently arranged funnels young people to educational destinations according to their parents' resources far more than other countries do, and – for those who go to university at age 18 – into subjects determined very much by their social and economic background. Thus, the lower-paid and more caring professions rank towards the bottom of Table 8.1. Being accepted to take a degree in social work ranks lowest (86th); nursing is at 81st place, teacher training at 74th; and childcare would also be low if we had enough people taking a degree in it for it to even feature in the table (in Nordic countries it is studied at masters level).

Table 8.1 86 subjects ranked by polar 5 to polar 1 ratio, UK universities age 18, 2019

Rank	Polar 1	Polar 5	Polar 1	All students	Ratio	Degree accepted to study in UK in 2019
1	4.23%	50.78%	95	2,245	12.00	L7: human and social geography
2	4.65%	51.16%	30	645	11.00	A2: pre-clinical dentistry
3	4.83%	46.90%	35	725	9.71	D1: pre-clinical veterinary medicine
4	5.15%	50.00%	35	680	9.71	Q8: classical studies
5	5.05%	47.05%	270	5,345	9.32	L1: economics
	5.32%	46.36%	230	4,325	8.72	L7 & F8 combined: all geography
6	6.02%	51.20%	50	830	8.50	R9: European languages and literature
7	6.54%	47.06%	50	765	7.20	RR: combinations within European languages
8	6.34%	45.32%	335	5,285	7.15	A1: pre-clinical medicine
9	4.46%	30.36%	25	560	6.81	B5: ophthalmics
10	6.67%	44.10%	65	975	6.61	V5: philosophy
11	6.49%	41.59%	135	2,080	6.41	F8: physical geographical sciences
12	7.21%	45.19%	75	1,040	6.27	Y: combinations of social studies/business/law with languages

Table 8.1 *(Continued)*

Rank	Polar 1	Polar 5	Polar 1	All students	Ratio	Degree accepted to study in UK in 2019
13	7.01%	41.82%	135	1,925	5.97	Y: combinations of social studies/law with business
14	6.12%	36.05%	45	735	5.89	F6: geology
15	7.06%	41.00%	290	4,110	5.81	L2: politics
16	7.60%	44.13%	285	3,750	5.81	Z: combinations of 3 subjects and similar arrangements
17	6.45%	36.13%	50	775	5.60	F7: science of aquatic and terrestrial environment
18	7.27%	36.82%	80	1,100	5.06	N3: finance
19	7.39%	35.80%	95	1,285	4.84	K2: building
20	8.14%	37.74%	360	4,425	4.64	G1: mathematics
21	8.51%	38.65%	120	1,410	4.54	H8: chemical, process and energy engineering
22	8.69%	39.26%	455	5,235	4.52	N2: management studies
23	8.89%	40.00%	60	675	4.50	Y: combinations of languages
24	8.65%	38.78%	135	1,560	4.48	LL: combinations within social studies
25	8.84%	37.83%	285	3,225	4.28	Y: combinations of social studies/business/law with arts/humanities
26	9.35%	40.00%	540	5,775	4.28	V1: history by period
27	9.10%	38.40%	365	4,010	4.22	H3: mechanical engineering
28	8.29%	34.46%	160	1,930	4.16	H2: civil engineering
29	9.27%	37.86%	290	3,130	4.08	F3: physics
30	8.84%	35.99%	205	2,320	4.07	B1: anatomy, physiology and pathology
31	7.61%	30.98%	70	920	4.07	D4: agriculture
32	9.38%	37.50%	60	640	4.00	Y: combinations of physics/mathematics/computer sciences

(Continued)

Table 8.1 *(Continued)*

Rank	Polar 1	Polar 5	Polar 1	All students	Ratio	Degree accepted to study in UK in 2019
33	9.38%	36.42%	380	4,050	3.88	C1: biology
34	9.09%	34.32%	200	2,200	3.78	N5: marketing
35	9.94%	36.77%	530	5,330	3.70	N1: business studies
36	10.25%	37.63%	290	2,830	3.67	Y: combinations of languages with arts/ humanities
37	9.93%	36.14%	265	2,670	3.64	H1: general engineering
38	9.57%	33.91%	220	2,300	3.54	K1: architecture
39	10.13%	34.97%	310	3,060	3.45	F1: chemistry
40	10.47%	35.39%	500	4,775	3.38	Q3: English studies
41	10.07%	33.68%	145	1,440	3.34	H6: electronic and electrical engineering
42	10.25%	33.50%	205	2,000	3.27	H4: aerospace engineering
43	11.03%	35.29%	75	680	3.20	VV: combinations within history and philosophy studies
44	11.11%	34.87%	145	1,305	3.14	Y: combinations of physics/mathematics with social studies/ business/law
45	11.30%	34.46%	100	885	3.05	L6: anthropology
46	10.75%	32.64%	285	2,650	3.04	C7: molecular biology, biophysics and biochemistry
47	10.84%	32.79%	630	5,810	3.02	NN: combinations within business and administrative studies
48	9.74%	27.01%	285	2,925	2.77	N4: accounting
49	11.84%	32.03%	425	3,590	2.71	W3: music
50	10.70%	28.79%	275	2,570	2.69	B2: pharmacology, toxicology and pharmacy
51	10.04%	26.25%	130	1,295	2.61	C9: others in biological sciences
52	11.54%	29.80%	740	6,410	2.58	W2: design studies
53	12.14%	31.07%	125	1,030	2.56	C3: zoology

Table 8.1 *(Continued)*

Rank	Polar 1	Polar 5	Polar 1	All students	Ratio	Degree accepted to study in UK in 2019
54	11.34%	27.53%	140	1,235	2.43	Y: combinations of social studies/law
55	12.30%	29.53%	910	7,400	2.40	I1: computer science
56	12.11%	28.13%	155	1,280	2.32	P5: journalism
57	12.65%	28.77%	1660	1,3120	2.27	C8: psychology
58	12.11%	27.21%	425	3,510	2.25	P3: media studies
59	13.64%	30.30%	90	660	2.22	WW: combinations within creative arts and design
60	12.67%	28.02%	1485	11,725	2.21	M1: law by area
61	13.61%	30.00%	415	3,050	2.20	W6: cinematics and photography
62	13.29%	29.11%	105	790	2.19	Y: combinations of arts/humanities
63	11.48%	25.14%	105	915	2.19	B8: medical technology
64	12.18%	26.24%	615	5,050	2.15	B9: others in subjects allied to medicine
65	12.96%	27.23%	640	4,940	2.10	L3: sociology
66	13.44%	27.97%	305	2,270	2.08	N8: hospitality, leisure, sport, tourism and transport
67	13.77%	27.29%	285	2,070	1.98	Y: combinations of science/engineering with social studies/business/law
68	12.68%	24.88%	130	1,025	1.96	M2: law by topic
69	14.23%	27.64%	175	1,230	1.94	Y: combinations of science/engineering with arts/humanities/languages
70	13.49%	25.12%	145	1,075	1.86	W1: fine art
71	13.51%	24.66%	200	1,480	1.83	Y: combinations of medical/biological/agricultural sciences
72	14.42%	25.80%	450	3,120	1.79	W4: drama
73	14.25%	24.97%	1130	7,930	1.75	C6: sport and exercise science

(Continued)

Table 8.1 *(Continued)*

Rank	Polar 1	Polar 5	Polar 1	All students	Ratio	Degree accepted to study in UK in 2019
74	13.35%	22.89%	420	3,145	1.71	X1: training teachers
75	16.09%	25.29%	140	870	1.57	I3: software engineering
76	14.60%	21.17%	100	685	1.45	I2: information systems
77	15.89%	22.43%	85	535	1.41	II: combinations in computer sciences
78	17.48%	23.79%	180	1,030	1.36	D3: animal science
79	16.53%	21.49%	100	605	1.30	W5: dance
80	15.28%	19.82%	505	3,305	1.30	X3: academic studies in education
81	17.01%	19.23%	1150	6,760	1.13	B7: nursing
82	19.20%	20.40%	240	1,250	1.06	F4: forensic and archaeological science
83	20.27%	20.95%	150	740	1.03	L4: social policy
84	19.14%	19.47%	290	1,515	1.02	M9: others in law
85	21.84%	19.16%	285	1,305	0.88	I6: games
86	21.53%	14.85%	435	2,020	0.69	L5: social work

Notes: Polar 5 are small geographical neighbourhoods where the most educationally and economically advantaged fifth of young people in the United Kingdom reside, and Polar 1 are the neighbourhoods where the most disadvantaged fifth live. Data are rounded to the nearest five in the original source files to preserve anonymity. A combined geography total added (unranked). Data first published here: https://blog.geographydirections.com/2020/08/21/geography-and-the-shifting-ratios-of-inequality-university-a-levels-and-gcses-in-2020.

Source: Kernohan (2020).

Jobs in care are relatively cheap jobs. In June 2020 it was revealed that a 2.5 per cent GDP investment by the government in care – increasing the numbers working in care to 10 per cent of the employed population, as in Sweden and Denmark – and raising the pay of all care workers to the real living wage would create 2 million jobs, all at the real living wage (De Henau & Himmelweit 2020). This would increase the overall employment rate by five percentage points and reduce the gender employment gap by four percentage points. In a comparison made in that report with a similar-sized investment in construction, the authors found not only that the Treasury would recoup 50 per cent more in direct and indirect tax revenues from investment in care but that investing in care would also create nearly three times as many jobs – over six times as many for women and 10 per cent more for men. And, since investment in care is greener than construction, a care-led recovery would be a green-led recovery.

Although the report's authors did not make the point, had they chosen to look at the finance industry as their comparison (rather than construction), they would have found that only slightly more jobs would be created – and that is before the merit and value of the jobs is even considered.

What may change after the height of the pandemic?

At first, not much may appear to change as the pandemic subsides. However, at the university level many more students will now have begun studies in September 2020 in UK universities, as exam grades were based on teacher predictions of how the students would have performed "on a good day". At the very least, this will help reduce youth unemployment in the autumn of 2020; at most, it will widen horizons and possibilities. It will also bring the day closer when it is realized that the English student loans system is unsustainable, because these students will not be being paid an amount in future that would repay the loans.

The United Kingdom, and most especially England, needs to look again at how universities across the mainland of Europe are organized and financed. On 26 July 2020 it was announced that the UK government would be bailing out up to 13 UK universities that were at immediate risk of insolvency as a result of the pandemic and the way in which UK universities had been marketized and privatized. However, the government initially was offering only loans to institutions. This is no long-term solution.

At schools and further education colleges more students will be studying for A levels and other qualifications in the two years ahead, more doing what they have chosen to do than ever before, thanks to the huge uplift in GCSE results that occurred in August 2020 when the exam board results were not used.

More children doing what they have actually chosen to do is a very good thing. However, they will be struggling to do this in the mess of semi-privatized academy chains and other aberrations that were created by government ministers in the last decade or so in a desperate attempt to bring a market into state education. In a time with fewer and fewer resources available as international trade reduces, this will simply be too expensive a situation to continue to tolerate.

At the height of the mess in education in the United Kingdom is its extremely elitist system of private education, which shuts the vast majority of young people out of a privileged education system. At the same time, it uses up a huge proportion of funds, general school staff, teachers, teaching assistants, playing fields, buildings and money on a very small number of young people, most of whom do not actually need any extra help and would do perfectly well in the state system. Given the depth of the recession we are in, it will be interesting to see the extent to which some of these schools become, in effect, nationalized as parents cannot afford to pay the fees in future. Fewer extremely affluent school students are also expected to be flying in from abroad in future as the after-effects of the pandemic rumble on.

Governments in future will also need to consider the proliferation of private nursery provision that made childcare for younger children so very expensive. During the pandemic many such nurseries insisted that parents carry on paying even though they would or could not take their children. In other countries childcare is arranged differently and is not commodified to this extent. Here it is a source of great personal profit for the owner of a private nursery, who often pays the employees very lowly too. In the past there were more imaginative forms of childcare in the United Kingdom – and more cooperative ones as well (including both playgroups and summer play schemes, which I was employed in a long time ago). We need to learn not only from other countries; we can also learn from our past.

Older adult education is often forgotten, and it is only an afterthought here. But with possible mass unemployment, with more leisure time in the "new normal", we should look at it again. If shopping for things you do not really need is to stop being the great recreation and spending activity it once was; if people are to have time freed up from commuting; if the very elderly are going to have to isolate more often for some time to come; perhaps the very least we can do is begin to provide more older adult education. The pandemic has taught us how to teach remotely, but not (yet) how to teach well remotely.

One final point: we have to remember the disadvantage we have over where we are starting from. I am a human geographer, and, as mentioned above, Table 8.1 shows that my academic subject now collects together more young people from a privileged background than any other – and, in fact, by 2019 more than it had for many years. The pandemic will have altered that. A level grading by teacher opinion means that we geographers do not expect to head this table when data for 2020 are made available in 2021. However, when the two parts of geography (human and physical) are combined, there is just one large mainstream school subject that is even more exclusive in its intake of students. That subject ranks fifth in the table; it is economics. We should not expect economics graduates in the United Kingdom to have a wide knowledge of education – in fact, they are even more narrowly educated in terms of their experiences of living in different areas of the country than are geographers (both types combined). Better policy is going to have to be drawn up by a wider range of people than simply social scientists from the most elite of social sciences!

Further reading

Blanden, J. 2009. "How Much Can We Learn from International Comparisons of Intergenerational Mobility?", Discussion Paper 111. London: Centre for the Economics of Education, London School of Economics.

Collini, S. 2020. "English universities are in peril because of 10 years of calamitous reform". *The Guardian*, 31 August. Available at: www.theguardian.com/commentisfree/2020/aug/31/english-universities-peril-10-years-calamitous-reform-higher-education.

De Henau, J. & S. Himmelweit 2020. "A care-led recovery from coronavirus: the case for investment in care as a better post-pandemic economic stimulus than investment in construction". London: Women's Budget Group. Available at: http://wbg.org.uk/wp-content/uploads/2020/06/Care-led-recovery-final.pdf.

Dorling, D. 2017. *The Equality Effect: Improving Life for Everyone*. Oxford: New Internationalist.

Dorling, D. 2019. "Jubilee 2022: defending free tuition". London: Progressive Economy Forum. Available at: www.dannydorling.org/?page_id=7340.

Kernohan, D. 2020. "% POLAR4 Q1 vs % POLAR4 Q5: 2019 cycle". Public Tableau, 6 July. Available at: https://public.tableau.com/profile/david.kernohan#!/vizhome/Principalsubject-POLAR/Sheet1.

Morris, T. *et al.* 2018. "Examining the genetic influences on educational attainment and the validity of value-added measures of progress". *British Educational Research Journal* 44 (5): 727–47. Available at: https://bera-journals.onlinelibrary.wiley.com/doi/full/10.1002/berj.3466.

OECD 2013. *OECD Skills Outlook 2013: First Results from the Survey of Adult Skills*. Paris: OECD Publishing.

OECD 2019. *Education at a Glance 2019: OECD Indicators*. Paris: OECD Publishing.

Ofqual 2020. *Awarding GCSE, AS, A Level, Advanced Extension Awards and Extended Project Qualifications in Summer 2020: Interim Report*. London: Ofqual.

Wilkinson, R. & K. Pickett 2009. *The Spirit Level: Why More Equal Societies Almost Always Do Better*. London: Allen Lane.

PART III

REFORM OF CORPORATE GOVERNANCE, INDUSTRIAL STRATEGY AND FINANCE

9

An ownership revolution

Will Hutton

Britain needs an ownership revolution. It needs its privately owned companies to be driven by a constitutionally entrenched purpose beyond profit making, to which all its stakeholders, including anchored investors, are committed. It needs many more firms to be diversely owned either as employee-owned companies, mutuals, co-operatives, trusts or partnerships, with sound constitutions that ensure their good governance and management. It needs more and better social ownership of assets it believes should be used to deliver the public good, which would otherwise be unobtainable. To secure all this, it needs vastly enlarged pools of dedicated capital to support the revolution – in particular, sovereign and citizen wealth funds alongside a reorganized and repurposed asset management industry. This ownership revolution is the precondition for achieving every worthwhile economic and social aim. There is no prospect of more justice, rising living standards and greater fairness without it. Ownership reform should be front and centre of our economic and political debate.

Ownership is fundamental. It is owners who shape the constitution of enterprise, and, in consequence, firms' agility, innovative capacity and productivity. It is the character of ownership that confers trust and commitment between all the firms' stakeholders. It is owners who give the green light to investment, employee participation and voice, customer engagement and the full acceptance of responsibilities to the environment. It is not enough in the twenty-first century to follow Milton Friedman's famous and much-quoted statement that the social responsibility of business is to increase its profits, so long as it stays within the rules of the game – a qualification that Friedman's critics often put aside as they seek to damn him.

But even accepting the qualification, Friedman's argument in wrong. Of course, no business is sustainable without profit; but owners are part of society, too. It is therefore not enough simply to follow the letter of the law around an overriding goal to maximize profits, arguing that the legal rules of the game completely and totally capture all society's preferences. That is to absolve business of all responsibility for the society of which it is part, claiming that achieving social and public good is only the government's provenance and government is all-seeing. Both claims are self-evident poppycock, and excuse owners from using their prerogatives well. For, in shaping the constitution of enterprise, owners dictate the character and shape of production, goods and services, work, pay and trust relationships between employee, consumer and manager. In any good society, it is only if profit follows purpose that the temptations to do bad or cut corners are obviated; it is purpose that, by having a human and moral dimension, ensures good conduct. Of necessity, it falls to the state to create a framework of law in which companies embrace their stakeholders and commit themselves to social and public objectives, as part of their commercial purpose laid out in their constitutions. It is the recasting of contemporary capitalism.

It all begins with public limited companies (PLCs) – the cornerstone of any capitalism. These are public only in the limited sense that their shares are quoted on public stock exchanges, and that they meet the listing, audit, reporting and legal requirements for being publicly traded. Listing a company's shares on the stock market allows it to raise equity capital through issuing more shares, while offering investors the comfort of being able to sell their shares to other investors, if need be, thus raising cash as required – while all the time knowing that minimal standards are being observed. These are good principles; and all advanced economies have an exchange where shares are issued and traded with accompanying listing requirements.

However, the open question associated with listing in a British context is: to what degree have companies, as constituted under current company law, become slaves to the time horizons, expectations of rates of return and financial priorities of investors over all other stakeholders? There is abundant evidence of a mismatch between the expectations of investors and those of companies: investors tend to have shorter-term time horizons and expectations of fast-growing and high returns; and they are constantly mindful of the possibility of exit, by selling these shares if their expectations are disappointed.

Different capitalisms offer different solutions to this problem. Some privilege founder shareholders with disproportionate voting rights (the United States, Canada); others encourage large anchor or blockholder shareholders, who have privileged access to information not available to investors at large (Germany, Japan, some Nordic countries); and others encourage shares to be held in blocks by foundations and trusts (Denmark, the Netherlands). The aim is to offer a buffer between the inevitable short-termism of financial markets and managers' concern about developing a durable purpose and strategy.

The United Kingdom is the outlier. To privilege any shareholder in any way above others is outlawed. Nor are any responsibilities expected of shareholders to the companies they own. British companies have no anchor shareholders but, rather, a multiplicity of disparate institutional investors (200 or more is typical) who own the bulk of the equity, none of whom are powerful enough to anchor a strategy and all of whom are free to exit at will. Against their priorities, there is little buffer. The United Kingdom ranks bottom of the international league table for lack of blockholder investors. As a result, investment, innovation and training strategies are subordinate to meeting investors' short-term profit expectations. British companies are particularly exposed to takeover, so that extensive sections of British business are either wholly foreign-owned (there are no British-owned building material businesses, for example) or they become especially exposed to the global rise of the $4 trillion private equity industry.

Private equity companies use borrowed money, whose interest is allowable to offset tax payments on profits, to buy companies in a "mortgage-and-flip-it" model. Their target companies are those that are asset-rich, to allow the collateralization of immense debt; they have strong cash flows to service the debt; and, in the short term at least, they can withstand swingeing reductions in both their headcount and spending on innovation and investment. Their investors want their cash back within ten years or less; so private equity's aim is to sell the underlying company on – with an apparent increase in profitability – to a trade investor or another private equity company, or back to the public markets, within that time frame. Examples are Melrose's acquisition of GKN; SoftBank's acquisition of the Cambridge-based creator of silicon architectures, Arm, which could have been Britain's Intel or Google; and Macquarie's acquisition of Thames Water. None have prospered: GKN was dismembered; Arm was sold on after four years to Nvidia; and Thames Water was sold on after being plundered for a decade, during which the delivery of clean, cheap water was secondary to routing profits through tax havens. Indeed, this "privatization of the private" has become one of the driving forces of British capitalism, extracting rather than creating value, leading the drive to contractualize work in short-term or zero-hour contracts while enormously enriching the partners and directors of private equity companies. Private equity acts directly to impose value extraction strategies and as an indirect enforcer of them across British business, for fear that, if it does not, it might succumb to private equity takeover.

But there is no axiomatic reason why the terms of ownership, with directors having a fiduciary obligation to maximize short-term profits and sell to the highest bidder in takeovers, should be the foundation of any capitalism – so allowing these developments. In fact, most successful companies around the world are those that pursue clearly defined and visionary social purposes over time, from which they make profits. It is by ensuring that companies have intrinsic social purposes, binding on all stakeholders – shareholders, directors and employees alike – that they mobilize their full potential and build trust, loyalty and success. Capitalism, correctly structured and incentivized, is a formidable vehicle for wealth creation. But it will not self-organize itself into these structures. That has to be done by the state.

The prize is great. The few companies that currently exemplify a different capitalist model – stakeholder capitalism – outperform other companies on a variety of dimensions. They are good places to work, have the capacity to innovate and invest, are genuinely committed to environmental sustainability and generate long-term returns. Purpose forms their "north star", providing the values and compass that hold the company together in good times and bad, and allowing commitment to innovation and investment on the basis of long-run success. This is why great companies set such store by their purpose statements, whether eBay and its purpose to create "a global trading platform where practically anyone can trade practically anything", or Unilever with its purpose to make "sustainable living commonplace"; Infosys to "navigate your next"; John Lewis proclaims its purpose to be "the happiness of its members"; Severn Trent's purpose is to be the most trusted water company, serving its customers and communities. These are not airy, rhetorical PR statements but invocations of the human spirit to do the best for their society – and which the companies do their very best to live in practice. The task is to make these the generality – not the exceptions.

As a first building block, companies should be legally required to declare their purposes in their constitutions, and to report regularly to their owners, the public and appropriate regulatory bodies on how they are fulfilling them.

This is a revolution, but the foundations have been laid in some existing company law and practice. Section 172 of the 2006 Companies Act (New Labour's small step in the direction of stakeholder capitalism – but a step nonetheless – taken after a six-year review of company law and two years of subsequent dithering over the legislation) requires a director of a company to act in the way that,

> in good faith, would be most likely to promote the success of the company for the benefit of its members as a whole. In so doing, directors have regard (amongst other matters) for:
>
> (a) the likely consequences of any decision in the long term,
> (b) the interests of the company's employees,
> (c) the need to foster the company's business relationships with suppliers, customers and others,
> (d) the impact of the company's operations on the community and the environment,
> (e) the desirability of the company maintaining a reputation for high standards of business conduct, and
> (f) the need to act fairly as between members of the company.

In addition, following representations by the Purposeful Company, the 2018 Corporate Governance Code requires those companies that voluntarily sign up to write a strategic report in which these section 172 issues are systematically addressed. In particular, they are required to state their purpose, values and strategy – and how they are achieving them. The Code is applicable to all companies with turnover in excess of £36 million and/or that have more than 250 employees. Thus, British and UK-based companies cannot complain that the proposal to incorporate around a declared purpose comes out of the blue. The ongoing difficulty is that too many directors do not know about these provisions; and, in any event, they regard them as being trumped by the higher fiduciary obligation: to maximize returns to shareholders. By hardening section 172 and the provisions of the Corporate Governance Code into law, so that companies are required to incorporate around a declared purpose, fiduciary obligations will become redefined as securing the success of the company so that it benefits all its members. No longer can there be confusion. Companies become purpose seekers. Every three years shareholders will be required to assess the purpose, and reaffirm their commitment in a vote – a "say on purpose".

This redefined public company becomes the foundation for other ownership reforms. Many of the contributions in this volume are inspired by the work of John Maynard Keynes; but Keynes's prescriptions went well beyond the radicalization of macroeconomic policy and extended to issues of ownership. In his 1926 essay against laissez-faire, Keynes argued that

> in many cases the ideal size for the unit of control and organization lies somewhere between the individual and the modern State. I suggest, therefore, that progress lies in the growth and the recognition of semi-autonomous bodies within the State – bodies whose criterion of action within their own field is solely *the public good* as they understand it.
>
> (Keynes 1972 [1926]: 291, emphasis added)

Keynes was arguing not for the monolithic state-owned and directed companies on the model of Attlee's nationalizations of coal, steel and rail but for the creation of a network of smaller, semi-autonomous companies, committed to the public good, but sitting between the individual and the state.

It is in this Keynesian tradition that the United Kingdom should commit to creating a new generation of "public benefit" or "public good" companies, whose constitutions go further than just incorporating around purpose and that are consecrated to meeting declared environmental, social or public objectives. A regulated utility or a social media provider, for example, would incorporate as a public benefit company, declaring its purpose as, say, "to deliver the best water possible at the cheapest price" or "to inform, educate and entertain" (the founding mission of the British Broadcasting Corporation [BBC]). In such companies, customers and employees would be represented on the board. Similarly, a British Broadband Corporation would commit to delivering nationwide free broadband.

The shareholder-value-maximizing PLC model, accompanied by "light touch" regulation, should never have been applied to privatized utilities and public networks. It was always a disaster waiting to happen – and so it proved. Profit targets and high dividend payouts have consistently overridden the interests of the public. Thames Water, mentioned above, is an especially egregious example. Until its recent change of ownership it built up sky-high debts and distributed vast dividends to its then private equity owners via a tax-efficient vehicle in Luxembourg. British Telecom's (BT's) investment in high-speed broadband has been slow and inadequate; and few would argue that the first target of the private rail operators has been high-quality passenger service. Indeed, the Johnson government looks set to abandon rail privatization completely after a series of debacles and scandals. Covid-19 has finally put paid to the myth that rail companies could be considered anything other than providers of a key public service: Under the newly announced "emergency recovery management agreements", they have been made de facto wards of the state, with their revenue losses funded by the taxpayer until 2022. This is to be succeeded by the reinvention of the rail operating companies as subcontractors holding concessions in return for an annual fee, rather than the existing seven-year franchise holders. But the problem will remain the same. Unless concession-holding companies are incorporated to deliver public good within a new framework of company law, their directors will continue to put profits before service delivery.

Public ownership should be redefined: the aim – as Keynes argued – is to create organizations whose owners are committed by law, regulation and their articles of association to delivering public good as their foundational purpose. This can be achieved not necessarily by the state owning 100 per cent of the share capital but, rather, by the state taking a "foundation" share in any organization that it believes should be dedicated to delivering public good. The provision of water, gas and electricity are obvious examples – but so are public transport and broadband communications. All should be incorporated as a public benefit company (PBC), declaring that their purpose is to promote the public good while seeking to make a reasonable surplus, and no more. The "foundation" share would give the government the right to appoint independent non-executive directors to guarantee that that purpose was being pursued. These companies would be required to remain domiciled in the United Kingdom for tax purposes, and not to use tax havens to shelter profits on which UK tax should be paid. Their non-executive directors would report regularly to regulators, explaining how the public interest was being achieved.

PBCs on this model would combine the best of the public and private sectors. Investors would invest in them as an asset class whose risks lay between investments in higher-risk PLCs and very low-risk government bonds: holding a franchise or contract to provide vital public goods would make them less risky than the general run of companies, so their returns would be commensurately lower. Private investment would obviate both the need for expensive public ownership of equity (it is estimated that it would cost more than £200 billion to fully nationalize all current privatized industries) and the ongoing provision of taxpayer funding, except in particular circumstances when even commercial funding for low-risk but low-return projects was not forthcoming. The model could be flexed. It would always be open to the state to own 100 per cent of the equity, if there was risk of consistent losses or need for lumpy, high-risk investment. A condition of qualifying as a public subcontractor could be to be incorporated as a PBC, so that, for example, only public benefit companies could contract to provide care for the elderly. Private equity firms provide 13 per cent of all UK care home beds; and four out of the largest five deploy tax havens through which to route revenues. This problem could be solved at a stroke if a care home contract could be held only by a PBC. The tax breaks favouring private equity should be gradually phased out.

Nor should the ownership revolution stop there. Employee ownership in Britain is paltry. Mutually owned employee ownership trusts (EOTs), in which the majority of the equity is held by the workforce, could, with much stronger tax incentives to encourage the transfer of ownership and allow workers to credit company shares to their pension funds, be vastly expanded. According to the Institute for Public Policy Research, EOTs could employ 3 million people within a decade. Co-operatives and mutuals could be expanded to employ over 1 million, especially if encouraged by a network of supportive institutions. Difficulty in raising external finance is the major constraint confronting co-operatives: a capital development fund and co-operative bank specializing in lending to co-operatives are imperatives to their growth. There should be major concessions on inheritance and capital gains tax for individuals establishing EOTs, mutuals and co-operatives. What characterizes all these ownership forms is a community of purpose between the owners and the enterprise. The evidence, as James O'Toole argues in his magisterial *The Enlightened Capitalists*, is that they outperform traditional capitalist enterprise.

It is this community of purpose that is needed in parallel with the stakeholder companies created by company law reform. They, in their turn, will need a majority of "anchored" shareholders, who embrace their declared purpose. This implies both new pools of capital from which such shareholders can be drawn – and a new approach by asset managers. In Germany and Scandinavia, companies typically have a few core, anchor shareholders – "blockholders" – constituting a critical mass of the voting rights, who, in effect, both control the company and provide it with long-term loyalty. Britain should use every tool in the policy locker – tax, regulation, law and the creation of new pools of capital – to foster more investor blockholders. For example, it should be blockholders and other long-term shareholders who vote on a company's future during a takeover; only those shareholders on the register at the time a takeover is launched should vote – not proxy agencies, and certainly not the motley bunch of arbitrageurs and hedge funds that recently settled GKN's fate. They sold it to the asset stripper, Melrose, having bought it after the bid was announced, only to make a turn by selling to the highest bidder – careless of the company's future.

Existing company owners and asset managers need to be required to take "intrinsic purpose" seriously. Britain's £7 trillion asset management industry does not remotely do this at present. The long-term stewardship of companies is not in the mainstream culture, business model or legal obligations of the owners of British shares and asset managers, the majority of whom are now foreign: British long-term pension funds and insurance companies now own less than 10 per cent of British quoted companies. In any case, many of the 40,000 pension funds are too small to undertake the stewardship expense of gathering information, quizzing managements and engaging with strategy. Although some foreign owners of British shares are signalling a welcome interest in supporting long-term value generation, this is far from common – and, again, expensive to do properly.

To reform this system, asset management companies should be required to declare their purposes as businesses, organize their business model appropriately (e.g. the Brunel Pension Partners have a management accord setting out the principles by which they want their funds managed) and report regularly on how they set about delivering it. The 2019 Stewardship Code requires asset owners and managers to declare their approach to stewardship as part of their definition of their purpose, and to report systematically on it. Signature is voluntary. As a first step, the newly established Audit, Reporting and Governance Authority, which replaced the former Financial Reporting Council, should require mandatory adherence to the Stewardship Code, and insist on full explanations when its provisions are not complied with.

Three additional measures are required. Too much stewardship is contracted out to proxy agencies, whose collective votes on everything from executive pay to the terms of a takeover can be decisive. They are subject to little oversight. Reform is vital. Proxy agencies should be required to sign and observe the terms of the Stewardship Code. Certain votes – say, on purpose, executive pay and takeovers – should not be contracted out to proxy agencies but, instead, reserved to the ultimate owners. Similarly, those votes should be retained by the ultimate owners when stock is lent for any purpose.

Second, forms of collective action by institutional shareholders should be actively boosted. Stewardship is expensive. A levy should be imposed on all asset management companies, to properly fund the Investors Forum – the fledgling institution set up for asset managers to coordinate interventions – so that it has the resources to engage with companies if, for any reason, they are in trouble or needing targeted assistance. There needs to be a wholesale overhaul of fee structures: the current lack of transparency and disclosure means that excessive percentages of customers' investment assets are creamed off by an industry of "financial planners", agents and custodial intermediaries who add little or no value, but use resources that could be deployed for genuine stewardship activity. In addition, the fee structures encourage the formation of multiple new subscale funds capitalizing on passing fads, but few large enough to divert sufficient resource to engage in worthwhile stewardship. There are fast-growing asset management houses, such as Vanguard, which offer low fees, but only because they are passive investors whose portfolio just reflects the stock market index. Thus, the only way they can improve performance is by better stewardship rather than over- or underinvesting in any particular company. They should be encouraged to do just that. Finally, to boost engaged stewardship, there should be investor-safe spaces, where management and shareholders can share information, secure in the knowledge that there is no risk of being prosecuted for collusion or acting in concert.

Last, new sources of finance are essential. Local authority pension funds are being merged to create "super-funds"; they should give mandates only to investment managers who subscribe to company stewardship objectives. Pools of savings should be made to work for the good of both the saver and the wider economy. Fast-growing so-called defined contribution private pension funds are set to grow to over £500 billion by 2030. If a fifth of their assets were earmarked for purposeful investment, up to £100 billion of new equity capital would be available for purposeful companies over the next decade. In addition, a citizens' wealth fund should be created from the receipts of the sale of public assets, rather than lost in the general maw of public revenues, alongside revenues from a tax on dividends (a "scrip tax"). Like the sovereign wealth funds of Norway and Singapore, this fund would be managed in Keynesian style, by an independent board, as an autonomous organization on behalf of the public. Singapore's Temasek has established an enviable track record of being an anchor for long-term, engaged and supportive investors. The citizens' wealth fund would aim to reproduce its success.

Proposals of this type even five years ago would have seemed outlandish. Today the mood is changing. Whether it be the American Business Roundtable or the World Economic Forum, there is a growing acceptance that the firm driven only by the desire to maximize shareholder value has had its day. The results are baleful: an overpaid management class and companies that, by and large, underinvest and under-innovate. It is time for an ownership revolution.

Further reading

Edmans, A. 2020. *Grow the Pie: How Great Companies Deliver Both Purpose and Profit*. Cambridge: Cambridge University Press.

Keynes, J. 1972 [1926]. "The end of laissez-faire". In *The Collected Writings of John Maynard Keynes*, vol. 9, *Essays in Persuasion*, D. Moggridge (ed.), 272–94. London: Macmillan.

Mayer, C. 2018. *Prosperity: Better Business Makes the Greater Good*. Oxford: Oxford University Press.

O'Toole, J. 2019. *The Enlightened Capitalists: Cautionary Tales of Business Pioneers Who Tried to Do Well by Doing Good*. London: HarperCollins.

Purposeful Company n.d. "Evidence reports". Available at: www.thepurposefulcompany.org

10

Industrial strategy for post-Covid Britain: a renewed public purpose for the state and business?

Suzanne J. Konzelmann and Marc Fovargue-Davies

There is no doubt that the UK economy will take a big hit from the Covid-19 pandemic. Estimates of its actual impact vary, but, at the time of writing, most commentators put the figure at between 11 and 14.5 per cent. To put that into perspective, following the 2007–09 financial crisis, between the first quarter of 2008 and the second quarter of 2009 the UK economy shrank by a little over 6 per cent, and it then took five years to regain its pre-crisis size. The sheer scale of the Covid-19 impact means that the state's support for the recovery will need to include an industrial strategy – something that Britain has not seen in over 40 years.

The nature and effectiveness of that strategy will largely depend upon the relationships between government and the various industrial sectors; much will also hinge on the question "What are companies actually for?". From Margaret Thatcher's election in May 1979 until very recently, the answer was a very definite "Making profits and delivering value to shareholders". But fallout from recent events, reminiscent of the interwar years, proves that it is just not that simple.

Beyond profit: the question of corporate purpose

Part of the United Kingdom's response to the 2007–09 financial crisis was to bail out financial institutions deemed "too big to fail". The fear was that, had they *not* been rescued, the resulting damage would be more than purely economic. The social dislocation resulting from account holders having no access to funds, losing their savings or being unable to pay their mortgages – plus the consequences of increased unemployment caused by the "Great Recession" that followed – would have been enormous.

The bailouts were therefore a de facto admission that businesses are indeed about more than profit. If that message needed any more reinforcement, it came in the form of admissions, by every government since 2008, that the economy needed rebalancing, with a new emphasis on manufacturing. We have yet to see any action, though. As it stands, the government's proposed post-pandemic recovery programme offers a lot of infrastructure investment; but, inexplicably, both industrial strategy and a business bank remain absent.

With trust in both government and big business currently hitting new lows, pressure for change is building again. Concern about environmental sustainability and high levels of social and economic inequality has inspired new ideas about corporate purpose, not only in academia but in business and policy-making circles as well.

In Britain, for example, since 2015 Will Hutton and Clare Chapman, then a director of BT, have engaged with leading UK companies through the Purposeful Company initiative, gathering evidence that corporate purpose adds value, issuing guidance for putting it into practice and pressing for changes in policy, regulation and law. One outcome can already be seen in the new 2019 UK Corporate Governance Code, which requires all companies with a premium listing to report on corporate purpose.

In the United States, too, business leaders are calling for companies to put "purpose" before profit. In 2018 Larry Fink, CEO of BlackRock, one of the world's largest asset management companies, sent an open letter to the CEOs of major corporations. With "governments failing to prepare for the future", Fink wrote, "society is increasingly turning to the private sector and … demanding that companies, public and private, serve a social purpose". Fink reiterated his argument about government failure and society's demand for companies "to address pressing social and economic issues" in his 2019 letter, emphasizing the "inextricable link" between corporate purpose and profit.

Seven months later the Business Roundtable, a group of CEOs of major US corporations, issued a "Statement on the Purpose of a Corporation", with 181 signatories. It still expressed confidence in the "free market system" but appeared to abandon the idea that a corporation's purpose is primarily to maximize profits for its shareholders, committing instead to prioritizing the long-term interests of all stakeholders. In

2020 Fink again urged companies to "embrac[e] purpose and serv[e] all stakeholders", linking this with "long-term profitability".

Fink's argument is strongly reminiscent of the policy debates of the interwar period, when voters' confidence in capitalism was also at a low ebb. During the Great Depression that followed the 1929 Wall Street Crash, both Britain's John Maynard Keynes and America's Adolf Berle argued that the social and economic role of companies involved far more than a short-term focus on the bottom line. Keynes went so far as to maintain that the age of laissez-faire capitalism had passed – not least because of the damaging effects of "dog eat dog" competition on the wider economy. Those who authorized the 2008 bank bailouts seem to have thought the same.

However, the interwar debate produced positive reforms; and the effect on the postwar British economy was profound. Large parts of industry – though far from all – were nationalized; the financial services sector was effectively regulated; and the state played an active role in the economy, with the objectives of economic stability, full employment and stable prices, rather than a single-minded focus on economic growth. The result was unprecedented improvements in living standards and economic equality, the steady reduction of public debt and the disappearance of financial crises – all things that are again on the wish lists of politicians and voters alike.

Unfortunately, it did not last. During the 1970s and early 1980s the social, economic and political consequences of stagflation, in no small part a result of two OPEC oil price shocks and the absence of a forward-looking strategy by either state or industry, encouraged a return to laissez-faire capitalism and wholesale privatization.

British companies respond to the Covid-19 national health crisis

Clearly, then, a good old-fashioned economic crisis can be a catalyst for highlighting systemic weaknesses, and sometimes driving change – in one direction or the other. This brings us back to the 2020 pandemic, which has also revealed the disastrous cost of an obsession with privatizing everything in sight, regardless of practicality. However, the pandemic has also shown that British industry and the state can cooperate effectively, in much the same way that, a century earlier, Keynes and Berle speculated they could.

The National Health Service is one of the few remaining institutions of the postwar consensus to have at least partly survived the privatization programme; and it is the core of the nation's response to the pandemic. Its purpose is mainly social; but, as well as healthcare, it is also a major employer and a large consumer of goods and services. Its economic role is thus secondary.

However, as a result of privatization, those goods and services (excluding drugs and medication) are now supplied through an arcane network of contracts and suppliers, rather than the NHS itself. Driven more by the pursuit of private profit than provision of a vital health resource with a social and public purpose, these contractors also have little or no experience of the health or medical sector. Until 2018 the supply chain was largely operated by DHL (a parcel delivery organization), and subsequently by Unipart, whose original purpose was distributing spare parts for British Leyland. Unipart operates a "just in time" model, difficult to scale quickly and entirely unsuited to dealing with a pandemic, when much larger amounts of equipment have to be made available immediately. Worse still, pandemics cause a spike in global demand for that equipment, making it harder to come by and more expensive. Even when these supplies *were* made available through the NHS's global supply chain, a significant proportion turned out to *not* be fit for purpose; both personal protective equipment from Turkey and ventilators from China had to be rejected.

By the middle of March 2020, albeit without admitting as much, the government recognized that the NHS's privatized supply chain had broken down. Most newspapers failed to grasp the fact that this was a private sector issue – and simply reported it as an NHS failure. However, it had far more in common with the breakdown of the security arrangements for the 2012 London Olympics, when G4S failed to provide the contracted-out resources. In both cases, public resources in the form of the military were brought in to clean up the mess. The army's assessment of the NHS supply chain was scathing, with senior officers describing it as "knackered" and incapable of matching supplies to demand.

As well as calling in the military, a call went out to UK manufacturers to see what could be made locally, rather than imported. The response by manufacturers and other specialists, including Formula 1 (F1) teams, medical companies and universities, revealed not only a willingness to contribute but also an ability to react extremely quickly, cooperate with both each other and government and mobilize high-performance networks of specialists. When new products emerged, the designs were often open-sourced, for others around the world to use without charge. Corporate purpose became a reality.

UK-based F1 teams immediately formed a collective, pooling their technical resources and initiating "Project Pitlane". They also established functional networks with medical companies, other manufacturers and universities. Although F1 teams are not normally in the business of mass production, motor racing demands extremely rapid conceptualization, design and prototyping – crucial assets for the new networks.

One of those networks, comprising the University of Southampton, NIHR Southampton Biomedical Research Centre, Kemp Sails, INDO Lighting and McLaren, developed the prototype of a revolutionary form of PPE – a respirator hood capable of reliably protecting NHS staff treating Covid-19 patients – in less than a week. As Professor Paul Elkington put it: "The engineering team have rapidly developed something really simple yet effective which can provide further protection and resolve some of the supply chain issues associated with disposable PPE." By the middle of April University Hospital Southampton had ordered 5,000 of the new respirator hoods, which were already in use by frontline staff, having entered high-volume manufacturing in under a month. Even before the new design received final approval by regulators, it was available on an open-source basis.

Another network, this time including University College London (UCL) and F1 engine specialists from Mercedes AMG HPP, set out to mass-produce a continuous positive airway pressure (CPAP) device, far simpler to manufacture in volume than a full ventilator. Reverse-engineering an existing, already approved product moved the new product into production even more rapidly, because of the shortened regulatory approval phase, with 10,000 units being delivered during the first month. Again, the designs and manufacturing instructions were open-sourced for global use. Many other British companies, large and small – including Jaguar Land Rover, Rolls-Royce, Catapult, JCB, Burberry and Private White VC – have also contributed their skills, individually or as part of a network.

This response to the Covid-19 pandemic has also highlighted clear divisions in the UK economy. Whereas high-value producers, such as those identified above, supported the collective cause, other sectors have been far more reticent. Finance, for example – so recently the recipient of huge public bailouts – has yet to return the favour.

There are also companies, such as those in the NHS's global supply chain, that do *not* create value but make their profit through cutting overheads to the barest minimum, and frequently beyond. This sector has contributed significantly to low wages and poor working conditions, precarious employment and the infamous zero-hours contract. Worse still, it *does not even* deliver the goods, leaving the public sector to pick up the pieces.

It is inescapable, then, that economic recovery from the pandemic – as well as developing a more vibrant and positive society – will be better served by encouraging more businesses with a sense of corporate purpose. Industrial strategy therefore needs to reflect that, as Britain needs more businesses and jobs that add significant value, and a lower proportion of obsessive cost-cutters that do not. Post-pandemic strategy also needs to reverse counter-productive privatization in essential public service areas, such as health, education, housing and care, that are currently subject to firms focused on cost, with no stake in the United Kingdom beyond profit.

The state as part of a high-performance network: UK Olympic sport

The part played by high-performance networks in Britain's response to the Covid-19 pandemic demonstrates the importance of the right vision, motivation, resources and people – as well as effective relationships. It also raises the possibility that such an approach might be an effective way to evolve industrial strategy for the United Kingdom. Imagining the government as part of a focused, success-oriented, high-performance network might well require a significant conceptual leap for most; but it has been quietly doing exactly that, for the last 24 years.

Why would you want the government on your team? Because there are some things only government can do, such as developing a supportive policy and making changes to the legal framework, corporate governance code, regulation and, potentially, the use of public funds.

None of this can be done by the private sector, but it does not mean that the state should be running the show; the Covid-19 design and manufacturing networks were "expert-driven", with each member contributing his or her particular expertise to support a common vision. That is how government should fit in, too: as a member, not as the boss nor a disinterested spectator.

Back in 1996 the then Conservative prime minister, John Major, first took an interest in British Olympic sport, resulting in a rapid, complete and sustained transformation in performance – plus a brand-new industry sector, which by 2014 was already contributing nearly £30 billion a year to the UK economy.

It all started after the 1996 Atlanta Games, at which the "Team of Shame" put in the United Kingdom's worst ever Olympic performance. That team included many stellar athletes, such as Roger Black, Steve Redgrave and Ben Ainslie. So why was there just the one gold medal? The problem was that, like UK industry now, Britain's athletes were not competing on a level playing field. Many of their rivals had the equivalent of an industrial strategy for sport, allowing them to fully develop their talent. The United Kingdom had no strategy at all.

Major might have been a keen sports fan, but he was not well qualified to decide what extra support Olympic sport needed, so he engaged with those who did. Actually having a policy at all was a clear step forward. Next came the single institutional change – the creation of UK Sport as the strategic lead body, focused solely on elite sport – through which the government could engage with all those institutions that supported Britain's elite sport development.

UK Sport is an unusual government body; there are no civil servants, since it is run by sportspeople, many of them former world champions. To date its two CEOs have both been women, internationally successful in team sports. UK Sport has also managed to avoid "capture", by either government interests or those of the sport governing bodies, clubs and universities that make up the rest of the expert-driven network. This network has continually evolved through the leadership of UK Sport. But that leadership does not happen in isolation; it is based on the best that each network member can contribute. UK Sport is also notable for working with technology partners such as BAE Systems and McLaren – who, as we have already seen, know how to perform in an effective network.

There was also some extra cash. Although you cannot do without it either in industry or in sport, it is still not difficult to invest in the wrong way. The value of an expert-driven network, with targets agreed in discussions that include government as a network member, is that funds are, more often than not, productively invested. Having to account for public funds brings not only a strong focus on success but also ever-improving professionalism, especially in corporate governance. As a result, UK Sport's average cost per medal is significantly less than many of its rivals.

Government can also remove or change unhelpful legal restrictions. Before Tony Blair's government changed the rules about how public funds could be invested, Olympic sport was handicapped by the requirement that public money could be spent only on facilities. Once that was lifted, funds could be spent on whatever the sport governing bodies thought was required to win. They were free to financially support athletes, who therefore no longer had to juggle training with employment; and they could fund the best coaches, sport medicine and science, and sport research and innovation. This is where many of the jobs in the new £30 billion elite sport sector have come from: secure, skilled jobs that pay appropriately.

The Olympic sport network has now evolved across nearly a quarter-century and several changes of government. It has created a new industrial sector and has moved the team from 36th to second in the world rankings; it is also currently the only team in history to improve its performance following a home Games. Not a bad return on the state's investment; but might its greatest value yet turn out to be the inspiration for how government can become part of an expert-driven network for industry?

The current debate about corporate purpose

The current debate about corporate purpose is largely a result of the return of laissez-faire capitalism since the late 1970s, along with its economic and financial instability, and increased poverty, inequality and environmental damage. It centres on the relationship and balance of power between the private sector and the state, and, as a result, the question of regulation.

Following the Second World War many states took a key role in their economy; the problem of managerial power was tamed and companies served an accepted public purpose. Across the industrialized world, this resulted in rising living standards and the absence of financial crises. But the 1980s brought a decisive shift in power towards the private sector and markets. In returning to laissez-faire, all the factors that had created the difficulties of the interwar years reappeared, with predictably similar results.

The contrasting perspectives on corporate purpose as it has evolved from the interwar years to today are also striking. The debate has narrowed, with concern about the relationship between firms and society – centrally important to Keynes and Berle – virtually disappearing. Today's business leaders do make the link between companies and the economy; and they talk about the other stakeholders, alongside shareholders. But most stop short of integrating corporate purpose with the broader interests of society as a whole, seeing stakeholder interests as primarily economic.

A notable exception is the Purposeful Company, which, in defining "intrinsic purpose" (Purposeful Company 2018), contends: "We are recovering the idea that business exists to pursue a purpose that benefits society." In its June 2020 response to the UK government's Business, Energy and Industrial Strategy (BEIS) Committee's post-pandemic economic growth inquiry (Purposeful Company 2020), it reiterated the view that – rather than having profit as its end goal – "[i]n a purposeful company, *creating value for society* is the end goal".

A cynic might argue that the motivation behind some of the moves by large companies to embrace their own version of corporate purpose is an attempt to avoid more stringent regulation. But history demonstrates that significant and positive change is possible – although achieving it will require a better and, above all, honest balance between the private sector and the state.

Conclusions

As the United Kingdom begins to emerge from lockdown, we will soon – hopefully – enter the post-Covid-19 recovery phase. What happens next will depend to a large extent on how government sees its own purpose.

For the last 40 years or so that has included stepping back from the economy, privatizing as much as possible and prioritizing the financial services sector. However, all the usual tools of traditional liberalized capitalism were tested to destruction in the last major recession – and now the United Kingdom, along with the rest of the world, is faced with a recession at least twice as deep, and likely to cause even more damage to economic and social infrastructure.

In this situation, it is hard to see how government can avoid major change. Like many institutions, the focus will be on recovery and development for a considerable time to come – which means a common purpose. It may well be that some institutions are born with a purpose, while others have a purpose thrust upon them. But, nonetheless, purpose there must be.

Fortunately, there are some excellent examples, for the government playbook, of how – and how not – to get things done. Clearly, inappropriate privatization, which can cause political embarrassment and huge extra costs, needs radical reassessment. But it is equally clear that the state can help get things done – and done well. High-performance networks supported the response to the pandemic, whereas the "knackered" privatized NHS supply chain broke down.

The way these networks developed and performed demonstrates a way forward for developing industrial strategy. Government has already participated in such a network, with the aim of transforming international elite sport competitiveness – and succeeded. It is not a blueprint for industry, since industry needs different things from elite sport. But the only way to find out is to engage. After all, without John Major starting the ball rolling, would Britain's Olympic performance have improved?

As we have seen from the long-running debates about corporate purpose, it usually takes a crisis, or a succession of crises, to catalyse change. It is worth noting that the economic and social advances of Clement Attlee's 1945–51 Labour government came on the back of two world wars, several financial crises, a world depression and a pandemic. It all sounds far too familiar for comfort. But the message is clear: the sooner you start the process of change, the more you will have to work with. Put simply, the time for change is now.

Further reading

Konzelmann, S., V. Chick & M. Fovargue-Davies 2020. "Shareholder value or public purpose? From John Maynard Keynes and Adolf Berle to the modern debate", Working Paper 520. Centre for Business Research, University of Cambridge. Available at: www.cbr.cam.ac.uk/fileadmin/user_upload/centre-for-business-research/downloads/working-papers/wp520.pdf.

Konzelmann, S., M. Fovargue-Davies & F. Wilkinson 2018. "Britain's industrial evolution: the structuring role of economic theory". *Journal of Economic Issues* 52 (1): 1–30.

Purposeful Company 2018. "The Purposeful Company Taskforce intrinsic purpose definition". London: The Purposeful Company.

Purposeful Company 2020. "Response to the BEIS Committee's post-pandemic economic growth super inquiry". London: The Purposeful Company. Available at: www.biginnovationcentre-purposeful-company.com.

11

Restoring pensions collectivism: a new public pension for the UK

Craig Berry

The impact of Covid-19 on UK pension provision has been, and will be, profound. Yet, just like the impact of Covid-19 on society in general – public services, the economy, our democracy, etc. – it is an impact that is significantly worse as a result of decades of mismanagement, corporate influence and ideological myopia in UK pension policy. I argue that a (wilful) misunderstanding of the elementary nature of pension provision among UK policy-makers is part of the explanation, creating myriad market failures that the state is intervening to mitigate and that would have been unnecessary had the system been designed more coherently around state-led provision in the first place.

Although the UK's pension problems pre-date Covid-19, the pandemic provides a useful, but tragic, illustration of the system's frailties. These frailties, of course, depend on whether the form of provision in question is (collectivist) defined benefit or (individualized) defined contribution provision. In defined benefit provision, a severe economic shock does not directly impact upon member outcomes, but falling asset values create funding deficits, and make employers less able and/or willing to compensate for shortfalls, which jeopardizes future provision. In defined contribution provision, member outcomes are entirely on how their own invested savings perform in capital markets – and those closest to retirement are acutely affected, as they have little or no time to recover from a period of poor returns. In the absence of any other safe haven assets, pension institutions tend to flock to government bonds – yet gilt yields are at historically low levels, in part as a direct result of macroeconomic policy.

The centrality of investment returns to UK pensions indicates that the country's provision has always been highly financialized. This has shaped understandings of a "crisis" associated with population ageing. The expectation that employers guarantee defined benefit outcomes – as the ratio of active, working-age members to retired members drawing a pension income has declined – has driven the rollout of defined contribution provision, whereby individuals alone shoulder the longevity risks. However, although there is nothing inherently wrong in adjusting provision to social and economic conditions, it should be noted, first, that large-scale collectivist pension provision in the private sector emerged during a period of rapid population ageing in the UK and, second, that the longevity gains of recent decades are now showing sustained signs of going into reverse. The demographic crisis in UK pension provision has been, at best, overstated.

Moreover, from the state's perspective, although the Pension Protection Fund has been established to support members of insolvent defined benefit schemes, the impact of population ageing on defined contribution provision – such that scheme members cannot even share longevity risks among themselves – is of far greater concern. Individual pension pots are being stretched too far, leading to a greater reliance on the state pension and welfare provision more generally (as well as informal carers) to sustain an acceptable standard of living in later life. Perversely, all evidence of underperformance in individualized provision is invariably treated as grounds for further individualization, both to insulate the state and employers from liability for any loss and in service of a flawed worldview in which individual pension savers are conceived as rational and informed market participants.

We need to start thinking about pensions differently. Pensions are not simply about deferred consumption – i.e. putting some of our income aside now for a time when we are less able to earn a living in the labour market. This definition assumes that pensions are about preparing for a known future, and, furthermore, that the mechanisms of intergenerational cooperation required to enable deferred consumption – an intricate process of capital de- and rematerialization – remain stable over time. Instead, pensions are a mechanism for coping with the certainty of uncertainty – i.e. the knowledge that the social and economic conditions required to sustain the pensions of tomorrow will be different from whatever we forecast today.

This forgotten origin story is why all large-scale pension provision requires an institutional guarantor – a temporal anchor – to ensure that outcomes will accord approximately with expectations. In UK defined benefit provision, it is a role traditionally expected of employers. This has given way to the hazy notion that individual self-interest and rationality can be relied upon, in place of concrete duties upon employers, as cross-temporal constants; this is perhaps the quintessential gamble behind the notion that defined contribution provision represents a sustainable future.

In practice, the state plays the role of temporal anchor for the vast majority, with even the UK's meagre state pension representing the bulk of retirement income for most people. This is a role the state must embrace more generally. Although it seems that the political conditions for a radical uplift in state pension entitlements remain elusive, the consistent failings of private pension provision may see support grow for an enhanced state role in providing workplace pensions in place of the private sector. Ultimately, and in short, a new public pension is required. This scheme would not remove the individual's responsibility to save for his or her retirement, but it would ensure that individuals are actually appropriately rewarded, and remunerated, when they do so.

State of confusion

As defined contribution provision becomes firmly embedded in the UK workplace pension landscape through "automatic enrolment", its flaws and failures are mounting. First, although the defined contribution revolution has increased enormously the coverage of workplace pension schemes, contributions are drastically lower than in defined benefit schemes. Too few employees or employers contribute more than the mandatory minimums specified in auto-enrolment legislation. Even in a best-case scenario, after a lifetime of saving most auto-enrollees will accumulate a retirement income that functions as a limited supplement to the state pension.

Second, many millions of people are excluded from even this system. Since contributions are made only on a qualifying band of earnings, and do not commence until an individual reaches the "earnings trigger" in a single job, the lowest-paid and those with multiple jobs are significantly disadvantaged. This inequality of course overlaps with the chronic inequalities of class, gender, race, etc. that are in the UK labour market. The self-employed – a group that has grown significantly since auto-enrolment was imagined (and seen average earnings fall) – obviously have no right to employer contributions, or automatic access to any workplace scheme.

Third, management charges and transaction costs are borne directly by scheme members in individualized pensions. Of course, this issue highlights one of the paradoxes of defined contribution provision: it may be that the investments that deliver the best returns – and therefore maximize retirement incomes – simply cost more to operationalize. Recent governments have acted to cap administrative charges, outlaw some of the most unjustifiable additional charges and increase transparency in transaction costs. But these regulations are no substitute for effective governance at scheme level – and better governance clearly costs more. Generally speaking, defined contribution in the UK is governance-lite, and becoming more so, precisely because the challenging investment environment – which regulators cannot influence – has focused political attention on charges and costs. Policy-makers can act in this domain, but nothing they do will make more than a marginal difference to outcomes.

Fourth, another area in which policy-makers can intervene, but have chosen not to, is the "small pots" problem. As workers change jobs they are likely to be enrolled into a new workplace pension scheme each time, leaving behind millions of small, dormant pots. Scheme providers have so far resisted all efforts to allow dormant pots to be merged, since it would essentially mean forgoing pots upon which they can levy management charges.

Finally, defined contribution provision is marred by historically low annuity rates. Individuals are required to convert their savings pot into a regular income at retirement. Product choice is a complex, risky and irreversible decision, yet the main problem is that no annuity product – in an era of extraordinarily low interest rates – can deliver the kind of outcomes expected when auto-enrolment was established. The Cameron/Osborne government's response to this was "pension freedoms": removing the tax penalties associated with choosing not to annuitize your pot for defined contribution savers. This may benefit some of the wealthiest savers, able to keep their pot invested for longer (and access advice to secure the most lucrative investment opportunities) before annuitizing, but even this is a rather illusory rationale. In practice, the reform has severely weakened the annuities market upon which, even in its depressed state, the vast majority of auto-enrollees will depend.

There is scope for state intervention to fix or alleviate many of these problems. Obviously, policy-makers could legislate for higher contributions, and to widen the coverage of auto-enrolment to excluded groups. Furthermore, the state could essentially serve as the provider of all defined contribution schemes, displacing the private sector – a role envisaged by the cross-party Pensions Commission of the mid-2000s, which led to auto-enrolment (the recommendation for a National Pensions Saving Scheme was rejected by the New Labour government). The state is also well placed to provide annuities (another role that was explored, but not recommended, by the Commission), and, indeed, on a fiscally neutral basis.

These would, of course, be sizeable state interventions. However, the state is already intervening to prop up the private pension industry in myriad ways. First, although the notion of a state-run scheme for all auto-enrollees was rejected, New Labour instead established the state-owned National Employment Savings Trust (NEST). NEST is designed to provide workplace pension schemes to smaller employers whose business might be less profitable for the larger providers. Yet NEST is now, by far, the UK's largest pension provider. In essence, NEST exists to serve not citizens but, rather, the private pension industry, since it enables the industry to focus on more profitable market segments without being weighed down by public service obligations to offer their services to all.

Second, it is worth noting the colossal sums the state continues to spend on pensions tax relief (PTR), which was redesigned in the mid-2000s to accommodate the rollout of defined contribution provision. PTR (which means that pension contributions are made from pre-tax income) costs around £35 billion per year, or close to a third of the annual cost of the NHS in England (although some of this is recouped through income tax on pensions in payment). There is no evidence that tax relief serves to incentivize additional pensions saving. It is simply a subsidy, which means that providers and the asset managers they contract have a greater volume of capital to circulate and extract rent from. This does not mean that individual savers do not benefit from the subsidy too – especially given how low contributions are in defined contribution provision. But its benefits are heavily skewed towards higher earners, who receive relief at their marginal tax rate during their working life before becoming lower-rate taxpayers in retirement.

A new public pension

The encroachment of the state into private pension provision demonstrates that the limits of financialized pensions are being reached. Utilizing the state to support collectivism, rather than simply compensate for the failures of individualized provision, is essential. The UK should establish a new publicly organized occupational pension – in addition to the existing state pension, and potentially replacing most privately run provision. In some ways, the new scheme would simply replicate the State Earnings-Related Pension Scheme (SERPS), which represented a state-run defined benefit scheme for those unable to access a decent occupational pension in the private sector. However, the new public pension could operate on a voluntary rather than mandatory basis, or, as with auto-enrolment, allow individuals to opt out once enrolled. SERPS was replaced by the State Second Pension (S2P) by New Labour, in a creditable attempt to make the state pension system more redistributive. However, in so far as S2P represented a welfare entitlement rather than a scheme seen to be based directly upon private saving, it was vulnerable to orthodox fiscal conservatism; accordingly, it was abolished by the coalition government, in return for an uplift in the basic state pension.

The first step towards establishing a new public occupational pension would be to nationalize all, or most, legacy defined benefit schemes, including the Pension Protection Fund (which pays reduced benefits to members of insolvent schemes). The second step would be the reconstitution of NEST as part of the new scheme. Both these steps would help to capitalize the new scheme, alongside additional fiscal underpinning. The system would then quickly transition towards opening to new members and accruals. The scheme would, fundamentally, mimic the practice of saving for a pension privately, but there would be significant scope for policy-makers to provide for guaranteed outcomes, and introduce redistributive elements.

Ultimately, it would be necessary to consider whether the new scheme would replace or complement existing private pension provision. It is clear that a public scheme organized as a defined benefit pension represents a far superior proposition for individuals than the defined contribution schemes into which the vast majority of auto-enrollees are now contributing. The new scheme could be established on a notional defined contribution (NDC) basis, with the state committing to provide retirement incomes in proportion to the notional (and adjustable) investment returns that contributions, if invested, would generate, rather than accrued rights linked to individuals' earnings. If so, there would be a strong case for the new scheme (eventually) replacing existing private pension provision. The NDC model would be similar to the one the French government is seeking to introduce. Ironically, whereas the proposals represent a downgrade of entitlements in France, and have provoked fierce resistance, this approach would represent a significant upgrade in the generosity and security of UK private pension provision. We can expect its precise features to evolve over time, but the principle that the state should act as the temporal anchor for collectivist pension provision would be firmly established.

The notion of simply expanding the state pension to render all private pensions saving unnecessary is an attractive one. But one of the benefits of the approach suggested here is that it would allow for variable pension ages between the two systems; it may be that we bring the state pension age back down to 65, on the expectation that people combine receipt with part-time work before accessing the new public pension at, say, 70. There are other progressive reforms policy-makers could take forward even in the absence of the new system. First, as noted above, the state could continue to allow for privately run savings schemes, but provide annuities for all savers when they reach retirement. Second, incentives could be provided for employers to "level up" existing defined contribution schemes to "collective defined contribution" (CDC) provision, in which members share risks and access annuity payments internally within the fund, rather than having to "cash out" at retirement. CDC provision is now legally permissible, but, without state support, is generally expected to be used only to "level down" from more generous defined benefit entitlements.

The responsible investment fallacy

A potential downside of a new public pension is that it would deprive the economy of a set of "patient" capitalists in the form of pension funds – and defined contribution providers such as insurance companies – that tend to invest over the very long term, supporting the sustainable development of productive capacity, in alignment with their liability profile. Assets held by pension institutions in the UK outweigh the total value of annual economic output. However, this portrait of pension investment is, at best, outdated. The notion that pension funds can become responsible corporate stewards is highly flawed.

First, there is no reason to believe that pension funds are particularly enlightened shareholders. Funds rightly strive to maximize returns for their members, and, even when they take a broader view of what constitutes members' long-term interests, ultimately their legal duties reinforce a "shareholder value" approach to corporate stewardship.

Second, even if it were the case that pension institutions were able to exercise influence over corporate practice, investment strategies have become increasingly conservative and short-termist in orientation. This is in part a result of the closure of defined benefit schemes, unbalancing scheme demographics towards retired members. Conservatism is reinforced by regulation, which is focused on protecting funds' residual assets at the expense of curtailing the prospect of higher-return (but riskier) strategies. In defined contribution provision, conservative investment strategies are of course inherent in the financing model, since individuals have no temporal anchor to ensure that value is retained amid uncertainty.

Third, the rise of passive investment, exemplified by investment in index-tracking funds, demonstrates pension funds' focus in short-term income stability, in a very low-yield environment. Index tracking simply replicates the aggregate performance of indexes such as the FTSE100 or S&P500, essentially by buying shares in every company on the index; as such, it is inherently pro-cyclical. In this sense, prudent investment practices at scheme level add up to a rather reckless strategy at the aggregate level. All these trends are underpinned by the role and power of an increasingly concentrated asset management industry, which manages funds on behalf of pension schemes, but over which scheme managers have little meaningful control.

This is not to suggest that pension investment practice cannot support progressive goals, such as decarbonization; for example, asset managers such as BlackRock, and scheme providers such as NEST, have been vocal about climate change representing an investment risk. However, there are significant limitations to this agenda, especially in so far as climate risks are incorporated into investment strategies via greater "ESG" allocations ("environmental, social, governance"). There are concerns around the rather generous criteria by which firms may qualify as ESG investments; these criteria may, for instance, direct investment to technology firms that do not themselves directly rely upon fossil fuels but whose business model serves to reinforce carbon-dependent accumulation and environmentally destructive consumption behaviour.

The most sensible conclusion is that the public sector is far better placed than pension institutions, as currently constituted, to make long-term and large-scale investments for the collective benefit of society, the economy and our planet. That said, the new public pension could be organized on a funded basis, or part-funded basis, with the state acting as guarantor akin to the role employers traditionally play in defined benefit provision. In this model, some or all of the accumulated capital could be diverted to democratically organized citizens' wealth funds. Some have in fact suggested that such a scheme could be used to directly fund public investment, with the state effectively borrowing from – and therefore paying interest to – the fund.

Conclusions

Collectivism in pensions saving is not simply about sharing risks with other savers. Even the notion that it involves sharing risks with our employer, or the state, is too simplistic. Pensions collectivism requires an institutional mechanism by which the core purpose of pension provision – mitigating the failure of the future to resemble that imagined in the present – is embedded. The state can mandate private institutions, such as employers, to perform this function, but in a financialized, capitalist economy it is more sustainable for the state to perform or underpin this function itself.

However, regrettably, this understanding of pensions has been forgotten. Rather than designing provision around mitigating failed futures, the UK has gambled on a highly individualized and market-based form of provision within which outcomes for retirees depend acutely on our forecasted futures being realized. UK pension provision is therefore in great peril; to avert catastrophe, especially in the absence of much more comprehensive state pension provision, a new publicly organized occupational pensions system will be required.

It is possible that public provision would disable pension funds' existing role as patient investors. Yet this role is rather illusory. Furthermore, with pensions collectivism restored to its essential function of mitigating uncertainties around how economic change will impact on our ability to maintain living standards over the life course, we may be able to orient public and private investment practice more generally towards the kind of very long-term investment opportunities that, although riskier, have the greatest benefit for society, the economy and our planet.

Further reading

Berry, C. 2021. *Pensions Imperilled: The Political Economy of Private Pensions Provision in the UK*. Oxford: Oxford University Press.

Mabbett, D. 2020. "Reckless prudence: financialization in UK pension scheme governance after the crisis". *Review of International Political Economy*. DOI: 10.1080/09692290.2020.1758187.

MacNicol, J. 2015. *Neoliberalising Old Age*. Cambridge: Cambridge University Press.

12

When the invisible hand fails, the visible hand should step in! Urgent need for a UK National Investment Bank

Stephany Griffith-Jones

Keynes's letters to President Franklin D. Roosevelt clearly illustrate Keynes's firm belief that the main policy to help the US economy recover in a sustained way from the Great Depression was through increased public investment. In 1938 Keynes wrote to Roosevelt:

> It is true that the existing policies will prevent the slump from proceeding to such a disastrous degree as last time. But they will not by themselves maintain prosperity at a reasonable level – not without a large-scale recourse to the public works and other investments aided by Government funds or guarantees; ... namely increased (public) investment in durable goods such as housing, public utilities, and transport.

In an earlier letter to the president, in 1933, Keynes had written,

> In the field of domestic policy, I put in the forefront, a large volume of loan-expenditures under government auspices. It is beyond my province to choose particular objects of expenditure. But preference should be given to those which can be made to mature quickly on a large scale, as for example the rehabilitation of the physical condition of the railroads ... I lay overwhelming emphasis on the increase of national purchasing power resulting from governmental expenditure, which is financed by loans. Nothing else counts in comparison with this.

This is still, or even more, the case now. It was, to an important extent, true after the so-called Global Financial Crisis of 2007–09 and the subsequent eurozone debt crisis; it is also true in what seems to be, unfortunately the far worse current Covid-19 crisis.

One of the modern ways of increasing public, as well as private, investment is through funding by public development banks. By working with private banks and private capital markets, as well as other public institutions, public development banks can add leverage to public resources. Such leverage, facilitating a counter-cyclical response, is particularly valuable in times of economic crisis. Second, and crucially, public development banks provide valuable policy steering to help channel significant financial resources to key priority areas, such as the urgent green transformation and more inclusive growth. Relying on well-functioning public development banks was the policy, for example, of the European Union in the wake of the eurozone debt crisis, when the scale and leverage of the European Investment Bank was significantly increased to support higher investment in difficult circumstances – a sort of Keynesianism *sans dire*.

More generally, it is noteworthy that, irrespective of governmental policy orientation, large national investment banks have been an important feature of the financial sectors of most developed and emerging economies, especially the most successful and dynamic ones, such as Germany, France, China, India, South Korea and Japan. The United Kingdom has been an exception in not having such a large public investment bank, despite its evident need.

During and after the 2007–09 financial crisis the World Bank and regional multilateral development banks (MDBs) sharply increased financing. The largest MDB, the European Investment Bank, saw its paid-in capital doubled, and its role increased by the Juncker Plan, which generated €500 billion of additional loans from 2015 to 2020; a bigger amount is projected to be provided by its successor, InvestEU, in the 2021–27 period.

The fairly recent creation of two large MDBs, the Asia Infrastructure Investment Bank and the New Development Bank of the BRICS (Brazil, Russia, India, China and South Africa), also reflects the shift in the development finance paradigm towards a more balanced public–private mix. Furthermore, a significant number of European, African and Asian countries have recently created new national development banks, while others have expanded existing ones.

According to research carried out at the French Development Agency (Agence Française de Développement), there are more than 400 development banks in the world, scattered in all continents; they include multilateral, regional, national and subnational development banks. The magnitude of their cumulative assets amounts to more than $11.4 trillion, roughly the equivalent of 70 per cent of the assets of the entire US banking sector. Development banks make commitments each year of $2 trillion, or 10 per cent of the world's gross fixed capital formation. Based on a 20 per cent increase in their current activity, development banks could mobilize an additional $400 billion by the end of 2021 alone. The function of development banks is not just to mobilize their own funds but, equally importantly, to mobilize private finance. Such an effort could thus double the amount available for reducing economic decline and stimulating economic recovery, to an additional $800 billion.

If the United Kingdom created a National Investment Bank, it could participate in such a massive increase of financing, to fund investment in strategic sectors. If this was done soon, it could help the recovery of companies and jobs from the Covid crisis in a strategic way, giving support to priority sectors.

Indeed, both the Global Financial Crisis and, more recently, the Covid pandemic have shown clearly one of the key aspects of the great relevance of public development banks: their ability to provide counter-cyclical finance at large scale in difficult times, to fund working capital when needed – as currently under Covid. But, even in normal times, public development banks can provide long-term funds, to help maintain finance for key long-term investment in priority sectors, such as renewable energy, greener transport, health and other social sectors, as well as innovation. Because they benefit from government ownership, which allows them to make long-term borrowings at fairly low cost, public investment banks are ideally placed to fund projects that are environmentally or socially valuable but are too risky to be attractive to purely private finance, such as helping fund the so essential "Green New Deal".

This is in clear contrast with private finance, provided, for example, by private banks, whose lending is typically pro-cyclical, as they become more reluctant to lend during recessions than in normal or "good" times. One could say that private banks tend to be "fair-weather friends", providing finance willingly in boom conditions, when companies and households are less in need of finance, but withdrawing lending in bad times, precisely when additional funding is needed. This helps to accentuate crises and recessions, as is the case in the present Covid difficulties.

With regard to the Covid-19 response, Figure 12.1 highlights the different common measures quickly adopted by development banks, to facilitate their counter-cyclical response. These include (a) fast-track procedures to facilitate the approval of transactions, with some development banks issuing loans in less than 24 hours after requests have been submitted; (b) the provision of working capital for companies through loans, grants and guarantees, with particular emphasis on support to small and medium-sized enterprises (SMEs); (c) a standstill approach on existing loans – extended grace periods; and (d) additional lines of support for the health sector and governments, especially local ones.

Public development banks, such as the German KfW bank, have been at the forefront of expanding their lending and other operations, in response to Covid, with an amount of €100 billion extra resources committed! In terms of support for health, it is noteworthy that China Development Bank, of mainland China, had already by the end of February 2020 issued ¥27.2 billion ($3.8 billion) of emergency loans for epidemic prevention and control. When the invisible hand of private

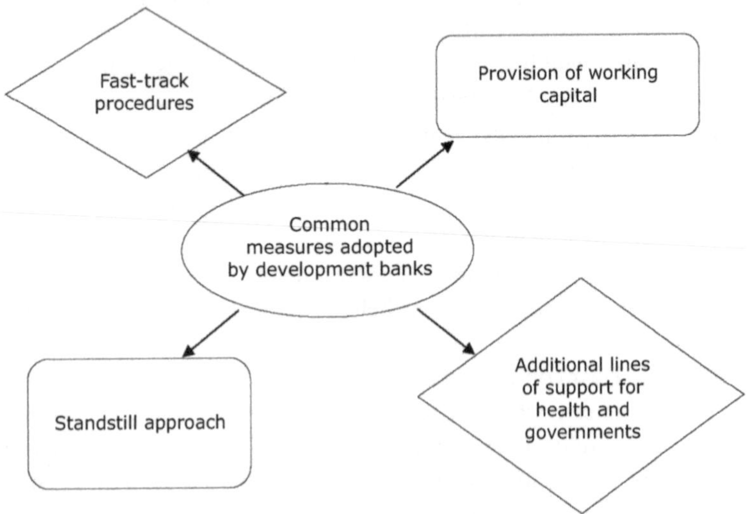

Figure 12.1 Initial measures adopted by development banks in response to Covid-19
Source: Griffith-Jones *et al.* (2020).

financial banks and markets does not act, or does not act sufficiently, then the visible hand of public investment and public development banks needs to step in.

The United Kingdom has been seriously handicapped in its economic response to Covid (as in previous periods of economic weakness, such as the 2007–09 financial crisis, as well as more generally) by the fact that it has a very small public investment bank, the British Business Bank, and the recently privatized former Green Bank. In fact, the United Kingdom is an outlier in Europe, among the G20 and worldwide, in not having a public investment bank at meaningful scale.

The inability to generate rapid counter-cyclical lending in economic downturns, as after the financial crisis and during the even larger Covid crisis, is one key reason why the United Kingdom should urgently create a National Investment Bank on a significant scale, as well as regional development banks (RDBs), as soon as possible. The 2019 Labour Party manifesto had a clear commitment to creating such banks, with a detailed blueprint for their establishment.

The other chief reason why a NIB is essential for the success of the United Kingdom, as well as other economies, is that such an institution would be, and is, a key policy instrument to help fund directly, and help mobilize additional funding for, the major investment needed to support the crucial structural transformation urgently required to ensure a more dynamic, low-carbon and just economy. Such a structural transformation points to the need for large-scale investment, often in new sectors or activities, over whose prospects there is inevitably a great deal of uncertainty. The private financial sector is often unable and/or unwilling to accept such a high level of uncertainty and commit resources, least of all if it is the only investor.

In the particular case of the United Kingdom, the commercial financial system has not performed well to support the real economy. It has been pro-cyclical, over-lending in boom times but rationing credit during and after crises. It has not sufficiently funded long-term investment in key areas such as green energy, needed to avert climate catastrophe and create green jobs, support innovative and small companies and fund infrastructure. Furthermore, private and public investment, already historically low in the UK economy, has fallen sharply since the 2007–09 crisis, to an important extent as a result of Conservative Party austerity policies. It is expected to fall further during the Covid crisis.

A particular source of concern is the fact that, for some time, the United Kingdom has been in last place among both the G7 and OECD countries, with the lowest share of investment in GDP.

Development banks worldwide are precisely aiming at helping to limit the massive damage to companies and jobs being done by Covid, supporting the recovery of the economy, and doing this – or trying to do this, as much as possible – in a way that would help to "build back better". This implies helping to give an important policy steer to achieve new social goals that have become clearer during Covid, such as shifting investment towards social spending, especially health and social care, but also directing investment into education, focusing on activities such as digitalization, and transforming the economy to a low-carbon one to be able to face the challenge of mitigating climate change.

The Labour Party supports the setting up of a National Investment Bank, initially aimed at addressing (a) the long-term funding gap for small and medium-sized enterprises across the country, emphasizing innovation and sustainability; and (b) the long-term funding gap for infrastructure investment in the country, including both physical and social infrastructure, with a particular emphasis on low-carbon infrastructure. However, the National Investment Bank's role was conceived as being much more than the financing of infrastructure and SMEs. Not only would infrastructure development need to support the decarbonization of the economy, but the NIB would also ensure that this be done using best practices. More broadly, the NIB was seen as supporting, in a major way, the financing of innovation, especially in areas of high priority for a sustainable and just transition.

The NIB was thus seen as much as a technical expert as a financier. It was with this expertise that the NIB would champion best practices. This would start with how it raises its funds – from local and global investors intent on supporting infrastructural renewal around clean technologies, decarbonization and social development – then move on to investing in small and medium-sized enterprises, the productive sector of the economy, and the promotion of SME business digitalization, sustainability and decarbonization.

The NIB was perceived as modelling itself on international best practice, especially of the many existing successful public investment banks (such as Germany's KfW), and thus would be expert in infrastructure project development, encompassing engineering skills, project management, planning and environmental sciences.

The NIB's other mission would be supporting small and medium-sized enterprises. It would provide financing, training, skills support and business information to SMEs. The institutional structure for this role was seen to require a reach into all regions of the United Kingdom, with a proposal for regional development banks connected to the NIB. This regional presence, and linking with local enterprise partnerships and their growth hubs, would support the development of a more focused and funded local presence. Combining local expertise, broad national overview of sectors and the use of data sciences would help the proposed NIB and RDBs bridge the information asymmetry normally faced by lenders to SMEs.

It is interesting that the Conservative government headed by Boris Johnson is reportedly planning to recreate a publicly backed Green Investment Bank to help fund the technologies and infrastructure needed to reach its legally binding 2050 net zero emissions target, according to the energy minister, Kwasi Kwarteng. This is potentially positive, although it is unclear if the bank's scale will be sufficient for the task. It also seems rather absurd to create a new Green Investment Bank only three years after the original Green Investment Bank was privatized. It is also noteworthy that the Chancellor of the Exchequer, Rishi Sunak, is reportedly drawing up plans for a possible new infrastructure bank to provide new funding for capital projects across the country, as well as to replace the significant funding previously provided by the European Investment Bank for infrastructure, which the United Kingdom is, regrettably, losing through leaving the European Union.

International experience indicates that there are key preconditions for making national development banks successful. These include: (a) autonomy in their decision-making, attached to transparent and competent governance, as well as highly skilled staff and management; (b) significant amounts of initial capital, provided by governments, to make a significant impact, both in terms of counter-cyclical impact in difficult times and to ensure that major investments go to strategic sectors; (c) using appropriate instruments to enable them to mobilize sufficient private finance, while channelling their funding to meet development objectives (indeed, it is vital to ensure that the instruments used, such as loans, guarantees and equity, are effective in mobilizing sufficient private finance, and do so in ways that allow the development bank to direct those resources to where they will have most development impact – implying sufficient policy steer – and in ways that do not imply excessive transfer of risk from the private financial sector to the public development bank, and ultimately to governments, so avoiding excessive public contingent liabilities); and (d) having local presence, which implies therefore the need for regional branches or regional development banks, so as to work closely with local companies, regional authorities and communities (this will also be an important instrument for supporting more disadvantaged regions – an important way to reduce the regional inequalities so prevalent in the United Kingdom).

The time for the United Kingdom to create a national investment bank is now! By not doing so, the UK economy will be left to face major challenges with one hand tied behind its back.

Further reading

Griffith-Jones, S. & J. Ocampo (eds) 2018. *The Future of National Development Banks*. Oxford: Oxford University Press.

Griffith-Jones, S. & P. Rice 2019. "Taking a national investment bank forward", working paper. London: Progressive Economy Forum. Available at: https://progressiveeconomyforum.com/wp-content/uploads/2019/09/Taking-a-National-Investment-Bank-Forward-4.pdf.

Griffith-Jones, S. *et al.* 2020. "Matching risks with instruments in development banks", Research Paper 170. Paris: Agence Française de Développement.

PART IV

Tackling poverty and inequality

13

Revive the commons!

Guy Standing

The commons are our collective heritage, our common-wealth, our public social and cultural amenities and institutions, our collective knowledge, our civil commons (epitomized by common law) and our traditions of sharing in society, epitomized by the old term "commoning".

The rights of the common people to access the commons and to share in its bounty were first set out in the Charter of the Forest of 1217, companion to Magna Carta. The Charter established that everybody has a right to subsistence and that the commons should make that a reality, providing, in the words of the old saying, "the poor man's overcoat".

Whereas in medieval times the commons related to the natural world – land, water, wildlife, minerals – the Charter's precepts of free and equal access and sharing also underpinned the public institutions and services built up over generations with public money and support. Like traditional commons, they have stood outside the market, as a free or affordable service for all citizens, not for private profit.

Throughout British history, rebellions and transformative moments have been about struggles to recover commons and systems of participative sharing. Now may be another of those moments. Many commons are of most value to those with low incomes, including the precariat, which has been disproportionately hurt by their plunder over the past four decades. The tragedy of de-commoning is that, as well as eroding social solidarity and respect for the ecosystems that sustain us, it has worsened inequalities in ways that orthodox economists ignore. The Covid pandemic has thrown into sharp relief the value of the commons and how society has been weakened by their erosion during the neoliberal era.

A progressive agenda worthy of the name must revive all forms of commons: natural, social, civil, cultural and knowledge. The discussion below illustrates how the five types of commons have been lost – and suggests what a progressive government should do about it.

The natural commons

Historically, waves of enclosure have depleted what was once common land on which commoners had rights, from roughly half of all the land in Britain in medieval times to 5 per cent today. This has resulted in one of the most concentrated landownership structures in the world, much inherited by a tiny elite. The largest private landowner is the tenth Duke of Buccleuch, who inherited 277,000 acres by virtue of being a descendant of an illegitimate son of King Charles II.

Making this even more inequitable, every year the duke and other large landholders have received millions of pounds in subsidies from the European Union's Common Agricultural Policy, which the government plans to continue outside the Union. The larger the landholding, the more they receive.

What is left of the land commons and commoners' rights remains under constant threat, from the erasing of footpaths and other rights of way to the earmarking of village greens for development to the leasing of forest land to private leisure companies. However, the plunder of the commons by privatization and commercialization, on top of austerity-driven neglect and decay since 2010, has removed common rights across the board.

The state of our public parks exemplifies the loss of commons through austerity. The government has slashed funding for the eight royal parks in London, given to the nation by Queen Victoria in 1851 for the public's "quiet enjoyment", obliging them to rent out large areas for rock concerts and other commercial events, such as Hyde Park's Winter Wonderland. The public not only lose access to these areas for long after the events have taken place, because it takes time for the grass to recover, they also lose their "quiet enjoyment" of the rest of the park as well.

The 27,000 public parks around Britain are also decaying as a result of huge cuts in local authority budgets. In a 2016 survey, only half the United Kingdom's public parks were reported to be in good condition; almost all had suffered cuts in funding, prompting commercial events to raise money and sales of land.

Elsewhere, the dire results of the privatization project launched by Margaret Thatcher in the 1980s are exemplified by the experience of the water industry. The 1989 water privatization subsidized the creation of nine English regional corporate monopolies, which proceeded to load themselves up with debt to boost profits, dividends and bonuses, while skimping on investment and maintenance spending. Ownership of the water and sewage system has passed into foreign hands, notably through private equity funds, set up specifically to make short-term profits and then disband. On one estimate, nearly three-quarters of the shares in England's water industry are foreign-owned, thereby syphoning the bulk of profits abroad. It is a colonization of our commons.

Meanwhile, untreated sewage is polluting our beaches and pouring into our rivers, not one of which is now safe for swimming. And massive leakages from elderly pipes mean that much of the treated water is wasted, pushing up consumer bills. Yet no one has been prosecuted, and the regulator, Ofwat, is even allowing the companies to determine their own fines!

Thatcher's woefully underpriced sale of North Sea oil rights was another act of self-inflicted colonization of our common-wealth. Her government dissipated the revenue on tax cuts for the wealthy, benefits for the unemployed (hit by its economic policies) and the Falklands War. The current government is using more public money to subsidize the cost of dismantling redundant oil rigs, which the oil multinationals could well afford after years of handsome profits.

Ironically, the China National Offshore Oil Corporation, a state enterprise, is now the biggest operator in the North Sea, accounting for a quarter of UK oil production. By contrast, Norway retained its North Sea oil as a commons. It has used the revenues to build what is now the world's largest sovereign wealth fund, benefiting all Norwegians.

And, although Britain is a world leader in wind generation, over 90 per cent of capacity is foreign-owned, a third in the hands of Denmark's Østrom. Offshore wind farms sit on the seabed leased from the Crown Estate, which receives a quarter of the auction proceeds (the rest go to the Treasury), under an archaic rule that all land belongs to the monarch. There is no direct benefit to the public from this plunder of the commons.

The social commons

The modern plunder of the social commons began with Thatcher's decision to grant council tenants the "right to buy" their home, at a hefty discount. Of course, this was popular with those renting council homes at the time and able to buy, many of whom profited further by selling on their homes at the market price or joining the swelling ranks of private landlords. But those homes were a social commons, an asset built with public money, belonging to society as a whole. Since then councils have been constrained from building more social housing to replace units lost. Today the council housing stock is the lowest on record, at under 2 million, from 5 million at the start of the 1980s.

The "right to buy" was accompanied by the growth of mass landlordism, aided by "buy-to-let" subsidies. The subsidies have been phased out, but not before producing over 2 million private landlords, some with numerous properties, overseeing 5 million units. Rents have soared and the shortage of affordable accommodation has reached crisis proportions, as the growth of homelessness bears witness. Contributing to the crisis in London and other cities are luxury property developments, priced out of reach to locals and used by foreign buyers as speculative investments rather than places to live.

Pressured by austerity cuts, local councils have invited commercial developers to overhaul housing estates, disrupting settled communities and providing scarcely any social housing. The government has also sold public land for private housing, although it was unable to tell the House of Commons Public Accounts Committee in 2015 how much the land was sold for, or how many houses had been built. All we know is that more of the commons has been squandered.

Separately, our towns and cities are increasingly being sold off to private investors, with the spread of privately owned public spaces. Streets, squares and iconic public buildings, as well as residential property, have passed into the hands of foreign property companies and financial institutions, as well as oligarchs, Middle Eastern sheikhs and Chinese billionaires and state corporations. Newly created Granary Square near London's King's Cross station, one of Europe's biggest urban open spaces, is now a private estate that can be hired for commercial events. Bishops Square, which includes Spitalfields Market and historic streets in east London, is now owned by J. P. Morgan Asset Management.

Private owners of public space can restrict what people can do there, or deny access altogether, preventing legitimate social and political activity. Thus, Occupy London was barred from demonstrating in front of the Stock Exchange in Paternoster Square, on the grounds that the square was privately owned by Japan's Mitsubishi Estate Company. Rights of commoning are denied.

Privatization and colonization have extended to many other aspects of our social commons. Nearly three-quarters of the care workforce are employed by private or voluntary entities rather than local authorities; three of the biggest care home chains are owned by private equity companies. Four Seasons Healthcare, a private equity-owned chain controlled by a US property investment group, operated 322 care homes until it went into administration in 2019, leaving 17,000 vulnerable elderly residents in limbo. This was just the latest in a series of private care home closures and bankruptcies. The disastrous record of care homes in the pandemic reflects the privatization and financialization of social care.

The "privatization by stealth" of the NHS, an integral part of the social commons, is proceeding apace, with the contracting out to private companies of an increasing number of services. These include not just back-office functions but medical services, including inpatient mental care and routine surgical procedures, such as hip replacement.

By 2018 non-NHS providers accounted for almost a half of NHS spending on community services, such as community nursing, health visiting and occupational therapy. Extensive outsourcing, coupled with financial stringency in the austerity decade, weakened the NHS for dealing with Covid-19. And the government will be under pressure to open more services to American healthcare companies in any post-Brexit trade deal.

Then there is the privatization of public transport services. A quarter of British households have no car, including half of those on low incomes. Rail privatization has been disastrous. Fares have soared despite continuing generous government subsidies, as have profits, much diverted abroad. Today two-thirds of Britain's rail operators are foreign-owned, including state-owned railways from Germany, the Netherlands and France. As for buses, deregulation alongside local authority budget cuts have produced chaotic, uncoordinated services and the withdrawal of unprofitable rural routes. This has left many households unable to travel to jobs, essential services and social activities. Another part of the commons has been lost.

The knowledge commons

The information, intellectual and educational commons have also been privatized and colonized. The government has cut funds for the

BBC, the closest the United Kingdom has to an information commons, notably by withdrawing its subsidy for free television licences for the over-75s; it has thereby forced the corporation to take the unpopular decision to reinstate the licence fee for all but the very poorest. The public broadcasting model, intended to serve the public interest with fact-based news and information, is under attack.

Australian-born Rupert Murdoch, now a US citizen, has led the colonization of the information commons. His ownership, through News UK, of *The Sun*, *The Times*, *The Sunday Times* and – until 2018 – Sky TV (now owned by Comcast, another US company) has enabled him to shape a right-wing political discourse in Britain. And in 2020, building on its right-wing TalkRadio station, News UK was reported to be planning a right-wing opinionated television news channel, in competition with a similar initiative linked to another US billionaire. The media regulator, Ofcom, which is supposed to ensure impartiality, has allowed TalkRadio and the LBC (originally London Broadcasting Company) radio station to abandon any pretence at balance, as long as they give airtime to alternative viewpoints elsewhere in the schedule (perhaps in the early hours of the morning). The regulator has failed to maintain the information commons.

The *Evening Standard* is owned by Alexander Lebedev, a billionaire ex-Soviet spy, dubbed "the spy who came in for the gold", whose son appointed as its editor the architect of austerity, George Osborne, the former Chancellor of the Exchequer. Not only has much of the print news media been colonized but social media – Facebook, Twitter and the rest – are predominantly controlled by US "Big Tech", which use devious tax avoidance schemes to pay trivial sums in UK taxes.

Other parts of the knowledge commons – the realm of ideas and inventions – are in no better shape. For generations the United States refused to honour UK and European copyright laws and bribed British workers to steal industrial secrets. But, once it had become the dominant economy, it put pressure on other countries to accept stringent intellectual property right laws, culminating in the passing of the global agreement on Trade-Related Aspects of Intellectual Property Rights (TRIPS) through the World Trade Organization in 1994, with the support of Britain and other European countries.

TRIPS has led to an explosion of patent filings worldwide, from around 1 million a year before TRIPS to 3.3 million in 2018. Patents grant applicants a monopoly on production for 20 years or more and are also used defensively to block competition. Meanwhile, copyright terms have been extended to ever longer periods, with authors now entitled to protection not only for their lifetime but for decades afterwards, with the royalties awarded to their heirs.

The British government has also supported the undemocratic Investor–State Dispute Settlement (ISDS) process, by which foreign capital owners can sue a government if, in their view, any policy change threatens their future profits. So far the ISDS has mostly hit developing countries. But, if a progressive government came into office in the United Kingdom, it could find the ISDS an impediment to restoration of the commons. Imagine what could happen if a Labour government tried to renationalize water.

The education commons are also being commodified, privatized and colonized. So-called public (private) schools continue to gain valuable tax breaks as charities. And the privatization of state schooling has advanced via "academies", "free schools" (sic) and "school–business partnerships", which permit individuals and companies, including foreign banks and multinationals, to influence what is taught and how.

The commodification of teaching is further eroding the educational commons, imposing uniformity and stifling creativity and the transmission of local vernacular values, the essence of the commons. Massive open online courses (MOOCs) are infiltrating the national educational system. Leading providers of these standardized "products" include the US-based corporates Coursera, which claims 30 million users globally, and Udacity, which operates in 119 countries. The so-called Khan Academy provides courses for schoolchildren, while Udemy, backed by global finance, offers 22,000 courses for adults.

Universities are drifting in a similar, commercialized direction, partly because of cuts in government funding. Today they not only increasingly try to sell themselves as a commodity, with expensive new facilities to attract high-fee foreign students; they have also delegated much of the teaching to an underpaid precariat, and outsourced services to private companies. The most glaring example is student accommodation, over 80 per cent of which is now provided by profit-making companies backed by considerable foreign investment, most prominently from Goldman Sachs.

The civil commons

Historically, common law was both universal and administered by government and agencies accountable to it and to the people. But recent governments have jettisoned fundamental principles of common law – equal treatment, proportionality and due process – in many aspects of the civil commons. Legal aid has been slashed and courts closed as a result of cuts in government spending, denying or restricting access to justice for many on low incomes. Meanwhile, justice services, from forensic analysis to immigrant detention centres, have been outsourced to profit-making companies.

About 15 per cent of all prisoners are in private prisons, five of which are run by French-owned Sodexo. Inevitably, private prisons try to minimize costs and maximize profits, leading to overcrowding, degrading conditions and a lack of experienced prison staff. Some have been so badly run that the government has been forced to take them over, stalling planned expansion.

The experience of privatized probation services has been even more dismal. In 2014 most of the probation service was privatized. One beneficiary was Working Links, owned by a German investment company, which also gained lucrative government contracts for welfare "services". It and other private providers performed so badly that in 2019 the government, in a climbdown, announced a return of probation to the public sector. By then a service that had taken decades to build up was in tatters.

Access to the law and protection against illegal acts are the essence of common law, with respect for due process, legal representation and the proportionality of punishment for misdemeanours and crimes, all enshrined in Magna Carta. All have been corroded, intensifying hidden forms of inequality. Thousands of actions that previously were not regarded as criminal have been made into crimes. These include the breaching of orders against behaviour deemed "antisocial" (such as noisy ball games), but which is not in itself criminal.

Moreover, social policy, notably in the form of Universal Credit, has made a mockery of due process and proportionality. Under Universal Credit, benefits can be withdrawn for trivial breaches of the onerous conditions, such as being five minutes late for an interview, on the decision of a Department for Work and Pensions (DWP) official, with no opportunity for the sanctioned person to be heard or have representation. Decisions on disability benefits by unaccountable bureaucrats, or, worse, employees of private profit-seeking companies charged with making disability assessments, can likewise deny vulnerable people vital benefits for many months until appeals can be heard, the majority of which have been successful.

The cultural commons

The arts, sport, the media, public libraries, art galleries, museums, concert halls and public places for performances are all part of our cultural commons. Public architecture, townscapes and landscapes also shape and constitute a country's cultural commons. In the 1970s half the architects in Britain were employed in the public sector, and local authorities had their own architects' departments, responsible for a vast range of public buildings as well as social housing geared to the needs and traditions of the local area. Today fewer than 1 per cent of architects work in the public sector, and it is left to foreign corporations and celebrity architects to reshape urban landscapes. They have jettisoned the historic character of cities, imposing an alien, often alienating skyline.

The library has been the depository of popular culture, at least since the establishment of the Great Library of Alexandria in the fourth century BC. In the United Kingdom, libraries do not simply lend books; they enable people without computers at home to access information and knowledge and to participate as digital citizens, as more and more government and private services move online. They also act as venues for the arts. Yet budget cuts have forced hundreds of libraries to close and others to restrict services and lay off staff.

Museums and art galleries, repositories of our common heritage, have been another casualty of austerity. Spending cuts have led to the extensive outsourcing of services, such as cleaning and catering, to private firms, often foreign-owned. They have also caused a drift towards the American model of dependence on private donations and sponsorship, giving decisions on what is displayed, and how, to multinational oil corporations or US banks.

Conclusion

Recent governments have aided and abetted the commodification and colonization of our commons. The claim that, following Brexit, this government is "bringing back control" and asserting national sovereignty is hypocrisy. The way to "bring back control" would be to reverse the privatization and commercialization of the commons, end austerity-driven neglect and develop a system for compensating commoners – all of us – for the plunder that has been allowed and subsidized by successive governments.

The story of plunder is a shift from enclosure to privatization, spurred by neglect during austerity. And privatization has paved the way for colonization by foreign capital, which has no accountability to the British government or to the British people. Private equity funds have been in the vanguard, and, although most of their money comes from abroad, including from sovereign wealth funds, a sizeable chunk comes from UK pension funds. The public's money is being used to take the commons from the public.

A Charter of the Commons is required, around which a public campaign can be launched. In *Plunder of the Commons*, the book on which this chapter is based, I have proposed elements for such a Charter. Others may have different priorities. Perhaps the Progressive Economy Forum can take a lead in bringing together groups wishing to see a revival of the ethos of the commons and draw up an agenda.

Above all, a mechanism is needed to compensate commoners for the illegitimate taking of the commons via enclosure, neglect, commercialization, privatization, austerity and colonization. A Commons Fund should be established, from which common dividends or basic incomes should be paid equally to all.

Further reading

Standing, G. 2016. *The Corruption of Capitalism: Why Rentiers Thrive and Work Does Not Pay*. London: Biteback.

Standing, G. 2017. *Basic Income: And How We Can Make It Happen*. London: Pelican.

Standing, G. 2019. *Plunder of the Commons: A Manifesto for Sharing Public Wealth*. London: Pelican.

14

The people's stake: inequality and "asset redistribution"

Stewart Lansley

Since the Second World War, attempts to deliver the social democratic goal of a more equal society have centred on a more comprehensive benefit system paid for by progressive taxation. It was a strategy that contributed to the peak equality achieved in the mid-1970s. Since then the strength of such "income redistribution" has been steadily weakened. The tax system has become regressive, taking a bigger slice of low than of high incomes, while working-age benefit levels have been sharply eroded. Alongside these changes, a series of shocks, many self-inflicted – from ever deeper recessions, deindustrialization and a decade of austerity to accelerating automation, Covid-19 and Brexit – have played havoc with family finances, livelihoods and pay. Today we have a mean and patchy benefit system pitched against a greatly heightened risk of poverty.

Britain needs a more equalizing tax/benefit system. But even a more progressive system of income redistribution would not be enough to tackle today's entrenched drivers of inequality. An effective anti-poverty and pro-equality strategy requires new measures of "asset redistribution" aimed at sharing the rising pool of wealth more equally. Wealth – which plays an increasingly central role in what the French economist Thomas Piketty has called a "force for divergence" – has long been the elephant in the room of anti-inequality policy.

Britain is an asset-rich nation, yet the revenue from capital taxes has been steadily falling and now raises a fraction of the total tax take. Outstripping the growth of incomes, the total level of national wealth has surged from around three times the size of the economy in the 1960s to approaching seven times today. Official data put personal wealth holdings at some £14.6 trillion, holdings that are increasingly concentrated at the top, reversing the long-term trends prior to the 1980s. They are a primary driver of today's institutionalized inequality. This is because the considerable returns from ownership (in the form of profits, rents and dividends) – returns that have for decades exceeded the growth rate of the economy – accrue disproportionately to the already rich. A tenth of UK households own 45 per cent of the nation's privately held wealth, while the least wealthy half own just 9 per cent.

Wealth is not just more unequally distributed than income. Much of the remarkable boost to personal fortunes since the 1970s has been both unearned and, too often, the product of damaging economic activity. A large chunk is simply due to over-inflated asset prices, often – as in the case of property – the result of poorly targeted state policy. Asset inflation – "growing rich in their sleep", as John Stuart Mill said of landlords – is good news for those sitting on tidy wealth piles, but it is bad news for the wider economy and those with little or no wealth. Much of the wealth boom has been the product of wealth transfer or extraction – enabled by heavily concentrated financial muscle – rather than of new wealth creation that brings benefits for wider society. Little of this boom has been harnessed for the public good.

A further chunk is attributable to the rolling fire sale of public assets: industrial, land and housing. Public wealth holdings today – from profitable state-owned enterprises such as the Land Registry to the land and property portfolios owned by public institutions such as the NHS and local authorities – account for a tenth of total national wealth compared with over a third in the 1970s. This deliberate depletion of the asset base once held in common has also greatly weakened the public finances: net *public* wealth (assets minus debt) has sunk from the equivalent of a half of national income to become negative today.

It will not be possible to achieve a significant dent in today's embedded inequality without measures to achieve a much more even spread of capital ownership and its gains. There are various alternative routes to this goal. One would be through a reform of existing wealth taxation that raises the revenue take. Another would be to give employees a stronger share in the ownership of private companies, through, for example, the promotion of alternative but greatly under-represented business models – from partnerships and co-operatives to mutually owned and social enterprises – that distribute primary economic gains more equally.

A citizens' wealth fund

Another, complementary but more direct approach would be the creation of a citizens' wealth fund, a collectively owned pool of wealth, owned on an equal basis by citizens. Such a fund would give all citizens a direct and equal stake in the economy, and offer a progressive and potentially popular way of managing part of the national wealth for the common good. With such a model, at least part of the gains from economic activity would be shared, including across generations, creating a new "counter force for convergence" – a force that would strengthen over time as the fund grew to become a larger constituent part of the economy.

The principle that a significant share of national wealth – natural and created – should be held in common has been advanced by a long line of thinkers, from the human rights campaigner Thomas Paine in the late eighteenth century to the Nobel laureate James Meade in the twentieth. For Paine, natural resources are the "common property of the human race". This idea should be extended to at least part of the pool of modern physical, productive and social wealth, "gifts of society as well as nature" – a pool that is essentially an inheritance from the efforts of previous generations. There have been various proposals over time for ensuring the greater social ownership of capital aimed at breaking up large concentrations of private wealth. In 1973, for example, drawing on the work of Meade, the Labour Party published an Opposition Green Paper, *Capital and Equality*. The paper called for society to establish a growing stake in capital through a national collectively owned fund. The study group behind the idea included the MP Barbara Castle, Nicholas Kaldor (economic adviser to the party's leader, Harold Wilson), and Lord Diamond, appointed to chair Labour's Royal Commission on the Distribution of Income and Wealth in 1975. Similar ideas were proposed in the 1980s by both the Social Democratic Party and the Liberal Democrats, yet no postwar government has attempted to implement any version of this idea.

A citizens' wealth fund would be a direct way of realizing this aim. It would socialize some of this accumulated historic wealth, most of it privately held by a business, landed and financial elite who had little or nothing to do with its creation. It would build the public asset base, thus strengthening the public finances, and mobilize part of the national wealth for the common good.

Such a fund, operating like a giant community-owned unit trust, would differ in a number of significant respects from the sovereign wealth funds – mostly financed by oil bonanzas – established by dozens of countries across the globe. Britain missed the opportunity to establish a sovereign fund from its own oil revenues. If it had done so, it would today have a fund close to the size of the giant $1 trillion Norwegian fund, the largest of the sovereign funds. Instead of investing the national oil bonanza in more sustained future prosperity, the United Kingdom chose a one-off, short-term boost to personal consumption. The creation of a citizen-owned fund from accumulated wealth pools would be one way of correcting this much-lamented historic failure.

Most existing sovereign funds operate with minimal transparency as little more than the investment arm of states. A model fund would be managed independently of government and the Treasury by a board of guardians, including representatives of government, business, trade unions and the public.

Although few existing sovereign funds act as a progressive force, there are several successful examples that offer important lessons for building a model fund. Most important is the Alaskan oil-based "Permanent Fund", which has paid a pioneering and highly popular annual citizen's dividend – averaging $1,150 every year – since 1982. In the early 1980s Shetland Island Council did a nifty deal with the oil companies, which agreed to pay annual disturbance payments in return for operational access to the North Sea. These payments were paid into the Shetland Charitable Trust. Now worth some £200 million (a significant sum for a population of 22,000), returns have been used to fund social projects from new leisure centres to support for the elderly. A similar fund was established by Orkney Island Council. These funds enjoy significant public buy-in. The Alaskan social dividend is high-profile and popular and has helped Alaska become one of the most economically equal of all US states.

In the early 1980s a scheme for local "wage earner funds", financed by an annual levy on shareholders, was implemented in Sweden. Devised by Rudolph Meidner, a key architect of the Swedish welfare state and head of economics at the Swedish Trade Union Confederation, this was a bold, if short-lived, experiment to take the country's model of social democracy to a further stage. The funds were, unsurprisingly, unpopular with business but, unlike the Alaskan approach, failed to win the level of public buy-in necessary for sustainability. This was in part because they were controlled by trade unions and the public lacked a direct stake in the funds. Implemented at a time when a pro-market new right was beginning to gain economic ascendancy, the scheme was closed by the incoming conservative coalition in 1991, by which time the funds had grown to be worth some 7 per cent of the economy.

Building a fund

A model citizens' wealth fund needs to build on these experiments. The power of such an approach depends on how the fund is financed and managed and how its gains are distributed. There is a strong case for initiating the fund with an initial endowment set at, say, £100 billion. Half of this could include the transfer of some existing publicly owned assets, including several highly commercial state-owned companies, such as the Land Registry and the Ordnance Survey – a transfer that would also protect them from privatization. A second element could include the issuing of up to, say, £50 billion of long-term government bonds. Some of these could operate a bit like the perpetual bonds advocated by the American financier George Soros. There has rarely been a better time to issue such bonds. Germany has recently issued a 30-year government bond with a negative yield. At today's near-zero interest rates (bank rate could yet become negative), this would be a highly cost-effective way of speeding the establishment of the fund. Such a method – the issuing of long-term fixed government loans – was used to finance the building of the new towns from the late 1940s, while the use of perpetual bonds or "consols" has a long history, especially in the United Kingdom and United States. The bond would be used by the fund to purchase more remunerative financial and physical assets to be held in the fund.

Additional funding would come from new levies aimed at raising, say, £50 billion a year on privately owned capital. This would involve the annual transfer of a small part of the current private wealth pool into the fund. The UK tax system falls disproportionately on income, while new levies on assets would be an effective way of recouping and redistributing some of the gains from unearned wealth accumulation. The combined revenue from existing capital taxes accounts for less than 2 per cent of total economic output. Although levies on wealth have proved unpopular, even among those who would be unaffected, their hypothecation into a fund owned on an equal basis by all citizens and used for explicit social benefit might well be a way of winning greater public support.

One of the most pro-equality approaches would be to source the fund in part through a new modest scrip tax, with the top 350 companies paying, say, an annual 0.5 per cent share issue into the fund (raising an estimated £12 billion a year). By diluting a tiny part of existing share ownership, part of the pool of institutional wealth would be gradually socialized, with the gains that now accrue to a narrow group of private owners shared across society. After a decade the citizens' fund would own 5 per cent of the stock of corporate capital, although a total limit – of, say, 10 per cent – could be set on the transfer.

Large corporations are, in essence, quasi-social entities, operating in interdependence with society. They enjoy significant state support, from an educated workforce and state-provided infrastructure to a system of "corporate welfare" in grants, subsidies and tax breaks worth some £93 billion annually (close to the total working-age benefit bill). This aid – along with the Covid-19 crisis-related handouts costing billions each week – comes free of conditions on tax dodging, employment practices or social responsibility. There is a strong case that such financial support should come with a proportionate equity stake that could be paid into the fund.

Socializing part of the ownership of companies in this way could be seen as an extension of company-based employee ownership and profit-sharing schemes already operated by some companies, albeit with two key distinctions. It would extend the principle of profit sharing across *all* medium-sized and large firms rather than within a small minority of firms. Second, the benefits would be distributed collectively rather than to individual employees.

In 2019 Labour's shadow Chancellor of the Exchequer, John McDonnell, proposed a company-based "inclusive ownership fund", with workers given a small ownership stake in the companies they work for, and an entitlement to a dividend payment up to a maximum of £500 a year. Although the businesses involved would gradually become part-owned by employees – at a rate of 1 per cent a year up to a maximum of 10 per cent – the proposal would have had a marginal impact on the goals of spreading capital ownership, and its gains, *across society*. Applied purely to companies with more than 250 employees, many of which already operate some form of employee shareholding, the plan would benefit only a tenth of employees, with the rest of the workforce – including the least-paid and least secure, the self-employed, those in small firms and working in the twilight economy and those working in the public sector – missing out. With the cap set at £500 per worker, only a small proportion of the dividends accruing to the firm-based fund would go to the firm's workers; the lion's share would go to the Treasury. A big part of the plan thus took the form of a disguised tax.

Other possible sources of finance include hypothecating the occasional levies on large companies – from corporate fines to one-off taxes (paid in shares) on windfall profits – for the fund. Examples of the latter include Labour's £5 billion 1997 windfall tax on the "excess profits" of the privatized utilities and the bank levy introduced in 2011. Other possible sources include new charges on merger and acquisition activity, a progressive tax on property values, raising the revenue yield from the new digital services tax on big technology companies such as Facebook and Google, and the introduction of higher rates on existing eco-taxes.

Figure 14.1 shows the size of such a fund after 10, 20 and 50 years. With an initial endowment of £100 billion, annual payments into the fund of £50 billion and a real rate of return of 4 per cent per annum, with payments starting at an annual rate of 4 per cent from year 10, the fund would be worth £712 billion in year 10 (matching the size of the current Norwegian fund, which began in 1996), £1.2 trillion in year 20 and some £2.67 trillion after 50 years.

To finance the fund, the aggregate annual tax take would rise by an amount equivalent to less than 2.5 per cent of GDP, mostly from the transfer of a small portion of personal and corporate wealth, leaving the bulk of this wealth untouched. This would yield a fund that would grow to represent over 60 per cent of the economy after 20 years and to a third larger than the economy after 50 years. A fund created in, say, 2021 would deliver annual returns of some £28 billion a decade later. These returns would double in size roughly every 15 years. A modest investment for a generation would build much greater resilience for the future. Less ambitious options – with smaller tax injections – would result in a smaller fund, and lower levels of payout.

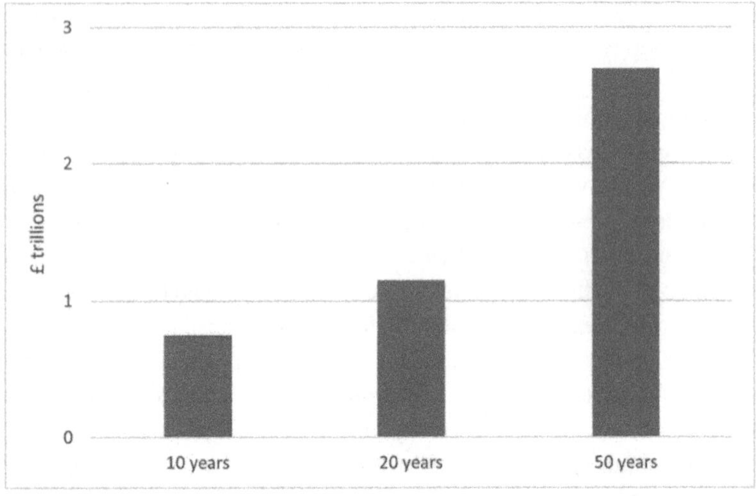

Figure 14.1 Size of citizens' wealth fund after 10, 20 and 50 years
Note: Assumes a 4 per cent per annum return and a 4 per cent payout from year 10.
Source: Lansley & McCann (2019).

A citizen's dividend and a basic income

Although the returns could be used to boost social investment, this would turn the fund into a state resource. To recognize the role of such a fund in socializing the wealth inheritance, there is a powerful case for returns to be paid directly to individuals as a citizen's dividend. An annual dividend would strengthen the current system of social protection and lower the risks associated with today's greater economic fragility. It could also be seen as a key step in the building of a weekly basic income (BI). Indeed, one possibility would be to start the process of introducing a BI scheme in parallel with a citizens' fund, by, for example, converting the current personal tax allowance – which costs around £110 billion a year – into a cash payment (see Stewart Lansley's chapter in this volume, Chapter 16). When the citizens' wealth fund is ready to start paying out, the returns could be used to raise the income floor already created by a starter BI scheme.

A citizens' wealth fund would transform the way the fruits of economic activity are shared. Such a fund does not offer a quick fix but a vision for a much more secure social future, paid for by a higher rate of collective national saving. It would help counter the dominance of "jam today" politics while providing some correction for intergenerational inequities that have been working against the young since 2000: it is younger generations and their children who would benefit the most.

There is nothing utopian about these ideas. There is a growing recognition of the case for using part of Britain's growing wealth mountain for building a better and more equal society while other nations have led the way in establishing wealth funds. Organizations that now back some kind of citizen's fund, if with varying degrees of radicalism and purpose, include the National Institute of Economic and Social Research, the Institute for Public Policy Research and the Royal Society of Arts, and there is now a renewed momentum behind the idea of a basic income for all. If the United Kingdom is to reverse the trends of the last four decades, it will need to tackle the institutional sources of inequality, and that includes an unacceptable concentration in the ownership of the country's mounting asset base.

A citizen's dividend offers a powerful new tool for social democracy, a twenty-first-century alternative to the top-down statism of old-style nationalization and the recent fashion for rampant privatization and uncontrolled markets. Although the lion's share of wealth would continue to be privately owned, a growing collectively owned wealth pool would act as a strong counter to the bloated power of capital. The fund would inject a new pro-equality bias that could transform the way we run the economy and society, and play a key role in any plan to reform Britain's inequality-driving economic model.

Further reading

Lansley, S. 2017. "Reversing the inequality spiral", *IPPR Progressive Review* 24 (2): 136–46.

Lansley, S. & D. McCann 2019. "Citizens' wealth funds, a citizen's dividend and basic income". *Renewal* 27 (1): 72–83.

Lansley, S. & H. Reed 2019. *A Basic Income for All: From Desirability to Feasibility*. London: Compass.

Standing, G. 2019. *Plunder of the Commons: A Manifesto for Sharing Public Wealth*. London: Pelican.

15

Over-leveraged households need debt relief

Johnna Montgomerie

The simultaneous shocks to human and economic health caused by the threat of a potentially deadly physical illness leave many households vulnerable to rapidly deteriorating financial security and stress. This combination of biological threat and social rupture have shaken the foundations of the macroeconomy. So far the response has been a huge monetary stimulus and fiscal rescue packaged for global corporations and national industries. This chapter makes the case for coordinated monetary and fiscal measures to provide debt relief targeted at households, not markets. Since the advent of neoliberal state policy in the 1980s, financial crises have become a regular feature of macroeconomic governance. Each successive crisis has brought more targeted interventions, initially to shore up markets, and then with systemic interventions to prevent economic collapse. Crisis intervention began with cutting interest rates and basic debt restructuring (i.e. Brady bonds) and gradually developed into large-scale liquidity injections (bailouts) and mass asset buybacks, which were rolled together as quantitative easing. The onset of the pandemic and the subsequent first lockdown created a new type of economic crisis, with origins in the human population, not imperfect markets. Yet the same set of unconventional monetary policies were immediately activated in response to the economic shock: interest rates cuts, direct liquidity injections and the mass selling of government debt as a safe asset. Unlike in the previous crisis, the UK government undertook a massive fiscal response, with the introduction of the furlough scheme, in which the government guaranteed up to 80 per cent of wages, and smaller programmes, such as the "Eat out to help out scheme" offering cash incentives to shore up demand in the hospitality industry.

This chapter explains how household debt relief provides a more effective way of stabilizing the macroeconomy in the short term, allowing medium-term structural reforms to shift the United Kingdom away from its long-standing dependence on debt-led growth. Providing debt relief for households involves the simple re-engineering of existing monetary and fiscal measures to target households, not markets, for state intervention. The monetary and fiscal measures outlined here can produce comprehensive debt relief for households struggling with debt repayments as a result of the pandemic. Debt relief will reduce individual hardship while generating a general uplift in the economy. Since debt is a pre-emptory (i.e. legal) claim on household income, debt relief works in the same way as an income tax cut, increasing disposable income by reducing the amount of cash flow going to repayments. This will lift expenditure by giving those households affected by the pandemic more of their income to spend, save and invest in the economy as well as reducing the psychological strain that financial difficulty causes. A sense of optimism amid the catastrophic economic shock will provide "relief" to those forced into hardship because of the virus. However, uplift will be only fleeting unless it is accompanied with structural economic reform seeking to prevent recurrent economic shocks and ever-growing inequality.

This Keynesian approach seeks to reduce the debt overhang to facilitate economic stability, and avoid another boom–bust–bailout–austerity cycle. The substantial debt stock, especially of private household debt, is a major source of protracted economic stagnation; and it is now combined with a once-in-a-century pandemic event just when the United Kingdom's political commitment to transitioning out of its long-standing economic relationship with the European Union (Brexit) takes effect. The cause of protracted stagnation in the United Kingdom is linked to persistently low productivity, increasing income and regional inequality, resulting from an over-reliance on financial services to drive GDP growth. These large macro-structural trends produce a condition of chronic debt dependence that fosters persistent "secular stagnation". After decades of public policy encouraging the build-up of all kinds of debt, the economy is trapped by the debt overhang. To put it simply, the UK economy operates on the basis of an overlapping set of dependences on debt. Financial institutions use debt as a major source of profits; households depend on debt to participate in the economy and sustain their standard of living; and governments depend on private debt to keep the economy growing and, when this strategy fails, use public debt to rescue markets. Debt relief for households is a direct way to break through the debt overhang, offering a new avenue of economic renewal that does not rely on yet more borrowing.

Debt relief can reduce harm and induce reform

Households are a central pillar of the UK privatized Keynesian growth model, in particular through the role that household debt plays in bolstering demand to drive GDP growth. This growth model is dependent on households' ability to maintain debt repayments, which convert present-day income into revenue streams directly into global financial markets. Income stability to maintain repayments and continued access to credit are paramount to the overall stability of the United Kingdom, and the wider global economy. The Money Charity publishes monthly statistics on private household debt in the country. In February 2020, at the cusp of the Covid-19 outbreak, the debt exceeded levels reached in 2008, right before the financial crisis hit. UK households owed £1,675 billion – the highest amount ever recorded, equivalent to 112 per cent of average earnings. These statistics demonstrate that the entire household sector is "under water", with debts exceeding incomes. From the macroeconomic point of view, in Q1 2020 households paid £139 million per day to financial institutions as interest payments. These flows of revenue are essential for the solvency of banks and the stability of financial markets. The daily conversion of flows of income into debt payments becomes a big problem when we consider the substantial income shock most households have experienced as a result of the pandemic. In September Citizens Advice reported its "estimate that 6 million adults in the UK have fallen behind on at least one household bill during the pandemic" (Citizens Advice 2020). This is an early indicator of financial difficulty that will have wider economic impacts.

Typically, debt problems are framed in terms of individual circumstances and/or the hardship of debtors. However, this point of view overlooks how the UK banking system and the government are dependent on households servicing their debts to underwrite overall financial market stability. The 2007 credit crunch that caused the 2007–09 Global Financial Crisis was caused by steady increases in default rates on sub-prime mortgage products in the United States. Sub-prime mortgages were a minute segment of overall global lending. Nevertheless, the rising default rates triggered multiple overlapping derivative contracts, traded multiple times over as assets on global financial markets. Thus, defaults on a small portfolio of loans has the potential to collapse global financial markets. The risk posed by Covid-19 is that income shocks of households will lead to rising loan defaults, which has the potential to be a catalyst for the deepest peacetime recession we have ever seen. Human suffering from the onset of a potentially deadly virus would be joined by that from an economic crisis. Debt is the pre-existing condition. Covid-19 makes visible how the UK economy is as sick as its people.

Even prior to the pandemic households faced income insecurity and financial fragility, caused, in part, by high levels of debt. People had jobs. But their incomes were stagnant over the past decade, jobs had become increasingly insecure and most people in work were also loaded up with debts. This has always been a blind spot for most economists and public policy-makers, because they frame the economic problems facing households in terms of the major economic problems in the 1970s, unemployment and the cost of living. In *Should We Abolish Household Debt?* (Montgomerie 2019), I show how a bailout package offered to households instead of to banks would stabilize the macroeconomy by ending chronic debt dependence. This chapter adapts this argument as a response to the economic shockwave caused by the spread of Covid-19 through the population.

Proposal: generalize historically low interest rates

In making my case for household debt abolition, I put forward the idea of a long-term refinancing operation (LTRO) for households. If credit is now publicly subsidized, then credit must operate not just as a source of private profit for a small group of rent-seeking agents but for the benefit of the wider public – part of a wider effort at structural economic reform seeking to ensure that credit serves the household and business sectors by facilitating economic activities that benefit society and distribute costs fairly between lenders and borrowers. Making low interest rates available to households, not just large institutional lenders, will make credit a small margin business providing the kind of patient, long-term financing that can build a vibrant economy.

In response to the economic shock, debt relief will have an immediate effect, but it will also ensure a long-term trajectory of reform away from a fragile debt-dependent growth model. Early on the Financial Conduct Authority (FCA) offered payment holidays on mortgages and consumer loans for the first six months (to October 2020) for households struggling with debt payments, but with interest still accruing. There are minimal forbearance arrangements in place. Emergency small business loans were offered for up to £50,000 but without favourable terms or much oversight, leading to concerns over mass fraud. Both measures are insufficient for coping with the fallout of sustaining a huge debt overhang in a pandemic-induced severe economic contraction.

Offering households low-cost loans to replace their current high-cost ones is a more sensible and long-term approach to managing the shock of the pandemic, and involves the routine process of establishing an LTRO funded by the Treasury and administered by the Bank of England. In brief, the benefits of an LTRO for households is that the March 2020 Bank of England cut to interest rates can be passed on to households; my proposal is to offer all debtors an exchange of up to £14,000 of outstanding debts for new zero-interest loans.

To understand how the LTRO works, begin with the rate of interest. Central banks have chosen to keep the overnight rate of interest artificially low since 2008, to ensure that there is plenty of credit flowing through the economic system. During the period from 1997 to 2007, the ten years before the financial crisis, interest rates were cyclical: they started high, fell, then rebounded. We know now that this ratcheting up of interest rates from 2005 created a larger pool of non-performing loans for banks. After 2008 short-term rates plummeted to below zero, and they have stayed there to the present day (at the time of writing). Long-term interest rates also slackened, which hurts long-term savers (such as households or their pension funds). Banks and other credit institutions expanded their margins by exploiting the preferential rate of interest offered by the central bank and the market rates they charge on loans, especially the very high rates that retail credit offers households. For example: credit card debts are 18 to 20 per cent, auto loans 4.5 to 6.5 per cent, lines of credit 3 to 6 per cent, overdraft facilities at major banks 33 to 50 per cent. Fringe financial products such as payday loans, logbook loans or door-step lending charge interest in the thousands of per cent

(1,000 to 5,500 per cent). The difference (or spread) between central-bank-quoted interest rates charged on credit and retail credit prices demonstrates the profitability of household credit products to banks.

My proposed LTRO focuses on redressing the stark hierarchy in the terms of credit (interest rate, length of loan and fees) for retail loans, or household debt. It would give households access to the equivalent of a 0 per cent balance transfer for up to the value of half median income – £14,000 per person in the United Kingdom. A household debt refinancing fund would use the same LTRO facility used by the central bank with the credit guarantees that were given to the financial sector in 2008: £2 trillion in the United Kingdom. Backed by credit guarantees, a newly established fund would offer households the ability to consolidate loans. At its most basic, long-term refinancing would provide the equivalent of half a year's median income to every borrower, paid back over seven years for consumer debt and up to 14 years for mortgage-related debts, subject to small administrative fees. These loan pools would be securitized and lenders would be able to access a simple debt swap from their current loan book for revenue claims. This would allow lenders to absorb the interest rate haircut (i.e. reduction in their anticipated future revenue) over the long term.

An LTRO would address the cumulative effect of carrying multiple debt obligations that are producing a generalized macroeconomic stagnation in the United Kingdom. By offering households the ability to consolidate and refinance their outstanding debts with low-cost long-term loans, an LTRO will generalize the benefits of unconventional monetary policy to the wider economy. Households could access the same form of debt refinancing already enjoyed by the financial sector, offering immediate relief to households by reducing the income-deduced costs of servicing debts. Securitizing the LTRO loan pools would offer lenders the ability to spread their losses over the long term. Setting a closing date for the securitized pools (seven years for consumer debts and up to 14 years for mortgage-related debts) would create an end point for debt dependence that should allow lenders to unwind their investments in continued household indebtedness.

Refinancing household debts will ensure that lenders, banks and financial institutions carry some burden. Banks have a licence to print digital money, which becomes a revenue stream in the economy. Credit contracts too are commodities traded many times over on global markets. If too much debt is causing wider economic problems and creating harm in society, then refinancing the existing debt stock to reduce the burden on household cash flow is the only way to reduce the harm debt causes to large swathes of the UK population. Publicly subsidized credit would play a useful role in the economy and improve the well-being of society.

Tensions and debates

Refinancing mortgage and consumer debts eliminates a portion of the revenue that lenders expect from charging higher rates of interest on retail credit products. The case against an LTRO for households is the same as the case against any attempt to ask financial institutions to take a haircut: short-term losses will cause a huge financial crisis. But the source of financial crisis lies elsewhere; such a crisis will happen no matter whether lenders take a haircut on household debt or not. Another argument against LTRO is the old "Banks will never lend again" refrain: refinancing to lower interest rates would give them no incentive to lend to households. But it is very doubtful that banks will not lend again, if their primary source of revenue is their profit from issuing loans.

The justification for a household debt write-down is far simpler than any objection to it: since lenders benefit from publicly subsidized low-interest credit, an LTRO for households ensures that low-cost credit is passed on to borrowers. Implementing fairness and equality in credit markets is not so radical in today's debt economy. A 0 per cent balance transfer deal for six months median income of outstanding debts gives households immediate relief at the same time as it spreads the losses incurred by lenders over the long term. Bail out households now, and banks will pay the costs later. A closing date for the securitized loan pool must be in place to ensure that debt-dependent growth ends, so that debt cancellation is not used to simply reset the same conditions – that is, the conditions for another debt boom.

Up until now the problem of the overindebtedness of households has been monitored by governments and financial regulators in a way that classifies types of debtors according to how well (or how badly) they are managing their loans. Typically this is done by creating benchmarks, measuring degrees of financial fragility, identifying problem debtors. Offering refinancing just to problem debtors with specific amounts of debt runs the risk that LTRO becomes an act of charity, not an economic necessity required to end macroeconomic debt dependence. It is better to target specific debt classes that cause economic distortions, such as mortgage debts that fuel the housing crisis and intergenerational inequality or student loans that saddle young people with high-cost loans even before they enter the workforce.

The reality of indebtedness, which is not easily grasped from aggregate measures, is that many households have multiple overlapping debts accounts: an overdraft; credit cards; a line of credit; a car loan; and a second mortgage on the home (if they own a property). Making long-term refinancing available to households allows those with the highest exposure to debt to consolidate loans. But those with small debts can also reap the benefits of refinancing. This approach will amplify the effects of debt cancellation throughout the entire economy, because more people will benefit from LTRO than if we just focused on bringing relief to the most indebted households.

LTRO lessens rent-seeking by lowering the interest rate, not the principal of the loan itself. The purpose is to make available to households the same low-cost credit that has been granted to banks. This would render the debt stock less of a burden on households and on the economy. Lenders and regulators view high-cost credit as being for short-term use by households; but this ignores how high-cost credit is used over the long term. A very large proportion of credit card holders carry a balance for over five years, and many people rely regularly on current account overdrafts. Similarly, payday loans are "rolled over" when a new loan is offered to cover the outstanding balance of the original loan. Offering households an option to consolidate and refinance their high-cost consumer loans will rectify the huge distortions caused by growing predatory indebtedness. The time shift of debt means that, for example, a loan for £45,000 issued in 2009 generates economic activity in 2009 when the newly created money is spent in the economy. However, there is also a long tail of higher interest payments, as households are bled dry into paying back the economic activity registered in 2009. Refinancing them will lessen the bleeding. A write-down of high-cost consumer debts can break the entanglements of debt dependence by hiving off the most expensive debts – those that are the biggest drag on household income and on the wider economy.

Strategy and implementation

Implementing debt relief as part of the Covid-19 economic recovery strategy is far less technical, in terms of procedures or mechanism, than it is political. All the regulatory processes and packages of measures needed to implement debt relief already exist and have been used extensively to support banks and financial institutions. Adapting or extending unconventional monetary policy to households requires no additional technical skill, only policy will. The critical paths to implementation need to focus on changing the macroeconomic policy frame, addressing the moral economy of debt that pervades public life and placing integrated debt relief among wider structural reforms of the domestic economy.

Transforming macroeconomic public policy frames was a key objective after 2008, when it was clear that most economists and policymakers did not "see it coming" when global financial markets collapsed and national economies in the United States, United Kingdom and Europe were sent into a tailspin. Despite the loud calls for change in the ideas that dominate macroeconomic policy-making, progress has been slow, and the limits of this approach are visible again with the Covid-19 pandemic. When it comes to households' financial fragility, even recognizing the heterogeneous nature of households would be a radical departure from current policy frames. More modest change would be to move away from a regimented focus on employment, inflation and consumer spending as functionally equivalent to the financial security of households. Macroeconomic policy frames must prioritize economic stability and household financial sustainability. Employment policy must address the problem of whether the income generated from employment is enough to service the huge debt overhang. Inflation policy must translate terms of credit into households' cost of living. Finally, registering growth from consumer spending in the current recovery should not ignore the costs of debt repayment over a much longer period, which produce substantial household financial fragility.

Changing the moral economy of debt is a more fundamental challenge. Morality is still considered the realm of religion or private life; the economy is about money and business. However, in the moral codes that govern economic life, the concept of a moral economy becomes clear. "Don't cheat, don't lie, don't hurt others; work hard and pay your debts, and you will live the economic equivalent of a 'good life' " – this is the moral economy of everyday life. At present the moral principles that govern debt say that public debt is a sign of bad government and private debt is a personal matter; as such, public debt is a source of debate and action, whereas private debt remains strictly about personal circumstances. This moral consensus ignores the reality that public debt is used to fund bailouts for some elite economic actors and impose austerity on the rest of society to pay for them. The extensive use of unconventional monetary policy in response to economic crisis establishes a moral economy of debt in which public debt liabilities, via the central bank's balance sheet, are rapidly expanding without moral debate at all. An engrained debt dependence creates a self-validating moral frame in which profits from credit are privatized within the financial sector, but losses generated from a debt-induced crisis are "socialized" via bailouts in which households absorb the short-term losses of the economic contraction and the long-term public debt liabilities of the bailout. In other words, lenders keep their profits and everyone else pays for their losses.

This moral economy of debt is reinforced by the view of the central bank as a technocratic agency that guards its independence from politics. The downside to central bank independence is a lack of democratic accountability to society, with no clear safeguards to ensure that the central bank's choices are not captured by private corporate interests. Central bank economists use their knowledge to design bailout packages in the belief that they are making rational and highly technical decisions about how to govern the economy. However, they are making value judgements informed by moral norms. Central bankers believe that banks are the best operators of the credit system and are "too big to fail". As a result, banks and the wider financial sector have received trillions in bailouts, guarantees and direct monetary financing from the central bank. This is a moral decision, not just an economic one, reflecting a value judgement about which sectors are worthy of saving through bailouts and which are not.

The common dictum goes: "If you owe $100,000, the bank owns you; if you owe $100 billion, you own the bank." The moral economy present in this dictum stipulates that "you must repay your debts" when you are an individual who owes debts to the bank, whereas the debts the bank owes other institutions are negotiable. It is not just individuals who owe debts to lenders. Governments and corporations, too, owe debts to individuals – by way of pensions and healthcare services, which have been reduced since the 2007–09 financial crisis. Many banks, to which individuals owe a great deal of money, are themselves technically insolvent: there are far more debt claims against them than revenue streams from the debts owed to them. The moral economy of debt is about determining which and whose debt promises are enforced and which and whose are cancelled. Therefore, a critical path to the adoption of debt relief for households is in the moral economy that permits debt restructuring as a necessary action under specific conditions.

Conclusion

Debt is at the centre of the contemporary political struggle. A debt relief agenda starts by building a consensus in which debt relief is part of an integrated progressive economic agenda with a comprehensive package of structural reform of financialized economies. The structural conditions created by debt-dependent growth were the cause of entrenched economic malaise before the pandemic and will continue to hold back any recovery, as debt obligations tie the entire macroeconomy to the past in material ways. There can be no moving on or reform without addressing the debt overhang. Coordinated debt relief for households requires political support and narrative, because money is politics. Private debt is a public economic issue over whether debt is creating wealth or harm. Addressing this issue requires abandoning the notion that indebtedness is the result of a lack of financial management skills or of an unreasonable desire to spend more than one's income. A growing number of households experience debt problems not because they lack financial education but because the entire economy is as dependent on debt as households are. A new set of priorities for governing the monetary system can be forged by addressing fundamental questions about the value of money, credit, debt and finance in the economy and society. What purpose does credit serve? How does credit generate well-being and distribute harm across society? Clarifying such matters will produce new norms to reorient monetary governance towards a path out of the cycle of recurring crisis, bailout and austerity towards a more stable and less indebted economy.

Further reading

Citizens Advice 2020. "Excess debts: who has fallen behind on their household bills due to coronavirus?". 8 September. Available at: www.citizensadvice.org.uk/about-us/policy/policy-research-topics/debt-and-money-policy-research/excess-debts-who-has-fallen-behind-on-their-household-bills-due-to-coronavirus.

Montgomerie, J. 2019. *Should We Abolish Household Debts?* Cambridge: Polity Press.

16

Reforming benefits: introducing a guaranteed income floor

Stewart Lansley

There are multiple faults with the existing system of social security, many of them exposed by the Covid-19 crisis. Millions fall through what is an imperfect, mean and patchy safety net. Benefit levels are below those in other comparable rich nations, and, for most of those of working age, less generous than in the past. The system has become heavily dependent on a complex system of means-testing, a long-term shift that is a fundamental turn from the original Beveridge/Attlee principles of universalism and collectivism. The system is not equipped to deal with today's higher levels of uncertainty and turbulence. It also fails the key test of constituting a robust defence against poverty: poverty rates are now close to record postwar levels, and heading higher.

Although Britain's benefit system for working-age adults has always come with some degree of work conditionality, these requirements are now applied with unprecedented severity. Since 2012 over 5 million sanctions have been issued, often for minor breaches such as missing or being late for a job centre interview. At one stage the Department for Work and Pensions was levying more fines than the mainstream justice system. These conditions and sanctions were suspended for a few months during the first pandemic lockdown, but they were then reinstated from July, albeit applied in what the DWP described as a "light touch" manner to take account of the impact of Covid-19.

Although a system of reciprocity – in which entitlements come with responsibilities – has been an important source of public support for collective social security, the combination of inadequate support and coercion undermines the vital principle of entitlement. What is the case for a return to sanctions in what is set to be the weakest jobs market for decades? The evidence shows that new claimants are actively seeking work, and that sanctions have largely failed to help the jobless back to work, instead pushing them deeper into poverty and ill-health.

Equally important, the principle of reciprocity is applied in a heavily one-sided way. Wealthy and poor citizens have long been treated by different standards, a built-in source of inequity that exacerbates existing divisions across society. Despite question marks about the source and wider impact of many top fortunes, and the growing mountain of unearned and lowly taxed wealth, lavishly paid corporate leaders and financiers mostly get a free ride from government. Today's business elite, free of the public scrutiny, "shame culture" and "othering" applied to those seeking benefits, have been handed a licence to secure an inflated share of national wealth, out of proportion to their contribution. In contrast, Britain's poorest citizens end up with low pay, insecure and dispiriting work and an often hostile press. Whereas the DWP is seen as alien by large numbers who seek its help, HM Revenue & Customs (HMRC) and the Department for Business, Energy & Industrial Strategy are – for the rich – essentially benign.

Runaway rewards for the rich and sanctions for the poor do not constitute a politics of the common good. The only time since 1945 that rights and duties have been close to alignment across society was in the "golden age", the immediate postwar decades, when the business class mostly accepted that corporate leadership came with obligations to employees and the local and national community as well as to shareholders.

A "guaranteed minimum"

The present system falls well short of delivering a "guaranteed income" despite this being one of the oldest ideas in the multi-century history of social policy. Late nineteenth-century social reformers joined earlier visionary thinkers to call for some version of a "minimum income" for all citizens. In the landmark 1909 *Minority Report of the Royal Commission on the Poor Laws*, dissenting members, led by the sociologist and historian Beatrice Webb, rejected the *Majority Report*'s emphasis on self-help and limited state support. Instead, they called for a radical, state-backed plan for comprehensive welfare provision as part of our common citizenship. At its heart was the idea of an entitlement to a "national minimum of civilized life".

More than a hundred years on, the hopes of these radical reformers have yet to be realized. The postwar model of social security set out to build just such an "income floor". Both Clement Attlee, Labour prime minister from 1941–51, and William Beveridge, architect of the welfare state, were committed to a universal and collective approach to social protection. They were strongly influenced by the *Minority Report*, which came to be viewed as a seminal moment in the history of social policy. In the postwar reforms, this floor was to be delivered by a combination of measures: a much more comprehensive system of collective national insurance; family allowances; full employment (for men); and buoyant wages. There was also the "safety net" of means-tested national assistance – a replacement, in effect, for the old Poor Law.

Although this new social contract with citizens was light years ahead of the patchy and widely hated prewar model of support, the new reforms were far from free of holes. Many, including most women, were not covered by national insurance, while the benefit levels were lower than even Beveridge's recommended, but mean, subsistence levels. The reformers hoped that, with the new national insurance scheme and economic buoyancy, national assistance would be a residual system quickly phased out over time. In the event, means-testing has come to play a much-expanded role. Today a combination of factors – from heavy reliance on means-testing to tough conditionality – means that the hope of an income floor has never been realized.

There are various possible routes to reform. One possible approach would be to revitalize the social insurance system so that it plays the more central role envisaged by Beveridge. However, below we examine two alternative approaches to reform being promoted by progressive thinkers. The first – a guaranteed minimum income (GMI) – is to retain a means-tested structure at the heart of the social security system but strengthen it by raising benefit levels and removing some of the existing restrictions. Such a model has been promoted by the New Economics Foundation (NEF) think tank.

The second would seek to realize the goal promoted by social reformers over centuries: the introduction of a modest income floor through a series of guaranteed, non-means-tested payments to all adults and children. Such a modest basic income scheme has been promoted by the think tank Compass.

A guaranteed minimum income

The idea of a GMI was presented by NEF as a temporary scheme to handle the Covid-19 crisis – "a new safety net to survive recession" – although others have called for the idea to become a permanent scheme. Central to the proposal is a significant rise in benefits – to £220 for a single adult and £322 for a couple per week – for those of working age. These levels are equivalent to the minimum income standard levels estimated by the Joseph Rowntree Foundation as necessary to secure a minimum acceptable living standard. The payments would replace Universal Credit, employment support allowance, income support, jobseeker's allowance and working tax credits. Under the plan, existing conditionality rules, sanctions and other restrictions such as the two-child limit would be lifted. The estimated gross cost of the scheme is some £3 to 4 billion per month, and would ultimately depend on the number of additional claimants.

Such a scheme would certainly raise the incomes of those in receipt of benefits and those applying for help. But it does so through a further hike in means-testing, and, at these higher benefit levels, a rise in the proportion of the working-age population entitled to claim. The goal of introducing a guaranteed decent income would hold only for those making successful applications. It would not benefit those who might (or should) be entitled but who fail to apply (a known problem with means-testing). Further, the proposal would involve a process of ongoing and complex assessment as circumstances change.

Another flaw with the proposal is that, although payments would be made to individuals, overall entitlement would continue to be on a household basis. This means that, for a couple, a change in circumstances for one adult would affect the income of the other adult; and neither would enjoy a genuinely independent entitlement.

The rise in benefit levels would also have a significant effect on the incentive to work for those who are unemployed and those in lower-paid work. It appears that those entitled to the GMI would, in effect, face a very high, or even a 100 per cent, marginal withdrawal rate. The unemployed would be significantly better off, but they would face a lowered incentive to find work. At the same time, those in low-paid work would be no better off from small increases in earnings, as increases in income would lead to an equivalent loss of benefit payment. These effects are likely to make the proposal politically untenable.

Because of these limitations, there are big question marks over how far the GMI scheme would deliver both the "guarantee" of the title and the goal of providing an "income floor". The proposal is likely to be expensive, involve mass, continuous means-testing and, by its big incentive problem at the margin, have a significant and unpredictable impact on employment levels and patterns.

A guaranteed income floor (GIF)

Contemporary proposals for a basic income come with varying degrees of radicalism. Some favour a full, "big bang" approach that would tear up the existing social security system and replace it with a generous system of payments – enough to live on. This approach has been pushed most fully by advocates of a utopian post-capitalist, post-work world. Such a scheme would be disruptive and expensive, involve many losers and have a negative effect on the incentive to work. It is difficult to see how such a full-blooded scheme could be implemented, at least in current circumstances.

An alternative way of looking at a basic income is that it would create a guaranteed income floor that, instead of replacing it, would be grafted onto the existing benefit system, sitting as a lower tier below it. Incomes and life opportunities would build from this base.

A GIF, as proposed by Compass, would pay a no-questions-asked, and initially modest, sum at proposed starter levels of £60 per adult and £40 per child per week. These starting levels could be higher (at extra cost) and could be raised gradually over time, through, for example (as suggested in Chapter 14), the annual dividends from a citizens' wealth fund. Under such a scheme, the benefit system would, for the first time, have a guaranteed and automatic income floor. For a family of four, this floor would be £10,400 a year. This guarantee involves no means-testing and is unconditional, and – as with the GMI proposal – would end the current system of sanctioning. It is guaranteed, secure and predictable and would not vary with work and earnings. Because there is no means-testing, the payment would not be withdrawn as income rises.

Modelling by Compass has shown that the proposed scheme is feasible, affordable and highly progressive. It would boost the incomes of the poorest families, cut child poverty by more than a third and working-age poverty by over a fifth, reduce inequality, strengthen universalism and cut means-testing.

A number of tax adjustments would be needed to meet the gross cost of a universal payment while making the tax system more progressive. These include the abolition of the personal allowance and its conversion into a cash payment, a rise in existing tax rates of 3p in the pound and a change in the current system of National Insurance contributions. Although other forms of funding could be used, these tax changes would ensure that the benefit of the basic income payments would be clawed back from better-off households.

It is sometimes claimed that an advantage of a means-tested GMI over a non-means-tested GIF is that, through such testing, the former concentrates the gains on those who need it most, while the latter spreads it evenly. But this ignores the overall distributive impact of such a scheme when taken together with the tax reforms that could fund it. As Figure 16.1 shows, together with the proposed tax changes, the distributional effects of a GIF are highly progressive. The largest gains are enjoyed by those in the poorest third, while there are small losses for those at the top.

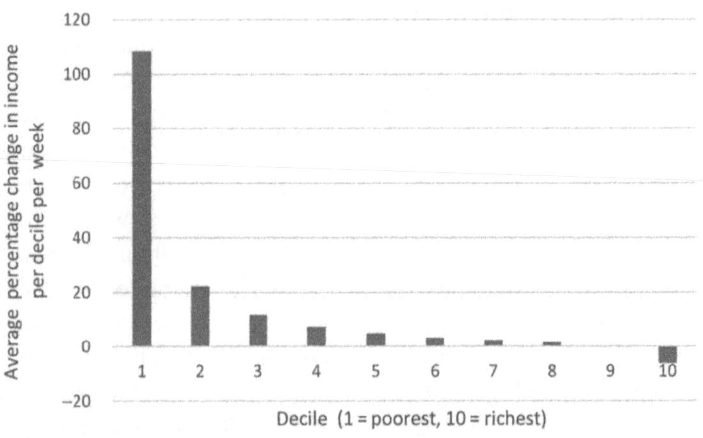

Figure 16.1 The distributional impact of a GIF
Source: Lansley & Reed (2019).

Even the sternest opponents of a basic income acknowledge its merits. It would provide, for the first time, a guaranteed and secure, no-strings-attached, minimum (if initially modest) income floor for all. Such a floor also has the potential to do much more than help fix a broken system of social protection and a fragile labour market, with the immediate gains strengthened by enhanced medium- and long-term dynamic benefits. A GIF would introduce a new and automatic anti-poverty force and bring much greater security to households in an increasingly fragile world.

One of these dynamic gains would be its potential to offer a new "charter for choice". Central to a basic income scheme is that it is non-prescriptive and non-judgemental: it would offer greater personal autonomy and flexibility between work, leisure (and let us not confuse leisure with idleness), education and caring. Some might choose to work less or take longer breaks between jobs. The guaranteed floor would help encourage entrepreneurialism and risk-taking, with some incentivized to start businesses. Some might take time to retrain, while others might devote more time to leisure, personal care or community support. Such a boost to choice has the potential to produce more social value, if currently unrecognized, than some existing paid work.

By providing an independent, albeit modest, income, a GIF would provide guaranteed financial support for the mass of unpaid work – from childcare to voluntary help – that is disproportionately undertaken by women and critical to the functioning of society. This would also correct for one of the injustices of the present skewed politics of reciprocity, with these contributions finally given recognition. Income predictability is known to be associated with improved health. With the greater income security provided, there would be steady improvements in mental health and well-being, an important and potentially significant strength of this approach. These are progressive changes with profound transformative potential, which would serve as the foundation for greater personal empowerment and freedom, and a springboard for more stable and fulfilling lives.

Comparing GMI and GIF

These alternative approaches need to be rated on cost, on how far they tackle the flaws with the existing system – low benefit levels, excessive means-testing, excessive conditionality, lack of predictability, high poverty count and a lack of a clear and robust income floor – and on their longer-term dynamic potential.[1] Both approaches have some strands in common. Both would end the disciplinary – and futile – sanction system aimed at pushing people into jobs, whatever their quality or stability. Both would raise incomes at the bottom. Both would cut poverty. But that is where the commonality ends. The two schemes offer very different visions of the future of income security.

A GMI would boost incomes for those on the lowest incomes, but via a permanent extension of means-testing, which could leave many of those entitled or in need missing out. It would not, therefore, provide the guaranteed income that is claimed.

A GIF would also raise lower incomes – thus reducing poverty – but through a route that would extend universality and, by reducing reliance on means-testing, tackle one of the primary flaws with the existing model. It would finally implement the idea of a "guaranteed income floor", albeit with an initially modest starting rate.

Under a GIF, the payment mechanism is clear, automatic and guaranteed. Under a GMI scheme, it requires personal application and assessment and a much larger and complex bureaucracy. The implications for work incentives are also very different between the two schemes. By introducing a "Plimsoll line" for incomes as part of building a new sense of common citizenship, a GIF would provide greater social resilience in an increasingly fragile age and a foundation on which individuals and households could build their lives and plan their futures.

Crucially, a GIF would, for the first time, create a dual-tier approach to benefit reform, with a guaranteed, automatic element creating an income base on which to build the means-tested element. This would create an entirely new and progressive system built around a guaranteed floor and means-tested top-ups. Over time the "Plimsoll line" could be raised, thus rolling back reliance on the means test. Whatever the approach, what is sure is the need for a fundamental reform of the

1. It is difficult to make precise comparisons between the two schemes on these measures. Although the Compass GIF scheme comes with detailed modelling on cost and impact, including its impact on poverty and the pattern of winners and losers, no such modelling is yet available for the GMI scheme.

current benefit system, which falls well short of what is needed in today's more fragile economy and poverty-driving economic and social model.

Further reading

Lansley, S. 2020. "Sanctions for the poor, runaway rewards for the rich". Transforming Society, 3 August. Available at: www.transformingsociety.co.uk/2020/08/03/sanctions-for-the-poor-runaway-rewards-for-the-rich.

Lansley, S. & H. Reed 2019. *A Basic Income for All: From Desirability to Feasibility*. London: Compass.

Stirling, A. & S. Arnold 2020. "A minimum income guarantee for the UK", policy briefing. London: New Economics Foundation. Available at: https://neweconomics.org/uploads/files/MIG-new.pdf.

PART V

A PROGRESSIVE RECOVERY

17

To restructure the British state, the international financial system must be transformed

Ann Pettifor

The Covid-19 crisis has demonstrated one important truth. The international financial system is designed on terms that suit the owners of capital, not on terms that suit nation states, or the majority of the population – as Geoff Tily explains in his chapter in this volume, Chapter 4. He writes that globalization is a system amounting to "internationalism on the terms of capital", whereas internationalism should be set on terms that benefit the majority – the people who labour by hand and brain. In this chapter, I contend that no reform of the state "for the common good" is possible under terms governed by the current international system of deregulated, globalized capital, constructed on the foundation of vast debts, costly credit and tax evasion.

During the Covid-19 crisis world leaders proved unable to convene an international summit to prevent the spread of the pandemic and to collaborate on a vaccine for the world's people. Some deliberately attacked the system of multilateral coordination to defeat pandemics, organized under the umbrella of the World Health Organization. However, central bank governors, led by the Federal Reserve, did work together and coordinate to save globalized capital markets from the economic consequences of the pandemic. Even while the governments of Trump, Bolsonaro, Modi and Johnson clowned around, grievously mishandling the crisis and causing thousands to die unnecessarily, technocrats at the Federal Reserve, the Bank of England and the Bank of Japan engaged in decisive, expansive and internationally coordinated action to save rentier capitalism. Big Wall Street and City of London financial institutions, corporations such as Apple and the world's airlines quickly became beneficiaries of central bank largesse.

As the Brookings Institution has carefully documented, whereas ordinary Americans faced unemployment and income loss, the Federal Reserve effectively nationalized Wall Street – and, with it, other financial entrepôts. It did so by cutting its target for the federal funds rate, the rate US banks pay to borrow from each other overnight, to a range of 0 per cent to 0.25 per cent and by purchasing securities. Between mid-March and mid-June 2020 the Fed's portfolio of private assets grew from $3.9 trillion to $6.1 trillion. It relaunched the Money Market Mutual Fund Liquidity Facility (MMLF), which backstopped money market mutual funds and massively expanded its repurchase agreement (repo) operations to channel cash into the money markets. As well as relaxing regulatory requirements, the Fed lent directly to banks from its discount window at rates lower than those charged during the Great Financial Crisis. On 23 March it established two new facilities to support highly rated US corporations. The Primary Market Corporate Credit Facility (PMCCF) allowed the Fed to lend directly to corporations such as Apple by buying new bond issuances and providing loans. And, under its new Secondary Market Corporate Credit Facility (SMCCF), the Fed was freed up to purchase corporate bonds as well as exchange-traded funds investing in investment-grade corporate bonds.

Trevor Jackson argued in April that the Fed's spectacular and unprecedented interventions in March 2020 were intended "to flood financial markets with cash as quickly as possible, so banks could keep lending, buyers of stocks could keep buying, and institutions *could keep making their debt payments*" (Jackson 2020, emphasis added). Far from deflating the by then global debt bubble, the Fed was intent on keeping debt and international creditors buoyant and solvent.

Covid-19 made utterly transparent the power and protection granted, above all, to private globalized capital markets, creditors, investors and speculators. Such internationally coordinated protection was not granted to the world's people or to the world's threatened ecosystems. By refusing to coordinate internationally to deal with the threat of pandemics, their impact on economies and the risks of climate change, world leaders abandoned their citizens, and effectively delegated leadership of the global economy to central bank technocrats and their clients in capital markets.

The temporary suspension of globalization

The pandemic arose in the first instance because of capitalism's destruction of nature to make way for profitable farming, mining and housing activities. These activities have stripped wildlife of habitats and brought societies into conflict with the animal world. The virus leapt from animal to human and was then spread worldwide by the very hallmarks of globalization: connectivity and integration. A single, globally interconnected and integrated market economy, governed effectively by the private authority of invisible financial markets and based on population growth and urbanization, dangerously escalates threats to human health. Professor Ian Goldin and Mike Mariathasan, in their book *The Butterfly Defect*, explained that more than 30 new disease-causing organisms have appeared in just the last two decades (Goldin & Mariathasan 2014). Coronavirus confirmed the threat and taught us that globalization acts as a passport for pandemics, turning airlines and international journeys into disease vectors. That is why the system of globalization had to be suspended for the duration of the pandemic.

The tragedy is that it took a pandemic, not civil society, to halt globalization in its tracks.

The left's blind spot

The failure to check *financial* globalization can be explained in part by the failure of progressive economists, politicians and activists to engage with the international sphere, in which globalization, capital mobility and Wall-Street-friendly central bank policies are promoted and defended. Instead, social democrats in Europe and the United States prefer to confine debates to the nation state and domestic policy priorities. Hence the focus on affordable housing, nationalization of the railways, poverty and homelessness – and, inevitably, the local environment. A classic example of the narrow focus of most progressives can be found in debates about taxation. Discussion and campaigns aimed at the tax-dodging of Silicon Valley platforms such as Amazon and Facebook, or of companies such as Richard Branson's Virgin, are conducted as if these companies can be coerced into obeying domestic tax law. Such hopes are utopian in a world system based on capital mobility – one specifically designed to enable Richard Branson of Virgin or Tim Cook of Apple to shift profits effortlessly across borders and into tax havens. This fact was starkly exposed recently when the EU General Court rejected the European Commission's attempt to recover €13 billion in back taxes from Apple, whose profits are protected by the tax haven that is Ireland, an EU member state.

Furthermore, the international system is designed to *oblige* nations to prioritize exports and to compete for foreign direct investment from global, private corporations – as part of what Keynes described as a "desperate expedient to maintain employment at home".

Social democracy's blind spot for the international financial architecture and its power over *domestic* policy-making has had other consequences. Not only does neglect of the international system let globalized capital markets off the regulatory hook, but globalization has also led to the rise of economic nationalisms. Globalization represents the tragic reversal of all that Keynes hoped to achieve at Bretton Woods: an international framework that would end nationalisms, international trade competition, high levels of domestic unemployment, low levels of aggregate demand and the consequent debt deflation. It was an attempt by Keynes and other economists to prevent the return of nationalisms and fascism by developing policies that increased domestic demand not by boosting exports and raising demand externally but by raising living standards at home: an inter-national system that would restore policy autonomy to democratic states and stability to the world's economies. Bretton Woods was an incomplete framework and, in some respects, unsatisfactory. Nevertheless, its ambitions were to be promptly and forcefully undermined by private European and American financial institutions.

The reality is that, today, all states are embedded in, governed by and subject to the international system of mobile, volatile, private financial markets – a system that has indebted and impoverished the many and raised political tensions, as reflected in the rise of nationalism. Millions of voters understand the nature of globalization, even while dimly aware of the monetary, fiscal or trade theories on which the system is built. This public awareness explains why some electorates have backed the election of "strong men" – politicians who offer "protection" from the very global markets that have stripped economies of jobs and income, while enriching rentier capitalists. Demands to "take back control" from these private markets by "building walls" and intensifying protectionism is what catapulted the governments of Trump, Bolsonaro, Modi, Duterte and Johnson to power.

It will not be possible for progressives to reverse nationalism, or reform or restructure the domestic state "for the common good", without a transformation of the governance of the international system. Such a transformation will require the restoration of *public authority* over private, deregulated, globalized capital markets and the restoration of policy autonomy to governments and their electorates; in other words, the restoration of economic democracy to the international system.

Progressive governments cannot mitigate and manage climate breakdown, energy insecurity and biodiversity loss in a world of global capital mobility and tax evasion. They cannot ensure "Medicare for all" or restore public health systems such as the NHS, for example, if global, mobile, tax-avoiding private equity firms are freed up by the international system (including its investor-biased trade rules) to compete with, and loot, local and central governments by imposing large debts and demanding high rates of return. And governments cannot overcome financial globalization's system of generating vast debts until the bias, effective subsidies and protections enjoyed by global mobile financial corporations – and "regulated" by private authority – are once again managed by democratic public authority. The management of taxation systems, exchange rates, interest rates and cross-border flows in the interests of the domestic economy is vital if democratic governments are to serve "the common good" by reducing indebtedness, stabilizing the public finances, increasing domestic demand, achieving full, skilled, well-paid employment and urgently tackling Earth systems breakdown.

States cannot afford to borrow to steady the economy if they do not simultaneously generate sufficient revenues through taxation to repay the sums borrowed and to stabilize the monetary system. To be clear, this does not imply that governments need tax revenues to pay for the necessary initial investment. As demonstrated in 2020, governments in possession of a central bank and sovereign currency, with sound tax collection institutions and policies, can, when necessary, raise vast sums – not just from their own central banks but also from pension funds and insurance companies. But to maintain and stabilize a nation's monetary system, and to ensure pension fund savings are protected, governments need ultimately to raise tax revenues to repay the initial finance. That is nigh impossible if states are obliged to operate within an international system of mobile tax-avoiding capital.

Transformation of the state?

How to achieve such a transformation? First and foremost, we need greater societal, academic and political understanding of the centrality – and negative impact – of the international financial system (disguised as "globalization") on domestic policy-making. The system is discussed in elite, niche circles, but not sufficiently understood by progressive political parties, trades unions, student groups and religious or community organizations. It can be changed only if there is greater public understanding of the real forces shaping globalization. Societies cannot transform that which they do not know of or understand. Spreading awareness of the way in which the globalized financial system exercises power over domestic policy-making is a vital first task for progressive forces – a task that must be undertaken with little help from an economics profession that remains aloof from such debates.

However, the major catch confronting states is this: policy autonomy over exchange rates, interest rates and cross-border capital flows can be achieved only by building a framework of international cooperation and coordination that prioritizes the domestic policy autonomy of all states. Such a system would be one amounting to "internationalism on the terms of labour", as Tily argues. Many will argue that, in today's world, generating international cooperation and managing global capital mobility are impossible, that the globalization "genie cannot be put back in the bottle". Such arguments are just a form of defeatism. They are contradicted by the worldwide rise of trade protectionism and strident anti-immigrant nationalisms – evidence that globalization can indeed be reversed, albeit in ways that are both harmful and reactionary.

For the international system to be managed in the interests of "the common good", progressive coordination and cooperation at the international level between state actors will be required. Such cooperation is anathema to the virulent nationalisms of Narendra Modi's India or Jair Bolsonaro's Brazil. But nationalisms must be overcome, and a spirit of internationalism fostered, if the international financial system, future pandemics and climate change are to be addressed successfully.

Building public and political confidence

There is a widespread sense of powerlessness in the face of global finance's great power. But societies would feel less powerless if there was greater understanding of the private financial system's utter dependence on the nation state: on public taxpayer-backed resources for the accumulation of wealth. The crisis of the Covid-19 pandemic has proved decisively that global capital markets are slavishly dependent on the largesse of publicly backed central banks, and in particular on the US Federal Reserve.

Important institutions of the state, including central banks such as the Fed and the Bank of England, are only able to undertake bailouts and the nationalization of capital markets because they derive their power to create new money ("liquidity", money market operations or QE) from a nation's taxpayers. Taxpayer power sustains and finances the *public* institutions that underpin the *private* monetary system. These include the nation state's legal institutions that uphold and enforce contracts; the tax collection system that regularly generates revenues – and will do so into the future; the currency-issuing central bank; the publicly regulated accounting system; and the taxpayer-financed legal system for the enforcement of contracts. No private financier can make capital gains in the absence of subsidies from these publicly financed institutions.

There are now an estimated 30.3 million taxpayers in the United Kingdom. In 2017, and according to the Tax Foundation, there were 143.3 million US taxpayers. In addition, governments impose property and sales taxes, together with tariffs or custom duties on imports. These regular tax collections (both current and future tax revenues) constitute the *collateral* that back up the UK, EU and US Treasuries. It is public collateral that gives authority to the actions of central bank technocrats, and effectively determines the value of currencies. Countries that lack a well-developed tax collection system and publicly financed institutions for managing the private monetary system (such as many in Africa) lack the public collateral needed for a strong central bank and sound currency.

In light of this knowledge, what is needed is, first, greater understanding of taxpayers' potential power and leverage over the private finance sector. Such understanding should lead to the formation of a new international union of workers, political parties, people and enterprises that regularly pay their taxes; a union that would spread understanding of the private global financial system's dependence on *public* resources – resources made possible by regular, law-abiding taxpayers. Such a union would empower citizens to impose conditions on the provision of a nation's public resources to the private finance sector, on terms and conditions that ensure that the private finance system is transformed from its role as master of both global and national economies to one of domesticated servant to nation states.

Fostering such awareness and cooperation will, in turn, require international leadership – the kind of progressive leadership that has hitherto been hollowed out by the dominance of globalized finance, the rise in unemployment and the collapse of skilled, secure and well-paid work. As noted above, these outcomes of globalization have alienated electorates and demoralized progressives.

In the United States and Britain, both the Tea Party and the Brexit Party, respectively, have succeeded in placing intense bottom-up pressure on right-wing political parties, transforming them. These activists have organized, seized and deployed political power, then demanded and achieved real, if harmful, change. But many activists and protesters, including the French *gilets jaunes*, actively resist political power, preferring to "remain unsullied by electoral politics, finding a community, an identity and a sense of purity in eternal protest", as Simon Kuper of the *Financial Times* wrote (Kuper 2020). The United Kingdom's Peoples' Vote alliance disintegrated, he explained, largely because, "thrilled by the narcissism of small differences", its leaders spent their energy infighting.

Some social democratic parties have been compromised by their perceived support for financial globalization. As a result of this apparent collusion with global capital, combined with the deliberate weakening of trade union power and rising private indebtedness, collective grass-roots political activism and pressure have withered away. Despite a record increase in the number of social protests worldwide, "the strongmen are (often literally) beating the protesters", wrote Kuper. As a consequence, social democratic parties have failed to organize effectively to seize and deploy political power. That can change only if pressure for radical change is applied on these parties by organized, progressive, *internationalist* forces and protests.

The Covid-19 pandemic is a moment of reckoning for globalization and our international financial system. It could also be a moment of transformation of the nation state – but only if forces on the left of society wake up to a fuller understanding of globalization as "internationalism on the terms of capital" and begin to build the political will to transform the international system into one based on terms set by democratic states and their people – broadly defined as labour.

Further reading

Goldin, I. & M. Mariathasan 2014. *The Butterfly Defect: How Globalization Creates Systemic Risk, and What to Do about It.* Princeton, NJ: Princeton University Press.

Jackson, T. 2020. "The sovereign Fed". Dissent, 16 April. Available at: www.dissentmagazine.org/online_articles/the-sovereign-fed.

Klein, M. & M. Pettis 2020. *Trade Wars Are Class Wars: How Rising Inequality Distorts the Global Economy and Threatens International Peace.* New Haven, CT: Yale University Press.

Kuper, S. 2020. "Will more bicycles really help green growth?". *Financial Times,* 20 February. Available at: www.ft.com/content/5af4d8b6-52b0-11ea-90ad-25e377c0ee1f.

Pettifor, A. 2019. *The Case for the Green New Deal.* London: Verso.

Pixley, J. & H. Flam (eds) 2018. *Critical Junctures in Mobile Capital.* Cambridge: Cambridge University Press.

18

Coronavirus and the national debt

Jan Toporowski and Robert Calvert Jump

Eighty years ago, on the outbreak of the Second World War, Keynes wrote a set of articles for *The Times* newspaper outlining how the British government could pay for the war effort without unduly restricting consumption. The articles were subsequently published as a pamphlet entitled *How to Pay for the War: A Radical Plan for the Chancellor of the Exchequer*. In it, he proposed "a plan conceived in the spirit of social justice, a plan which uses a time of general sacrifice, not as an excuse for postponing desirable reforms, but as an opportunity for moving further than we have moved hitherto towards reducing inequalities".

No apology is needed for recalling Keynes's pamphlet, in view of the scale of the Covid-19 crisis and consequences for the country. The essays collected in this volume cover many aspects of the crisis, and lay out a number of approaches for dealing with them. At the start of the crisis, during the first period of lockdown, the key requirements were the provision of medical support and, as in wartime, ensuring that the population could maintain their consumption of essentials. As the world moves forward, macroeconomic policies to deal with the longer-term economic consequences become more pressing.

In this chapter we discuss the financing of these macroeconomic policies. Specifically, we discuss their impact on the national debt, whether or not this poses a problem and what can be done about it. Much remains unknown, but what is certain is that the nature of the crisis requires a level of borrowing that has no precedent in peacetime. The limits this poses to policy, and how these limits might be overcome, will determine the course of the recovery.

Fiscal commitments

At the start of the Second World War Keynes argued that the central dilemma was how to conserve resources for military purposes while maintaining decent standards of consumption for the least well off. The outbreak of the Covid-19 crisis posed a rather different problem: consumption was compressed as a by-product of lockdown, and by the loss of income of many workers and large numbers of small and medium-sized enterprises. In 1939 government expenditure was boosted by spending for military purposes. Today's fiscal outlays have been boosted by the need to support consumption through furloughing, welfare payments and medical expenditure.

However, in another respect, there is a similarity between the situation of the country in 1939 and the present situation that has an important bearing on the consequences of the crisis. As in 1939, Britain entered the Covid-19 crisis with one of the highest levels of income and wealth inequality in western Europe. This is associated with elevated levels of poverty, principally because of the deregulation of Britain's labour market and welfare "reforms".

To attempt to mitigate the effects of the crisis, the UK government has implemented a number of policies aimed at maintaining incomes. These include the Coronavirus Job Retention Scheme, which has subsidized up to 80 per cent of the wages of more than 9 million workers, and the Self-Employment Income Support Scheme, which has provided grants to around 3 million self-employed workers. Business loans have been distributed via the Coronavirus Business Interruption Loan Scheme, the Coronavirus Large Business Interruption Loan Scheme and the Bounce Back Loan Scheme, which have collectively disbursed over £40 billion. At its peak, the Bank of England's Covid Corporate Financing Facility held more than £20 billion of commercial paper.

Households and businesses have also been supported by more straightforward changes to the tax system. Business rates have been suspended for 12 months in the retail, hospitality, leisure and nursery sectors, both VAT and self-assessment tax returns have been deferred and rebates for statutory sick pay have been made available to SMEs. The standard Universal Credit payment has been temporarily increased, as have Working Tax Credits and Housing Benefit, which, taken together, are expected to result in around £7 billion of additional social security payments in the 2020/21 financial year.

Whether or not these support schemes will extend to those most at risk of poverty remains to be seen. Increases in Universal Credit payments and Housing Benefit are welcome; but they do not come close to reversing a decade of cuts to social security. Excluded UK, a non-governmental organization formed in May 2020, estimates that over 3 million people have missed out on state support during the Covid-19 crisis. More generally, the army of precarious workers on non-standard contracts, many of whom lie behind the rise of in-work poverty, are highly unlikely to have received support and struggle to navigate the Universal Credit system.

Two things can be said with some certainty. First, the distributional consequences of the crisis will be highly regressive. Aside from its impact on poverty, the lockdown and social distancing have allowed salaried middle-class workers, many of whom have not been placed on furlough, to accumulate a large amount of savings. Recent policy announcements such as the Jobs Retention Bonus, in which firms will be paid £1,000 for every furloughed employee who returns to work, appear to be a straightforward handout to predominantly larger firms and their shareholders. A similar observation can be made about the Stamp Duty holiday, which will mainly benefit homeowners.

Second, the amount of borrowing used to fund the government's response to the Covid-19 crisis will be unprecedented in peacetime. Figure 18.1 reproduces three potential trajectories for the ratio of UK public sector debt to GDP from the Office for Budget Responsibility's latest *Fiscal Sustainability Report* (OBR 2020), in which a "downside scenario" implies a ratio of 120 per cent within the next five years. These trajectories are consistent with forecasts produced by academics and think tanks. As illustrated in Figure 18.2, the debt levels implied by the "downside" scenario in Figure 18.1 were last seen in Britain in the 1950s.

Financing the crisis

As the crisis progresses, government expenditure will need to be maintained to support private sector incomes. At the same time, tax receipts will fall with economic activity. A fixation on reducing government borrowing by increasing taxes or cutting expenditure, just because the immediate medical crisis has abated, will hobble the economic recovery. Maintaining high levels of government expenditure

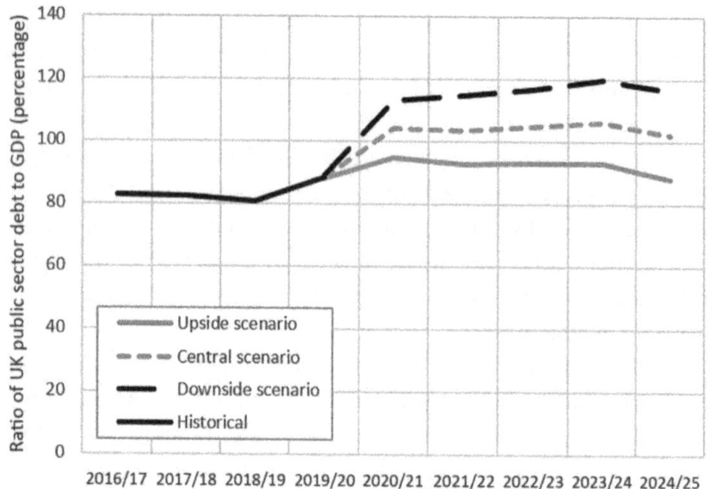

Figure 18.1 Ratio of UK public sector net debt to GDP, 2016/17–2024/25
Source: OBR (2020).

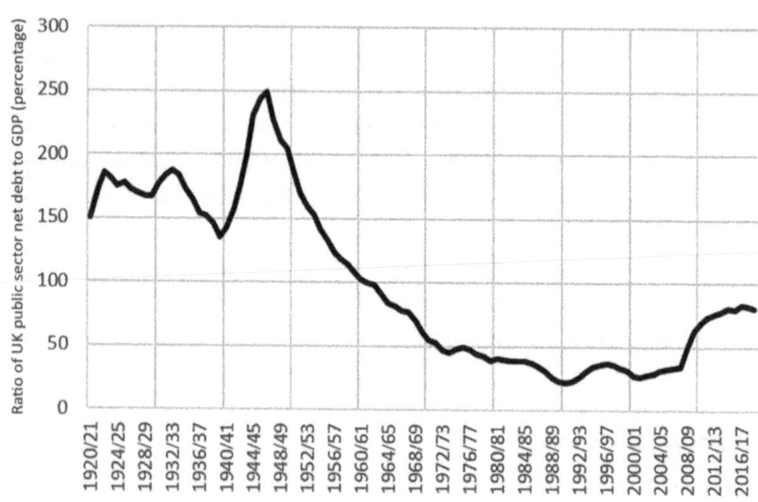

Figure 18.2 Ratio of UK public sector net debt to GDP, 1920/21–2017/18
Source: OBR, June 2020 "Public finances" databank.

amounts to a sizeable fiscal commitment. How the associated deficits and debt should be financed is an inevitable part of economic policy-making, and needs to be approached rationally rather than by resort to the banal precepts of household finance that have dominated politics for the last decade.

The obvious way of financing the crisis, and one that appeals to the dominant Treasury view, is by raising taxes. However, the amounts that can be raised by taxation are inevitably limited in the immediate future, and the prospects for a balanced budget are unrealistic. A second, more spontaneous solution is a transfer of financial risk onto the private sector, and the concomitant rise in private debt. This is part and parcel of any austerity strategy, but households and firms that have borrowed purely to survive the crisis will seek to repay that debt during the recovery. The only way to achieve this is by limiting expenditure, and thus the greater the private debt incurred during the crisis, the slower will be the recovery.

A third way of financing the crisis is by the creation of new money to cover the difference between government spending and taxation. In April 2020 the Bank of England announced a temporary extension to the Ways and Means facility, which is, essentially, the government's overdraft facility at the Bank, and – if used – is a type of monetary financing. More importantly, the Bank extended its quantitative easing programme, in which existing government bonds are purchased by the creation of reserves, by such an extent that it bought more debt than the government had issued during the initial phase of the crisis. Nevertheless, reserves pay bank rate and are still a part of the public sector net debt; and, since QE is a tool of monetary policy rather than fiscal policy, it could be wound down, or interest rates increased, if the country suffers an inflationary shock.

The final way of financing the crisis is by the sale of government bonds and similar debt instruments to the private sector. In comparison to increasing taxation, government borrowing has the advantage of maintaining private sector incomes over the crisis. In comparison to smaller firms and households, the government can access considerably lower interest rates, and thus, in principle, it is more efficient for the government to shoulder the increase in financial risk that arises from an event such as the Covid-19 crisis. Finally, in comparison to monetary financing, the sale of government bonds and other debt instruments has the advantages of absorbing any excess liquidity in the banking system accumulated by the salaried middle class and larger firms during the crisis, and increasing the stock of safe sterling-denominated assets for intermediaries and institutional investors.

Reinforcing the inherent benefits of bond financing is the fact that interest rates on all maturities of government debt are extraordinarily low, and have been lower than the rate of price inflation for some time. In real terms, this means that investors are paying the government to borrow, in which case it makes sense for the government to "lock in" low interest rates by issuing longer-maturity gilts. Long-dated gilts are, in a sense, like fixed-rate mortgages: if the interest rate on a 30-year government bond is 1 per cent, then the government pays 1 per cent on that bond for 30 years, regardless of how interest rates move in the future. Not only is bond financing inherently superior to other forms of financing large, unexpected increases in expenditure, at the present time it is also remarkably cost-effective.

Stabilizing the national debt

After the crisis has abated, and the recovery has taken hold, the government will either have to stabilize the ratio of public sector debt to GDP at the levels implied by Figure 18.1 or target a slowly decreasing ratio. This will probably require a primary surplus – i.e. a surplus of tax income over non-interest expenditure – but, as the vast majority of the bonds issued to finance the Covid-19 crisis will be issued at very low rates, any post-crisis primary surpluses are likely to be manageable. In fact, in the July 2020 *Fiscal Sustainability Report*, the Office of Budget Responsibility estimates that interest payments as a percentage of GDP will remain below 2 per cent until 2030, driven in large part by the bank rate and gilt yields remaining subdued over the same time horizon (OBR 2020).

It is possible to arrive at a formula for the primary surplus that stabilizes the public sector debt/GDP ratio. If we denote the primary surplus/GDP ratio by p, the interest rate paid on the public sector debt by r and the GDP growth rate by g, then the primary surplus that stabilizes the debt/GDP ratio at some level d is given by

$$p = \left(\frac{r - g}{1 + g}\right) d$$

which ensures that flows into the public debt (i.e. interest payments plus expenditure) and flows out of the public debt (i.e. tax receipts) stand in such a ratio that the public debt grows at the same rate as GDP.

Using this formula, Table 18.1 tabulates the primary surpluses required to stabilize the public debt at hypothetical debt/GDP ratios for hypothetical interest rates, in which we make the conservative assumption that nominal GDP growth is equal to 3 per cent (implying a historically low real growth rate of 1 per cent if the Bank of England meets its inflation target). As Figure 18.1 makes clear, long-term interest rates as high as 5 per cent do not require enormous primary surpluses to stabilize the public sector debt/GDP ratio at the kinds of levels implied by the top end of the estimates in the figure. Intuitively, stabilizing a large public debt requires a large amount of debt to be issued every year, as a growing economy requires a growing debt stock for the debt/GDP ratio to remain constant.

Thus, with interest rates either equal to or somewhat above their current levels, a relatively low primary surplus will be required to stabilize the debt/GDP ratio after the Covid-19 crisis has abated and the recovery taken hold. With the issuance of long-maturity bonds, these

Table 18.1 Primary surplus required to stabilize debt at hypothetical debt/GDP ratios and average interest rates, under the conservative assumption that nominal GDP growth is equal to 3 per cent

Debt/ GDP ratio (percentage)	**150**	−2.9	−1.5	0.0	1.5	2.9
	140	−2.7	−1.4	0.0	1.4	2.7
	130	−2.5	−1.3	0.0	1.3	2.5
	120	−2.3	−1.2	0.0	1.2	2.3
	110	−2.1	−1.1	0.0	1.1	2.1
	100	−1.9	−1.0	0.0	1.0	1.9
		1.0	**2.0**	**3.0**	**4.0**	**5.0**
	Average interest rate					

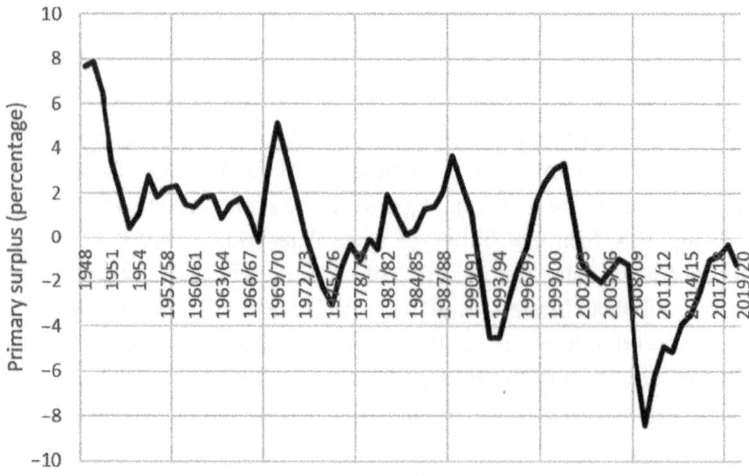

Figure 18.3 UK primary surplus, 1948–2019/20
Source: OBR, June 2020 "Public finances" databank.

low interest rates can be "locked in" in the same manner as a fixed-rate mortgage. And finally, as Figure 18.3 suggests, the government can in fact run a primary deficit indefinitely if interest rates remain below the rate of GDP growth. As shown in Figure 18.3, the higher primary surpluses indicated in Table 18.1 are similar to those run by postwar Britain up to the 1970s, and are certainly achievable once the Covid-19 crisis has passed.

It is also important to note that, although economists and commentators naturally focus on the primary fiscal balance, policy also needs to focus on the incidence of taxation and levels of expenditure, because these have an impact on well-being and economic growth. One of the reasons why ten years of Conservative austerity failed to reduce the national debt relative to GDP was precisely because public expenditure was limited overall, and tax rates on higher incomes were cut. The result was to slow economic growth and reduced overall well-being. With low interest rates, the sensible approach to the government debt is to maintain public expenditure, and raise taxes on wealth and higher incomes.

To summarize, government expenditure over the Covid-19 crisis ought to be financed by the issuance of long-maturity debt. Given likely debt levels, current interest rates and the likely future path of interest rates, the implied cost of interest payments on that debt will remain manageable. After the crisis has abated, and the recovery taken hold, small primary surpluses will probably be required to stabilize the debt/GDP ratio, depending on the interest rates that the public debt ends up being issued at. If the average interest rate ends up below the growth rate, then the government will not need to run a primary surplus, though it might choose to do so anyway to target a falling debt/GDP ratio.

Achieving a primary surplus

It remains to consider how a primary surplus might be achieved. As discussed above, the peculiarities of the current crisis make its distributional consequences particularly regressive. This means that wealthy households and larger firms will be in a considerably better position than low-income households and smaller firms following the crisis, reinforcing the inherent moral case for the use of progressive taxation. In fact, a case can be made that the taxation of wealth and profit income should form the basis for paying any interest rate costs on the public debt, since taxes that the wealthy pay towards government expenditure are received back as profits in the companies they own, or interest on the bonds they hold – sometimes individually, but more often via pension funds.

A government bond is simply a commitment for future taxpayers to pay future bond holders. A shift towards wealth taxation and higher taxes on profit income after the crisis would facilitate sustained government expenditure at a higher level, because the extra taxation required to pay the interest on any bonds issued to finance the crisis would fall on those with savings. In this manner, financing the crisis via the issuance of long-dated debt would not result in a further increase in inequality, and as noted above, would support GDP growth. The payment of interest on government borrowing through higher rates of taxation on the wealthy would merely redistribute income among the wealthy.

How much money could be raised by increased taxation of wealth and profit income? Information from HMRC and the Institute for Public Policy Research and independent research from Avinash Persaud, chairman of Intelligence Capital, suggests that an increase of Corporation Tax by one percentage point could raise £2.8 billion annually, a tax on non-pension assets could raise £6.9 billion annually and reforms to the United Kingdom's Financial Transactions Tax could raise £4.7 billion annually. Recent studies by researchers at the London School of Economics and University of Warwick (Advani & Summers 2020) suggest that a minimum tax rate based on the total amount of income and capital gains earned by high-net-worth individuals could raise £11 billion annually, and that £20 billion a year could be raised by taxing all income and capital gains at the same rate as earnings. If, as a conservative figure, financing the fiscal response to the Covid-19 crisis requires the issuance of £500 billion of bonds at a 3 per cent yield, then the extra interest payments will come to £15 billion annually. It would therefore be straightforward to fund these payments via progressive taxation.

Concluding remarks

What is a reasonable level for the national debt? There is probably no such thing as a single, "optimal" debt/GDP ratio, but it is the case that the debt/GDP ratio can be too high. As suggested by Figure 18.3, a required primary surplus greater than 10 per cent would be at odds with postwar fiscal policy in the United Kingdom, and would be politically difficult to sustain. However, the debt levels required to finance the Covid-19 crisis are nowhere near their maximum sustainable rates, and any primary surpluses required to stabilize them are completely manageable.

The United Kingdom entered the Covid-19 crisis with one of the highest levels of inequality in western Europe and a catastrophic record on poverty and deprivation following ten years of austerity. Shockingly, more than 1 million children live in households that earn less than 60 per cent of median household income, as it existed in 1997. These characteristics of society are likely to have been exacerbated by the peculiarly regressive distributional consequences of lockdown and social distancing, in which poorer households and smaller firms have seen their incomes fall, while the salaried middle class and larger firms have accumulated large amounts of savings.

The government should therefore finance the cost of dealing with the crisis by the issuance of long-term debt; and, once the recovery is assured, any primary surplus required to stabilize the debt/GDP ratio should be achieved by the imposition of taxes on wealth and profits. This will require a new political settlement based on both higher levels of taxes and a greater progressivity of the tax system as a whole. Although there is some evidence that the Conservative Party is moving in the former direction, there is less evidence that it is committed to progressive taxation. On the contrary, a vocal section of the Conservative Party is already exaggerating the economic stimulus to be obtained from reducing the taxation of wealth and higher incomes. In that case, the coming political battle will be over the progressiveness of the tax system as a whole, and how far the tax base should be tilted towards wealth and profit income.

Further reading

Advani, A. & A. Summers 2020. "Raising money from 'the rich' doesn't require increasing tax rates". London School of Economics and Political Science, 15 June. Available at: https://blogs.lse.ac.uk/businessreview/2020/06/15/raising-money-from-the-rich-doesnt-require-increasing-tax-rates.

Calvert Jump, R. & J. Michell 2020. "Inside the black box: the public finances after coronavirus", discussion paper. London: Institute for Public Policy Research.

Escolano, J. 2010. "A practical guide to public debt dynamics, fiscal sustainability, and cyclical adjustment of budgetary aggregates", Technical Guidance Note 10/02. Washington, DC: International Monetary Fund, Fiscal Affairs Department.

Keynes, J. 1940. *How to Pay for the War: A Radical Plan for the Chancellor of the Exchequer*. London: Macmillan.

OBR 2020. *Fiscal Sustainability Report 2020*. London: HMSO.

Toporowski, J. & R. Calvert Jump 2020. "The Covid-19 bailout and its financing dilemmas". Institute for New Economic Thinking, 30 June.

19

Progressive tax reform

Jo Michell

The Covid-19 crisis has thrown the fault lines of the United Kingdom's unequal and divided society into sharp relief. A decade of cuts has degraded state capacity, hampering the official response to the virus and exposing entrenched inequalities of income and wealth, deep divides in health and sharp geographical disparities. The scale of the interventions needed to place a floor under incomes during the crisis highlights the ineffectiveness of the social safety net provided by the British state.

There is little public support for the reshaping of the public sector that has taken place over recent decades. Survey evidence shows scant enthusiasm for either the long-run shift to greater tax regressivity or the post-2008 cuts to the public sector. In response to polling questions, the British public increasingly express a desire for greater state capacity and provision, alongside higher taxation to support that capacity.

Long-run demographic change adds to the pressure for reform of the British state. It is something of a cliché to argue that the British public desire Scandinavian-style public services alongside a US-style taxation regime – but the evidence increasingly shows that this is not a fair characterization: the British public want a state that works, and they are prepared to pay for it, especially if they regard the distribution of taxation as fair. Public attitudes to the loopholes and exemptions that allow those at the top of the income distribution to pay less demonstrate that people understand the unacceptability of those at the bottom facing higher marginal tax rates than those at the top.

If we are to face the challenges of the coming decades, from the pandemic and its aftermath to climate change, automation and ageing, a restoration of state capacity is essential and, indeed, inevitable. An effective state requires a stable, robust and fair tax base. Reform of the UK tax system is long overdue.

Vision for change

A new social contract between the British government and its citizens is urgently needed: a contract based on a well-functioning state that provides high-quality public services for all citizens without discrimination, protects the poorest and most vulnerable and provides a decent and comprehensive social safety net. This is what the majority of the British public say they want.

Such a transformation of the state can occur only alongside the fundamental reforms needed to deliver a stable system of taxation constructed on the principles of fairness and progressivity.

The Tax Justice Network has identified the four "Rs" of taxation: revenue, redistribution, repricing and representation. Tax supports government spending by providing the state with *revenue*, enables the *redistribution* of income and wealth and facilitates *repricing* to influence spending and consumption patterns. It also provides *representation*: all of us who pay our taxes demand accountability.

People are prepared to contribute to the capacity of the state if they understand that their contribution is well managed, proportionate and fair. The tabloid media constantly directs attention to the alleged benefit-scrounging neighbour with the curtains closed. Yet a far greater, if less visible, burden is caused by those on very high incomes paying some of the lowest effective tax rates. Big companies can dodge their obligations. The biases of the current tax system entrench gender and race inequalities.

Rationalizing and simplifying the system to remove what are, effectively, loopholes for rich individuals and large corporations will not only increase revenues for the exchequer, but also help to demonstrate to those on average incomes that the system is not rigged against them. This increases the feasibility of gradually increasing contributions from those who, while further from the top 1 per cent, are still reasonably well off and able to pay a bit more – as many tell pollsters they would in return for a well-functioning state.

Tax the wealthy properly

The United Kingdom's tax system disproportionately focuses on taxing labour income as opposed to capital income and wealth, further entrenching the high levels of wealth inequality in this country. Over the last 50 years the nation's wealth has risen from an amount equivalent to 300 per cent of GDP to 700 per cent of GDP, while at the same time wealth-related tax revenues have remained steady at about 3 per cent of GDP. Some wealthy people pay very low marginal income tax rates; for example, the average tax rate on someone earning over £10 million is just 21 per cent. There is an emerging economic view on how to tax the wealthy more and close some of the existing tax advantages that the wealthy benefit from.

Wealthy individuals can generate large incomes from investments in the form of dividends and capital gains. There are a range of generous tax allowances and rates that can slash the tax bills of people who profit from these sources of income. A first step would be to ensure that income from wealth is taxed at the same level as income from work by aligning tax rates on capital gains and dividends with income tax levels.

The United Kingdom desperately needs to update the way property is taxed. Council tax is 30 years out of date and the current system is deeply regressive. Stamp duty, which is levied when a home is sold, is progressive overall, but it penalizes those who need or want to move house. Both taxes should be scrapped and replaced with a progressive property tax levied on the value of the property. Under this reform the vast majority of people would pay less in tax, and it would be significantly more progressive than the status quo.

Money held in private pensions and other financial investments is highly concentrated among the wealthiest. Savers attract significant tax breaks, whether in the form of allowances on individual savings accounts, generous pension tax breaks or additional tax free allowances. This system needs to be reformed.

Finally, the United Kingdom should consider introducing an annual wealth tax. This would help tackle the underlying inequality in asset ownership. Countries such as Switzerland have a highly effective wealth tax that raises revenue and tackles inequality. A high-level group of academics are leading a Wealth Tax Commission to explore how to implement this in the United Kingdom. Any introduction of a wealth tax should be accompanied by reforms to inheritance tax, which is deeply disliked by the public and is riddled with loopholes that tend to benefit the wealthiest families.

End the race to the bottom on corporate taxation

The United Kingdom has been engaged in a damaging race to the bottom on corporate taxation. The headline rate has dropped from 30 per cent in the 2000s to 19 per cent in 2017, one of the lowest rates in the developed world, and significantly below the OECD average of 24 per cent. Low corporation tax rates create opportunities for tax avoidance by encouraging people to shift labour income into companies and so pay lower tax rates. Share ownership is concentrated in the hands of the wealthy, and so lower taxes on corporate profits benefit those who are already well off. What is particularly striking is that even the leading UK business groups do not support headline rates this low. In March 2021, chancellor Rishi Sunak signalled an apparent reversal of this approach, announcing that corporation tax would rise to 25 per cent from 2023. If this change comes into effect – without being offset by other policies – this would bring corporation tax into line with the OECD average and will significantly increase tax revenue.

As well as a low headline rate, the current corporate tax approach favours debt financing over equity financing. This encourages firms to load themselves up with debt, which can wipe out any corporate tax bill. This is a favoured tactic of private equity firms, and it often undermines otherwise healthy companies. The government should reduce the ability of firms to write off debt interest payments against their corporation tax liabilities.

The system of taxing multinational companies is a hundred years out of date and was designed for a period when international trade involved moving physical goods. This creaking approach to taxing global firms allows digital giants such as Amazon, Google and Facebook to pay very low rates of tax. The UK government has introduced a Digital Services Tax, but at most this is a sticking plaster, and does not deal with the underlying problems with the system. A progressive government should take a new approach (called unitary taxation) that would enable governments to tax the profits of large multinational corporations based on where they employ people, own assets and make sales. This approach should be combined with an effective minimum corporate tax rate, as is being discussed by the OECD. This would lead to a much fairer distribution of corporate taxes.

Clamp down on tax dodging

The United Kingdom has a major problem with tax avoidance and evasion. Estimates of revenue lost range from £31 billion a year to £90 billion. It is important to tackle this problem, both because of the money forgone and because significant amounts of tax avoidance and evasion undermine public faith in the tax system. The United Kingdom and its secrecy jurisdictions also undermine the tax systems of other countries. Curbing tax dodging involves three things: fixing structural problems with the tax system; providing better-quality data; and beefing up the enforcement of the rules by HMRC and Companies House.

Much tax avoidance is driven by companies and individuals exploiting weaknesses and loopholes in the system to legally pay less tax. For example, it is common for high earners to put their income through a company. This means that they pay significantly lower tax rates than if they were earning through the PAYE (Pay As You Earn) scheme. Fixing many of these structural issues with the tax system, as discussed in the sections above, would reduce tax avoidance.

The authorities and the public currently lack much of the information they need to spot and deal with tax avoidance and evasion. When it comes to multinational companies, it can be very difficult to identify where they make money and pay taxes. For this reason, the government should require companies to publish information on their activities broken down on a country-by-country basis. Companies already collect this information, so the extra costs would be minimal. HMRC, and other UK authorities involved in tackling tax evasion and financial crime, should be given automatic access to information on a range of financial transactions. This already happens on an international basis, so should be relatively straightforward to apply domestically.

Having the right information is just the first step. It is vital that the government invests in the authorities responsible for enforcing the rules. For example, HMRC has seen its budget slashed over the last decade. Evidence from Arun Advani (see Advani 2019) shows that audits by the tax authority typically bring in four times their cost. This should be a no-brainer for a government seeking extra revenue. Another part of the problem is that much tax evasion is carried out through companies. As Richard Murphy has shown, company regulation in the United Kingdom is pitiful, and many companies are allowed to disappear without paying the tax they owe. A beefed-up companies regulator would help close the tax gap.

Finally, tax avoidance and evasion are possible only because of an army of professional enablers, including accountants and lawyers, who design new schemes to help their clients pay less tax. The various professional regulators, and the government's financial crime authorities, need to do a much better job at holding these individuals to account.

Tensions

A number of objections could be raised to the proposals above. There are inevitable tensions with other progressive objectives. We briefly consider some of these possible objections and tensions.

A reasonable Keynesian objection is that raising taxes during a recession will further depress demand, causing output and employment to fall yet further; there is an emerging narrative that argues against tax rises for this reason. Although the Keynesian view is valid when considering the effects of increased taxation in isolation, tax reform should be part of a broader package including substantial state investment in a "Green New Deal", direct job creation measures, strengthening the social safety net and redistribution from rich to poor. The overall macroeconomic effect of such a package would be expansionary, not contractionary.

Estimates of the specification and size of a "Green New Deal" vary widely, but a conservative estimate could be that government spending would need to increase by the equivalent of 5 per cent of GDP. Estimates of spare capacity (labour market slack and underutilized capital equipment) also vary greatly (and suffer from serious methodological flaws in some cases), but 5 per cent of GDP is a large number relative to most reasonable estimates. Any package of investment commensurate to the task of dealing with the climate emergency could therefore quickly push the economy against capacity constraints and bottlenecks. Under such circumstances, some restraint in consumption expenditure – particularly the carbon-intensive luxury consumption of those at the top of the income distribution – is likely to be required to prevent inflationary pressure.

Tax restructuring should be part of a package of measures aimed at reversing the inequality that has been a feature of recent decades.

Redistribution will exert an expansionary influence, because those on lower incomes spend a greater share of their income than those on higher incomes. This effect is likely to be reinforced by the reduced uncertainty resulting from a functioning social safety net and reduced reliance on market forces for the provision of education, health and pensions.

An important area of debate and possible tension relates to the use of the tax system in facilitating the transition to a low-carbon economy. The roles of tax identified above include raising revenue to support the substantial public expenditures required, and the creation of incentives and disincentives for particular types of activity. It is widely accepted that taxation of carbon should play a role in the low-carbon transition. However, carbon taxation (or carbon pricing, as it is often called) needs to be part of a more comprehensive strategy for dealing with climate change, not least because such taxes tend to be regressive.

There is an important role for the tax system in directly penalizing polluting activities and/or providing subsidies to promote desirable activities that contribute to the low-carbon transition. There are potential difficulties here, in that some high-carbon activities cannot be avoided, such as the manufacture of steel and concrete. The most appropriate approach may therefore be to provide incentives in the form of subsidies and tax breaks to those businesses that meet environmentally friendly criteria alongside ending existing subsidies to the fossil fuel industry. Such a system will need to be carefully policed to avoid gaming and misreporting. This would need to be combined with serious regulation of carbon-intensive activity.

One argument commonly raised against progressive taxation is that it reduces incentives for wealth- and job-creating investment activity. The evidence accumulated over recent decades is hard to square with this claim: corporations have paid substantial sums in dividends and share buybacks while simultaneously cutting capital investment and borrowing on bond markets. Capital income as a share of GDP has risen at the expense of wages even as investment has stagnated. There is little evidence that a more progressive taxation system would serve as a disincentive to productive investment.

On the contrary, current tax structures provide incentives to misreport income types and, arguably, facilitate the accumulation of income streams that are better characterized as rents than the returns on capital investment. Business investment and job creation are ultimately driven by demand for the products sold by businesses. The reforms outlined above will raise overall demand for goods and services, stimulating investment and employment.

One potential issue with rationalizing the tax regime is the possibility of corporate relocation to appealing tax regimes – either of financial reporting by moving headquarters or of genuine economic activity. Part of the solution is international cooperation; governments must attempt to work with overseas counterparts to avoid a regulatory "race to the bottom". Attempts to tax large corporations can lead to retaliatory trade responses, as seen recently when the United States threatened to impose tariffs in response to a proposed European digital income tax. An emerging discussion emphasizes the importance of common minimum tax rates across borders to limit the appeal of financial reporting from tax havens. However, there is little evidence to support the view that actual economic activity is highly sensitive to tax regimes; firms instead regard tax as part of the cost of doing business in any particular country.

Where next?

The year 2021 is very different from 2010. Politically, there is little space for more austerity. Institutions at the heart of the economic establishment, such as the IMF, are calling on countries to spend now and worry about government deficits later.

Even before Covid-19 struck, the Conservatives won the 2019 general election in the United Kingdom on the basis of promises of more spending and a promise to "level up" forgotten parts of the country. It is hard to see a return to an era of significant government cuts. Given the demographic trends, it is highly likely that government spending will increase. In the medium to long run this means that taxes will probably go up to help support this spending. This represents a realignment of UK politics towards a more progressive approach to tax and spend.

Research into public attitudes by Tax Justice UK has found that almost half the people would be prepared to pay more tax themselves (Tax Justice UK 2020). The research also finds substantial support for higher taxes on the wealthy and companies. Support for these measures actually went up during the first Covid lockdown. Conservative and Labour voters all support a more progressive tax system.

This means that the time is ripe for the structural changes outlined in this chapter. It is important to make the case now for progressive tax changes, even if their introduction is staggered to avoid choking off demand as the economy recovers from the current crisis.

Further reading

Advani, A. 2019. "Uncollected tax revenue: who is underpaying and what we should do about it", briefing. London: Social Market Foundation. Available at: www.smf.co.uk/publications/uncollected-tax-revenue-underpaying.

Advani, A. & A. Summers 2020. "Raising money from 'the rich' doesn't require increasing tax rates". London School of Economics and Political Science, 15 June. Available at: https://blogs.lse.ac. uk/businessreview/2020/06/15/raising-money-from-the-rich-doesnt-require-increasing-tax-rates.

Murphy, R. 2008. "The missing billions: the UK tax gap", Touchstone Pamphlet 1. London: Trades Union Congress. Available at: www.tuc.org.uk/sites/default/files/documents/1missingbillions.pdf.

Tax Justice UK 2020. "Conservative voters shift in favour of tax rises under lockdown". 9 September. Available at: www.taxjustice.uk/blog/conservative-voters-shift-in-favour-of-tax-rises-under-lockdown.

20

A progressive recovery

Jan Toporowski

The announcement from the Office for National Statistics at the beginning of August – that economic activity in the United Kingdom contracted in the second quarter of 2020 by slightly over a fifth – can have come as no surprise to anyone who has observed the shutdown of high streets up and down the country and the furloughing of something like a quarter of the private sector labour force. Although much attention has been given to the loss of trade for large corporations in the travel business in Britain, such as British Airways, incalculable damage has been wreaked upon small and medium-sized enterprises, which actually employ the majority of workers in the private sector.

In this situation it is useful to take a long-term view, to see how previous disasters and policy errors have affected the economy. The benchmark for economic activity over the last half-century has been 1979. At the time the economy was recovering from the "oil price shock" of 1974, during which the price of oil (on whose imports Britain was then wholly dependent) had quadrupled, and the Labour government was submitting to the monetarist demands of the International Monetary Fund to restrict spending. It was also the eve of the government of Margaret Thatcher. Her brutal industrial policies resulted in the worst depression since the 1930s, mass unemployment and street riots.

Despite the efforts to attract international business – as showcased in the much-bragged-about Nissan car factory in Washington, County Durham – the economy took well over a decade to recover from that forced contraction in industrial production. The collapse of the coal industry, heroically resisted by the National Union of Mineworkers, was merely the most spectacular shutdown of productive activity. Even with the boost from Nissan car production, the motor car industry reached its postwar peak as long ago as 1972, when 1.92 million cars were manufactured; by 2016 production was 1.7 million, and was already declining (Brexit and all that) before the shutdown of car showrooms in March 2020. By then, too, the industry's structure had changed: car production had become "internationalized", with most car plants being foreign-owned. More importantly, an increasing amount of production was merely the assembly of components produced elsewhere, providing little value added in the United Kingdom because so much of a "British" car now consists of imported parts.

A modest Thatcherite recovery was hit again by the recession of 1991/92. It took the Labour governments of Tony Blair and Gordon Brown, on the eve of the 2007–09 financial crisis in the United States, to bring industrial production in Britain above the level it had reached in 1979.

The crisis hit British industry badly, not so much because Britain is directly exposed to US markets but because so much of British industrial production is controlled by large international corporations whose corporate culture is a never-ending festival of mergers and takeovers. This is how, for example, steel production in the United Kingdom fell into the hands of Tata International (owners also of Jaguar Land Rover), which had started life as a company operating wholly in India. Typically, such corporate restructuring is financed using bank borrowing, which is then refinanced into corporation shares or bonds. The capital markets had suffered from illiquidity since before the turn of the century, making new share issues difficult. When the money markets froze up in 2007 – making it impossible to roll over short-term borrowing – Britain's captains of industry did the only thing that could save their business: they drastically cut back their expenditure on plant and equipment.

Cutting back investment means a "saving" for the individual corporation. But for the economy as a whole it precipitated a decline of industrial production by some 15 per cent between 2007 and 2010. British industry has not recovered since then. The benchmark of 1979 remains a high point of British industrial endeavour.

This history of industrial neglect and consolidation lies at the core of British economic stagnation, even though it is not the full story. To get that we need to add in the rise and decline in North Sea oil production, itself masked by the fall in oil prices since 1980, followed since the 1990s by another rise until 2014. This, to some extent, replaced coal production (although never the employment provided in the mines). The other sector masking British industrial decline is the rise of services.

But this, too, is dependent upon the continued growth of not only the middle classes – employed outside industry and hence, in aggregate, little affected by the industrial business cycle, but also government employment and those bureaucratic hierarchies required for the maintenance of industrial control in conditions of fluid capital ownership and financial restructuring.

The Covid recession

The Covid recession is different from previous recessions – and not just in being a response to a "natural" infection, like the Black Death in the fourteenth century. Previous recessions were attributable to economic policy errors, or the way in which a capitalist economy normally functions. Unlike those economic contractions, the present recession is a consequence of the comprehensive measures being taken to prevent the spread of the disease. Production has fallen not because workers are falling sick by their machines but because they are being obliged to stay at home.

Home confinement has in turn precipitated a major fall in household consumption, visible at airports, theatres and retail resorts in our towns and cities. According to the ONS, in 2019 the average household in the United Kingdom spent nearly a third of its budget on travel, restaurants and hotels, and recreation and culture. These are now rare and risky activities. This contrasts with previous recessions – notably the recession that followed the 2007–09 financial crisis, the economic contraction of 1991/92 and the great deflation of the Thatcher years – which were almost invariably led by contractions in investment rather than falls in consumption,. The very British way of promoting private enterprise through mergers and acquisitions itself serves to discourage investment: whereas "synergies" and "shared overheads" are the battle cries of corporate raiders and investment bankers, the effective economies are usually obtained by disinvestment, such as shutting down production capacity that competes with more financially powerful or efficient capacity.

Moreover, with a welfare state that hardly meets the needs of the destitute, the present recession is exacerbating the inequalities that, as documented in the other contributions to this volume, were already indefensible even before the outbreak of Covid-19. The situation is deteriorating rapidly with the policy response to the crisis, which overwhelmingly favours the propertied classes and the salaried middle class. The material condition of the propertied classes has not been altered by the crisis; and it turns out that the labour process of the majority of the salaried middle classes depends upon online skills that may be easily located at home. This is not the case with manual workers, who have borne the brunt of the shutdown of manufacturing and non-essential retail and hospitality activities. The government has responded to this with the furlough scheme, providing a basic replacement income to workers temporarily laid off, or putting them on sick pay.[1] A lower segment of the population, the unemployed or self-employed, are thrown onto the mercies of a welfare system whose reforms over decades have been designed to reduce support and make it less accessible, despite the generous-sounding title of "Universal Credit". Finally, at the bottom is a shadowy stratum of refugees and illegal migrants, whose precarious legal situation prevents them from ever approaching an official body with a request for assistance.

This inequality has a distinct bearing on the progress of the infection and, hence, the likely duration of the recession. Poor people in Britain are overwhelmingly concentrated in urban areas, in overcrowded housing conditions that make it impossible for the sick to isolate themselves effectively. Inadequate welfare support forces them to go out to work, or search for it, in close proximity to potential sources of infection. In this way, poverty ensures the recurrence of Covid. In turn, the absence of a strategy to eliminate poverty reinforces reliance on measures that can only cripple the economy. What is being experienced has happened previously, although never on the same scale as today. The cholera outbreaks of the nineteenth century were similar: then it took more than half a century for the enlightened sections of the middle and upper classes to realize that the only way in which they could be safe in their urban redoubts was by eliminating housing poverty and providing clean water and sewerage facilities.

The Covid recession may be led by the fall in household consumption. But, less visible to the average furloughed worker, holidaymaker abroad

---

1. By the beginning of May over 6 million workers, or almost a quarter of the labour force, were receiving this basic income in place of their normal wages.

trying to return home in advance of new quarantine requirements or teenager trying to make sense of her examination results, has been the precipitous decline in private sector investment. This, as noted above, was the leading factor in previous economic contractions. Even before Covid arrived, private sector investment looked sickly, beset by Brexit concerns and the Johnson government's European negotiating strategy of "no-deal" brinkmanship. In the second quarter of 2020 business investment fell by over 30 per cent, a striking sign that household consumption may recover; but private sector economic activity will not get back to pre-crisis levels.

The Neville Chamberlain strategy of recovery

At the end of June 2020 the prime minister, on a visit to Dudley, West Midlands, was asked what his strategy for economic recovery was. Boris Johnson replied with another three-word slogan that he hopes to make memorable: "Build, build, build". Money was announced for road projects, hospitals, schools and housing. A few days earlier the Centre for Policy Studies had published a report by Sajid Javid, Johnson's first choice as Chancellor of the Exchequer, who had resigned just before the pandemic arrived. Javid's report, entitled *After the Virus: A Plan for Restoring Growth*, presented the pitch of the most influential part of the Conservative Party, for overcoming the Covid recession and the economic consequences of Brexit. According to this, the British economy is to be revived by deregulating the economy and cutting taxes and infrastructure spending.

But there is in fact no evidence that tax cuts or deregulation can persuade businesses to invest, if their customers and other businesses are not spending their money. And the promise of infrastructure spending is a proto-Keynesian acknowledgement of continuity with the policies of George Osborne and of the electoral debt owed by Conservative MPs to voters in former Labour constituencies in the West Midlands and the north of England.

But, even under Osborne, the policy was not new. It had in fact been pioneered in the 1930s by Neville Chamberlain, when he was Chancellor of the Exchequer in the National Government of Ramsay MacDonald (before Chamberlain became prime minister and then threw it all away by his ineffectual resistance to Hitler). Chamberlain had been Lord Mayor of Birmingham, his family fiefdom where his father Joseph Chamberlain pioneered the "municipal socialism" of public utilities financed by the city authorities. The National Government was reviled for reducing unemployment benefits. But Chamberlain also gave money to local authorities for council housing and public works. The open-air swimming pool "lidos", which are so admired today, were built by Chamberlain to relieve unemployment and improve the health of the nation. Herbert Hoover, the American president who was in office during the Wall Street Crash of 1929, also dabbled in public works before he was replaced by Roosevelt in 1933.

How effective is the strategy of reliance on public works? In the past it made, at best, a difference; but it did not provide a solution for economic depression: mass unemployment remained in the United Kingdom right up to the Second World War, when the call-up for military service eliminated labour surpluses. In the decade under the economic direction of Osborne and his successors, public works have made little impact upon the unemployment black spots of the West Midlands and the north of England. This, we are told by the political experts, is why electors in those areas voted in such numbers first for Brexit, and then for a Conservative Party that declared economic rejuvenation and welfare improvements to be natural outcomes of leaving the European Union, rather than of public works.

The most cursory examination of the labour process involved in public works reveals the reasons for their limited effectiveness. They employ prodigious quantities of young migrant labour, precisely because they are not permanent places of work. In the nineteenth century it was the surplus labour from Ireland and Scotland that built the canals and the railways. In the twenty-first century our public works have drawn in labour surpluses from eastern and southern Europe. Anyone venturing onto one of these sites would find themselves in a Tower of Babel, with workers speaking Spanish, Romanian, Bulgarian, Italian, Polish and Portuguese. They save up their relatively high earnings; or they send them back home as remittances. This much is obvious, except to politicians modelling high-vis jackets for media photographers.

Behind this partiality for non-British workers lie two dysfunctions of the British labour market that have never been effectively addressed by governments: a housing market that taxes young workers and is an obstacle to geographic mobility; and a technical training system that does not deliver the skilled workers the economy needs. These are the reasons why public works in twenty-first-century Britain cannot put the unemployed to work. Johnson's promises of hospitals, schools and infrastructure for the depressed regions can do little for the unemployed of those areas.

The progressive alternative

Public works have their place in any comprehensive strategy of economic recovery. But they are not enough; and they need to be justified by their social use value, rather than the business opportunities they provide for their contractors. The justification for a hospital or a railway line is the need for its facilities. The excesses of the old private finance initiative lay not only in their inflation of costs but also in their destruction of often still serviceable buildings. Public construction should be undertaken not just because it creates employment but because it is useful and greens our economy. Progressives and leftists can take this view because they know that there are also other ways in which jobs can be created; conservatives can rely only on the inflation of their proto-Keynesian public works to cover up their failures over poverty, employment and public services.

The most obvious other way of creating employment is through subsidized consumption, through such policies as the provision and extension of high-quality public services. The Covid pandemic has clearly shown the need for major investment in the social care sector. Other social needs that require public initiative are social housing and further education. We know who the key workers are. We should be providing decent housing for them, close to their places of employment, rather than requiring them to commute long distances, at risk of Covid and the jeopardizing of their family lives. Technical education is in need of major investment, not only to provide skilled workers and to change to skills of the unemployed but also to raise the status of skilled workers. The measure of social mobility should be the pay and respect afforded to engineers and technicians, rather than the number of students from state schools at the ancient universities.

A less obvious way of supporting economic recovery is through the redistribution of income, by means of welfare payments financed by taxes on higher incomes and wealth. Those on higher incomes will not miss the money. At worst, they will save a bit less, while businesses will benefit when welfare recipients spend the money that would otherwise be lying idle in the accounts of the rich. A start could be made by returning grants to students for staying on at school after school-leaving age, or for entering into technical education, and remedying the notorious parsimony of Universal Credit.

Finally, a policy measure that distinguishes the left or progressive approach should be the demand for accountability for public funds. Whereas Conservative politicians champion the interests of big business, with indiscriminate subsidies, deregulation and tax cuts, the left stands for transparency and pursuit of the public interest. The issue is of major importance, because it touches upon the question that has divided the Labour Party since the 1980s: the question of the socialization of the means of production. It has been thought since then that this question had been resolved in favour of private ownership. But the Covid crisis has seen the private sector place itself into the hands of the government. Every day the Treasury pores over requests for subsidies from the public purse. We take it for granted that our transport infrastructure and our key industries operate in accordance with the demands of the Treasury, rather than the financial targets of shareholders and directors.

The demand for accountability touches upon what we mean by the socialization of the means of production. Big business would like it to mean that the government "takes the risk" by covering losses and subsidizing profits. The leftist and progressive view should be that money is provided for a demonstrable social purpose; and this should be subject to democratic scrutiny. In Britain, such scrutiny is provided through trades unions, central and local government and the regional governments of Scotland, Wales and Northern Ireland. Union and workers' rights need to be strengthened to allow them to carry out this scrutiny effectively; and government inspectorates of employment and environmental protection need to be reinforced.

The urgent need for accountability goes to the heart of how British business operates. British business was mired in debt even before Covid drained its sales revenues. This is because a high proportion of formerly quoted businesses (high street names such as Boots and Pizza Express, as well as care home providers such as Care UK) are owned by private equity funds. These funds have traditionally operated in the shadows of the financial system, borrowing large amounts of money to take over corporations. The debt is then transferred onto the balance sheet of the company taken over in this way, with the company then being forced to sell off subsidiaries and "sweat the assets" (reduce employment to raise labour productivity) in order to repay the debt. For such businesses, government loans and subsidies offer new opportunities for debt management and refinancing balance sheets, to save on financing costs. The saving can then be "capitalized" and handed over as profits to owners and shareholders. To smaller businesses, the government offers low-interest Bounce Back loans for the express purpose of paying off bank debt.

Thanks to the Covid crisis, the government has become a supplementary financing facility for UK business, facilitating debt management rather than ensuring the maintenance of production and employment. Such diminished expectations are in sharp contrast to the 1930s, when, in the United States, Roosevelt gave financial assistance but to companies that gave commitments on workers' rights, employment and investment.

An assured recovery therefore requires more than just token public works. It needs comprehensive investment in public services, a progressive redistribution of income and democratic accountability for the large sums that are now being used to subsidize private enterprise. A party of crony capitalism cannot do this.

Further reading

Javid, S. 2020. *After the Virus: A Plan for Restoring Growth*. London: Centre for Policy Studies.

Kalecki, M. 1990 [1944]. "Three ways to full employment". In *Collected Works of Michał Kalecki*, vol. 1, *Capitalism: Business Cycles and Full Employment*, J. Osiatyński (ed.), 357–76. Oxford: Clarendon Press.

Labour Party 1945. *Let Us Face the Future: A Declaration of Labour Policy for the Consideration of the Nation* [the Labour Party manifesto]. London: Labour Party. Available at: www.labour-party.org.uk/manifestos/1945/1945-labour-manifesto.shtml.

Index